AF656202

Appropriate Technologies for Drought Prone Areas

Appropriate Technologies for Drought Prone Areas

Brindra Chauhan

RANDOM

RANDOM PUBLICATIONS

NEW DELHI (INDIA)

Appropriate Technologies for Drought Prone Areas

ISBN 978-93-5111-769-8

© Reserved

All Rights Reserved. No Part of this book may be reproduced in any manner without written permission.

Published in 2016 in India by

RANDOM PUBLICATIONS

4376-A/4B, Gali Murari Lal, Ansari Road
New Delhi-110 002
Phone : +9111-43580356, 011-23289044, 011-43142548
e-mail: sales@randompublications.com,
info@randompublications.com, randomexports@gmail.com

Reprint 2024

Type Setting by : Friends Media, Delhi-110089
Digitally Printed at: Replika Press Pvt. Ltd.

Preface

Drought is the most widespread hydro meteorological syndrome of 'prolonged period of water scarcity affecting natural resources, environment and, thereby, the people'. Environmental changes, viz. climate change, land-use changes an d natural resource degradation have aggravated drought occurrences and vulnerability, thus disrupting the normal socio-economic settings. All the regions of India suffer with drought incidences of varying periodicity, with 13 states repeatedly declared as drought-prone. Complexities of drought symptoms and impacts have sought for an understanding of an ecosystem approach for drought management, rather than as a hardcore meteorological discipline. Regions of Rajasthan, Bundelkhand, Karnataka and Orissa are typical examples of drought-related deprivation and resultant conflicts, whereas drought in states like Chhattisgarh, Punjab, Haryana, etc. are the result of improper agriculture practices and poor water management. In this article, the strategies of drought monitoring, data management, impacts and mitigation approach are critically assessed in the Indian perspective. Integration of drought management with the framework on natural re sources and climate-change adaptation at different levels have also been discussed. The terrible shortage of drinking water and life-saving irrigation to the field crops, particularly in the hottest period of the season, become the menace both for flora and fauna. Food grains and fodder for humans and livestock/domestic animals become the greatest problem among other problems of socio-economic life style of the poorest of the poor farming communities. Suitable farming technology and extension strategy need to be disseminated on war-footing in the drought affected areas of the country vis-à-vis in the neighboring countries.

– Author

Contents

1

Dryland Agriculture

BACKGROUND

The Rainfed/Dryland area under cultivation is about 85 million hectare which is 60 per cent of the total net sown area. The Sub-Mission on Rainfed/Dryland agriculture of the National Mission for Sustainable Agriculture attempts to devise strategies to make Indian agriculture more resilient to climate change. A number of technologies such as short duration drought resistant varieties, genotypes resistant to drought, conservation of initial soil moisture technologies and farming systems approach to Dryland farming etc are available. However, further research is required to develop more such technologies and refine them by testing for adoption. The Sub-Mission intends to support the convergence and integration of traditional knowledge and practices systems. The priority areas as conceived by NAPCC and by the Ministry of Agriculture are given below:

AREAS OF PRIORITY

- Development of drought and pest-resistant crop varieties and also encouragement/promotion of adoption of low input and water efficient agricultural technologies and existing stress tolerant varieties.
- Improving methods to conserve soil and water to ensure theirs optimal utilization.
- Generate awareness through stakeholder consulta-tions, training workshops and demonstration exercises for farming communities, for agro-climatic information sharing and dissemination
- Financial support to enable farmers to invest in and adopt relevant technologies to overcome climate related stresses.

STRATEGY

TECHNOLOGY ADAPTATION

The potential of rainfed farming system will be harnessed through farming systems comprising crop, livestock, horticulture, agro forestry, fishery, bio mass and alternate income generating activities. Region specific farming system models having low input sustainable agriculture for different rainfed agro ecologies, waterlogged/flood frequented areas and overstressed irrigated areas will be inventorised and promoted for its wider adoption.

Enhancing productivity of water with distribution and application of irrigation water using micro-irrigation, supplemental and deficit irrigation, less water demanding crop and varities, resource conservation tillage, improved soil fertility and *in-situ* moisture conservation practices and multiple water use based farming systems will be promoted. Farming system models when integrated with watershed development will reduce risk and improve resilience towards adaptation to climate change.

Declining productivity as a result of excessive fertilizer use, physical and agro-chemical soil degradation, excessive withdrawal of groundwater and inefficient water use are serious concerns. Knowledge dissemination about rational and efficient use of resources and incentivization for saving resources through labour and/or material for promoting conservation agriculture, on-farm biomass generation and incorporation, cover cropping with leguminous crops, tree based farming systems, efficient water and fertilizer saving practices, integrated nutrient management, adoption of stress tolerant varities, crop-livestock integration and bio-mass recycling should form part of policy and investment portfolio. Wider adoption of these interventions taken on mission mode would help in adaptation and mitigation of climate change.

On development front, a two-pronged strategy is suggested to cope-up with impact of climate change on Dryland agriculture, i.e.:

- Build the capacity of the primary and secondary stakeholders through various training programmes, workshops and exposure visits; and
- Strengthen the existing government programmes of watersheds, micro-irrigation systems, etc. and adopt relevant technologies to overcome climate change related stresses.

Among the most important approaches is the adopting of farming system which combines crop production with animal resource development, agro-forestry and resource conservation technologies. Attempt will be made for updating and inventorization of available region-wise technologies for farming system.

RESEARCH

The Sub-Mission will have a two pronged strategy, viz.:

- Short term and long term research on climate change; and
- Capacity building of scientists on research methodologies in climate change, demonstration/training of farmers through Model Field Units (MFU) on coping with climate change.

The strategies for addressing the themes of the Sub-Mission on Dryland agriculture are given in the following table:

S.No.	Theme	Strategy
1.	• Promotion for adoption of drought and pest resistant crop varieties • Improving methods to conserve soil and water different agro-climatic	Short term and long term research on adaptation and mitigation through a net-work mode: — Promotion of existing varieties suitable for zones at a faster pace. — Develop more technolo gies and refine them for adoption.
2.	Stakeholder consultations, training workshops and demonstration exercises for farming communities, for agro-climatic information sharing and dissemination	Capacity building of scientists on research methodology; training of farmers on technologies to cope with climate change and use agro-climatic information, through Model field units in 50 pilot districts.

Research will be carried out on specific projects under the umbrella of the over all programme by Institutions of NARS and few relevant Institutions outside through a net-work mode. Research on mitigation will cover identification of Germplasm, development of crop varieties, soil and water management, conservation agriculture, energy use efficiency, livestock and fisheries management to reduce the impact of climate change on productivity and to decrease the GHG emissions from agricultural livestock sector.

FINANCIAL OUTLAY

DEVELOPMENT

The details of the fund requirement for the various activities proposed are given in Annexure—IV. The following table gives a summary of financial outlays for eight years (during XI Plan (2009-12) and XII Plan (2012-2017):

S.No.	Activities	Financial Outlay (₹ in Crore)
1.	Training/ capacity Building	313.00
2.	Workshops	17.00
3.	Farmers Field Schools	50.00
4.	Financial Support to Farmers to overcome Climate related stresses in targeted area of 35.00 million ha.	12,000.00
5.	Efficient use of water and nutrients (40 million ha)	45,000.00
	Total	**57,380.00**

RESEARCH

The total cost of the research component is estimated to be ₹ 1383.0 crore for the 3 years of the XI Plan and complete XII Plan period. The year-wise and head-wise break up is given below.

(₹ in crore)

Component	XI Plan				XII Plan						Grand Total
	2009-10	2010-11	2011-12	Total	2012-13	2013-14	2014-15	2015-16	2016-17	Total	XI + XII
Short term and long term research in network mode	80	133	80	293	80	150	80	80	100	490	783
Cost of MFUs in 50 districts under KVKs	60	20	20	100	300	50	50	50	50	500	600
Total	**140**	**153**	**100**	**393**	**380**	**200**	**130**	**130**	**150**	**990**	**1383**

Note: The cost of one MFU is one crore for the full plan period. It is proposed to set up 100 MFUs during XI Plan and 500 during XII Plan, which will cover most of the KVKs in the country. These MFUs will serve as training and capacity building centres and operational research and providing feedback to the research Institutes on the adoption and mitigation technologies generated by the NARs.

PLAN OF ACTION

DEVELOPMENT

The action plan for the next eight years envisages human resource development to cope up with climate change through conservation and efficient management of natural resources.

For this, a bottom-up approach is suggested, which involves training of farmers mainly from the 100 core rainfed districts during the first phase, followed by trainers from 73 core rainfed National ARP zones out of the total 131 Agro-Climatic Zones.

These training programmes are to be supported by capacity building of policy makers, administrators to come-up with suitable guidelines and policies to deal with climate change.

The developmental effort needs a constant support of research for this, core researchers have to build their capacities through a three-week training programme.

All HRD programmes need to be in tune with global efforts. For this, exposure visit of higher-level officials are required.

The summary of activities proposed is below:

S.No.	Target Group	Training Duration (Days)
A.	Capacity Building	
	• Farmers (4,80,000)	5
	• Trainers (58,400)	7
	• Policy Makers, Administrators And Research Managers (1600)	3
	• Core Researchers (2880)	21
	• Exposure Visit (240)	14
B.	Workshops	
	• Workshop at District Level (100 Distt.)	03
	• State Level (Core Rainfed Zone-73 Zones)	03
	• National Level	03
C.	Farmer's Field School (one in each core rainfed distt.) in numbers	100
D.	Area in which financial Support to Farmers is proposed to be given to overcome climate related stresses (adoption of new verities of crops, minimum tillage, contingent plan measures, organic farming, water conservation, etc.)	35.00 million ha

Note: The figures in parentheses indicate number of participants Systematic plans be prepared for wasteland development from dovetailing funds from NREGA, SGRY, RKVY, etc. For this purpose, state level land development fund may be created and used. Such developed lands may be allotted to landless agricultural labourers, SC/ST farmers and their SHGs, with specific guidelines.

With a view to utilizing large fallow lands, states to develop and encourage land lease markets under their respective laws to optimum use of privately owned fallow lands. The lease system should ensure that the land owner does not risk of losing land, the cultivator has enough incentive to invest and continue his farming activity.

The studies of the Geo-spatial Data and Earth observation through use of communication technology and Remote Sensing Tools have shown the signs of climate change. It has also become possible to map, monitor and model the impact of climate change on earth resources and environment. Synergy of these will be suitably used in the implementation of proposed programme.

Water conservation, groundwater re-charge and rainwater harvesting by adopting appropriate technologies and funding mechanism. 12 lakh water harvesting structures in rainfed areas *i.e.* 3-4 structure in each village be taken up in mission mode.

To enable farmers to invest in and adopt relevant technologies to overcome climate related stresses, the additional activities such as introduction of new varieties of crops resistant to temperature, minimum tillage, contingent plan measures to mitigate effects of extreme weather events, organic farming for carbon sequestration, additional surface storages and groundwater recharge, etc would be undertaken for adaptation and mitigation of the adverse effects of climate change.

It is proposed to undertake these activities including farming system and livelihood support in about 5.00 million ha area in the already developed watersheds of X Plan at the ₹ 6000.00 per ha. The above activities will be also undertaken in the 30.00 million ha of Rainfed/Dryland areas in a period of 8 years (remaining 3 years of XI plan and XII Plan) at the rate of ₹ 3000.00 per ha. This will be additional to the existing unit cost norms under the existing watershed schemes.

Efficient Use of Water and Nutrients Application

The low water use efficiency, water scarcity and droughts will further aggravate the situation in rainfed areas due to climate change. Efficient water management of the available/created water resources is one of the key areas to address the water scarcity issue. The availability of nutrients is limited in rainfed areas due to the limiting soil moisture. Therefore, application of the fertilizers should be done in judicious manner for its potential use. The application of liquid fertilizer and soil amendments along with water application will not only helpful in providing nutrients to crop but also help in efficient use of soil moisture. For efficient water management and to encourage liquid fertilizer application, it is proposed to bring 30 million ha under pressurized and non-pressurized water application system in the remaining years of XI Plan and XII Five year Plan in the country.

The proposed targets and outlays are:

- Pressurized irrigation system (Drip/Sprinkler) in 20 million hectare
  - Assistance up to ₹ 25,000 per hectare or 50% of the actual cost whichever is lower for installation of drip/ sprinkler systems including water lifting devices in 10 m. ha. (Total cost ₹ 25,000 crore).
  - Assistance up to ₹ 10,000 per hectare or 50% of the actual cost whichever is lower for installation of drip/sprinkler system to the farmers who have the tube-wells/ water lifting devices and other infrastructure excepting the application system, in 10 m. ha. (Total cost ₹ 10,000 crore).
- Non-pressurized irrigation system in 10 million hectare

Developing distribution system through box and conduit systems and pre-fabricated water conveyance system in 10 m. ha is proposed for improving the water application. Farmers would also be advised for adopting ridge and furrow method of irrigation, raised bed method of farming, field Bunding and levelling etc. for efficient use of water. Assistance to farmers up to ₹ 10,000 per hectare or 50 per cent of the actual cost whichever is minimum will be supported (Total cost ₹ 10,000 crore).

In addition, following also are to be suitably adopted:

- Model codes on drought, floods and good weather be prepared bringing out short term and long term mitigation measures, such as ensuring availability of quality seeds, planning for crops/varieties resistant to heat, floods, etc.
- The National Seed Grid will be strengthened to ensure supply of seed across the country as per area specific requirements.
- Issuance of Soil Health Pass Book to each farmer with soil testing advisories within next five years.
- Bio-fertilizers, liquid fertilizers and compost should be included in the subsidy regime. Their production and marketing needs to be undertaken in an organized manner.
- Guidelines may be put in place for rotational grazing, scientific lopping and pollarding and conserve fodder resources.

RESEARCH

Considering the 4th assessment report of the IPCC released in 2007, the impact of climate change on Indian agriculture is expected to be more severe than realised earlier. Particularly, Dryland agriculture is likely to face more risks and uncertainties due to predicted changes in rainfall patterns and increased droughts. Sectors like livestock production and fisheries are also likely to be significantly affected. While the impacts of climate change are regional and global, the adaptation and mitigation measure have to be evolved locally by blending traditional wisdom and modern technologies. Although many of the technologies developed by NARS in the past like short duration varieties and soil and water conservation measures are potentially useful for adaptation and mitigation, the scale and magnitude of the problem cutting across all sectors requires an exclusive and dedicated research programme.

The indirect effects of climate change on water resources are likely to be more significant than the present. Likewise, soil organic carbon and other basic soil processes will be affected. A comprehensive research programme is therefore required which should address natural resource management issues, development of crops and cropping systems that cope with increased temperature and rainfall aberrations, energy efficient production technologies and crop management practices which reduce the emission of green house gases.

The Sub-Mission on Dryland agriculture intends to address these critical gaps in addition to studying the effects on livestock, fodder production and fisheries in a comprehensive manner. Strategic research be taken up for evolving suitable cropping systems for various agriculture climatic conditions to enhance yield levels. The Sub-Mission activities will form part of overall activities of the National mission on Sustainable Agriculture which in turn will work in coordination with other missions like water and energy under National Action Plan on Climate Change.

The suggested research programmes such as cataloguing of germplasm of crops, livestock and fisheries evolving short duration varities, study of pests and diseases with respect to weather relationships and use of micro-organism based technology will be taken up for adaptation and mitigation. The details are at Annexure—IV.

COLLABORATING AGENCIES

Development: Adoption of Technologies

Past experience has shown that working in partnership and in a consortium mode has proved to be more effective, resulting in cost reduction and resource sharing by avoiding duplication. It is, therefore proposed to develop strong linkages with National Organizations like ICAR, ISRO, IMD (NCMRWF), NRSC, SAC, NABARD and other institutions and NGO's and Line Departments besides improving the existing linkages with SAUs. It is also proposed to strengthen linkages with international organizations like CGIAR Institutes, UNDP, FAO, WMO, etc.

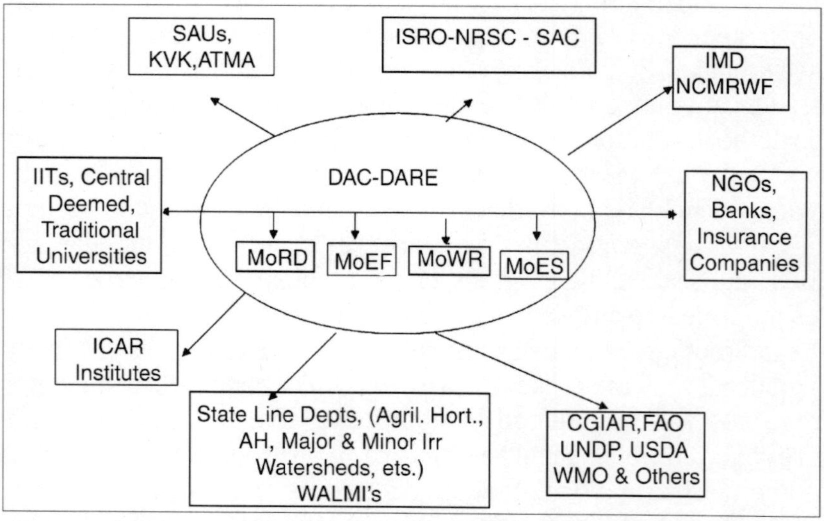

Fig. Proposed Linkages and Collaborating Institutions

In the coming years, linkages are to be strengthened further to exploit the synergistic power of institutions and organizations to cope up with climate change.

The following figure depicts an illustrative outline of proposed collaboration.

DRYLAND IN INDIA

CONCEPT

Indian agriculture is predominantly a rainfed agriculture under which both dry farming and dry land agriculture is included. Dry faring was the earlier concept for which amount of rainfall (less then 500 mm annually) remained the deciding factor for more then 50 years. In modern concept, dry land areas are those where the balance of moisture is always on the deficit side. In other words, annual evapotranspiration exceeds precipitation. In dry land agriculture, there is no consideration of amount of rainfall. It may appear quiet strange to a layman that even those areas which receive 1100 mm or more rainfall annually fall in the category of dry land agriculture under this concept.

To be more specific, the average annual rainfall of Varanasi is around 1100 mm and the annual potential evapotranspiration is 1500 mm. thus the average moisture deficit so created comes to 400 mm. this deficit in moisture is bound to affect the crop production under dry land situation ultimately resulting into total or partial failure of the crops. Accordingly the production is either low or extremely uncertain and unstable which are the real problems of dry land in India.

The success of crop production in these areas depends on the amount and distribution of rainfall, as these influences the stored soil moisture and moisture used by crops. The amount of water used by the crop and stored in the soil is governed by the water balance equation: ET = P-(R+S). When the balance of the equation shifts towards right, precipitation (P) is higher then ET, so that there may be waterlogging or it may even lead to run off (R) and flooding.

On the other hand, if the balance shifts to the left, ET becomes higher then the precipitation, resulting in drought in the various severity. Taking the country as a whole, as per meteorological report, severe drought as large area is experienced once in 50 years and partial drought in five years while folds are expected every year in one part of the country or the other, especially during rainy season. In fact the balance of the equation is controlled by the weather, season, crops and cropping pattern.

STATUS

Out of 14.2 million ha of net sown area in the country, rainfed agriculture is practiced in 95 million ha (67 per cent). Nearly 67 m ha of rainfed area falls in the mean annual precipitation range of 500-1500 mm.

The average annual rainfall of the country is 1200 mm amounting to 400 million ha meter of rain water over the country's geographical area (329 m ha). However, the distribution across the country varies from less than 100 mm in extreme arid areas of western Rajasthan to greater than 3600 mm in NE states and 1100 mm from east coast 2500-3000 mm in the west coast. The broad area of the summer monsoon activity extends between 30^0 N to 30^0 S and from 30^0 W to 16.5^0 E. the detail information on rain fall and monsoonal pattern in India has been summarized in the following table:

Table. Rainfall and Monsoonal Pattern in India

Season/Period	m ha m	Percent
Winter (Jan-Feb)	12	3
Pre-monsoon (Mar-May)	52	13
South-west monsoon (Jun-Sept)	296	74
North-east monsoon (Oct-Dec)	40	10
Total for the year	**400**	**100**

Rainfed farming comprises about 91 per cent area of coarse cereals (sorghum, pearl millet, maize and finger millet), 91 per cent pulses (chickpea and pigeon pea), 80 per cent of oilseeds (groundnut, rape seed, mustard and soybeen), and 65 per cent of cotton. Also, about 50 per cent area under rice and 19 per cent area under wheat is rainfed.

During the past 25 years there occurred significant changes in the area and yield of imported crops of rainfed farming areas. The area under coarse cereals decreased by about 10.7 million ha and most of this was under sorghum. The area under oilseeds increased by 9.2 million ha and most of this increase was due to irrigated rapeseed and mustard and soybeen. The total area under pulses and cotton remained constant but more of cotton became irrigated and shifts in the area under occurred from one agro-ecological region to others. Area under chickpea in the northern belt decreased but increase in the central belt. This change occurred due to increase in area under rice-wheat cropping system which displaced chickpea and also pearl millet to a great extent and maize to a small extent.

According to the present concept, there are 128 districts in the country which face the problems of dry land of these 25 districts covering 18 m. ha of net area sown with 10 per cent irrigation receive 375-750 mm rainfall annually spread over Central Rajasthan, Saurashtra region of Gujarat and rain shadow region of Western Ghats in Maharashtra and Karnataka. Twelve districts have irrigation covering 30-50 per cent of the cropped area and do not pose serious problems. The remaining 91 districts covering mainly Madhya Pradesh, Gujarat, Maharashtra, Andhra Pradesh, Karnataka, Uttar Pradesh, parts of Haryana, Tamil Nadu etc., represent typical dry land area. The total net sown area in these districts is estimated to be 42 million hectares of which 5 m ha are irrigated. Rainfall in these districts varies from 375 to 1125 mm. therefore, more and more efforts are to be made for enhanced and stable production in these areas so that the recurring droughts do not stand in the way of meeting the growing food demands.

It is not that no attention has been paid in the country towards the development of dryland farming. Efforts were made right from 1923 to improve crop yields with the establishment of a research projects at Manjari in Maharashtra and later at Solapur, Bijapur, Raichur and Hagari in Deccan and Rohtak (Haryana) in the north. An All India Coordinated Research Project for Dry land Agriculture was launched by ICAR in 1970 in collaboration with Government of Canada and later Central Research Institute for Dry land Agriculture (CRIDA) was established in 1985 at Hyderabad. These projects generated technology, which, if followed, can bring marked improvement in cropping intensity, productivity and stability in production.

Problems

In dry land agriculture, scarcity of water is the main problem. Apart from the low and erratic behaviour of rainfall, high evaporative demand and limited water holding capacity of the soil constitute the principle constraint in the crop production in dry land area. Yield fluctuations are high mainly due to vagaries of weather, often much behind the risk bearing capacity of the farmers. It is surprising to a layman that even humid areas with 2000 mm of annual rainfall not only suffer from moisture stress, but also face drinking water scarcity. Monsoon starts in the month of June and ends in last week of September or sometimes in the first week of October.

Most of the rainfall is received during this period. With undulating topography and low moisture retention capacity of the soil, major portion of the rain water is lost through run-off, causing erosion and adding to the waterlogging of low lying areas. After the rain stops, very little moisture is left in the profile to support plant growth and grain production.

In dry land area deficiency and uncertainty in rainfall of high intensity causes excessive loss of soil through erosion which leaves the soil infertile. Owing to erratic behaviour and improper distribution of rainfall, agriculture is risky, farmers lack resources, tools become inefficient and ultimately productivity is low.

Vertisoles have high clay content and high moisture retention capacity. Owing to its swelling and shrinking characteristics, permeability is low and hence the rate of infilteration of water is minimum. This causes more surface and high soil loss from the top layer owing to surface erosion. It is estimated that 68.5 tones/ha per year soil is lost from*vertisoles*. Due to high clay content it develops cracks during Rabi season at flowering stage of crops.

Alfisols are, by and large, light textured soils which have low moisture holding capacity but high water intake. The rain water falling in such areas gets soaked up and saturates the profile. The soil water percolation is more and therefore, is lost for crop use. Owing to faster intake of water in the profile the surface run-off is limited and soil loss from erosion is low (3.05 t/ha/year). Soil crusting is a common problem in low rainfall areas.

Entisols are generally loamy sand or sandy loam. Depth in these soils is not a constraint. These soils have very low clay content and hold water up to 200 mm per meter of soil profile. Its nutrient holding capacity is poor. In low rainfall areas monsoon cropping is practiced and in high rainfall areas double cropping is possible.

Submontane soils are medium in texture and depth is medium to deep as well as moderate in clay content. Moisture retention capacity is high (300 mm/m. profile). These soils are poor in nitrogen but in other nutrients. Phosphorous may be limiting in high production system. Due to high rainfall double cropping is possible in these soils.

Sierozems are extremely light soils, effectively depth being influenced by the $CaCo_3$ concentration in soil profile. Its moisture holding capacity is low (150 mm water.m). Sierozemic soils are low in nitrogen and sometimes inadequate in phosphorous. Subsoil salinity is common. These soils are mostly monsoon cropped, except in deep sandy loams where post-monsoon cropping is also possible. Crusting is very frequent.

IMPROVED DRYLAND TECHNOLOGY

The improved techniques and practices, which have so far been generated and recommended for achieving the objective of increased and stable crop production in dryland areas, have been summarized in following lines.

CROP PLANNING

The farmers of the dry land areas, prior to the development of dry land techniques, were growing a crop either on rainwater in kharif or on conserved soil moisture during the winter. The crop varieties grown when moisture is sufficiently available. Such varieties have low genetic potential for yield. Selecting suitable crops and varieties capable of maturing with in actual rainfall periods will not only help in enhancing production of a single crop but in intensifying the cropping intensity. Many criteria have been laid out for selecting a crop variety for drylands. The capacity to produce a fairly good yield under limited soil moisture conditions is the most desirable criteria. The duration of kharif crops/varieties should not normally exceed the number of rainy days. In other words, crop varieties for dryland areas should be of short duration, through resistant tolerant and high yielding which can be harvested with in rainfall periods and have sufficient residual moisture in soil profile for post-monsoon cropping.

Under dry land agriculture determination of length of growing period (LPG) *i.e.*, moisture availability of a given soil type, provides better index than total rainfall based crop planning. LPG is defined as the period when the moisture and temperature regious are suitable for crop growth and the period is determined by the FAO method (1983). The LPG is computed as the sum of the period when P is more than 0.5 PET plus time taken to utilize stored soil moisture (assured 100 mm) after P falls short of PET. For example 'Nagpur' and Ratnagiri in Maharashtra receive mean annual rainfall of 1120 mm and 2500 mm, respectively but LPG determination indicates that both the places have LPG of 210 days in deep black soils. Therefore, both the places are suitable for single long duration on a short duration crop with a relay rabi crop.

PLANNING FOR ABERRANT WEATHER

Dryland agriculture is subject to high variability in areas sown, yields and output. These variations are the results of aberrations in weather conditions, especially rainfall. Delays in normal monsoonal pattern causes problems of timing and the organization of preparatory tillage and other initial activities for commencing cultivation processes for the season. Such monsoonal delays have repercussions on the programme of activities for the entire agricultural year.

Even after the onset of monsoon and the commencement of planting, there may be monsoonal withdrawal causing moisture stress on plants and creating difficulties in the adoption and timing of approval cultural practices ultimately causing reactions in yields and outputs. Some crops are highly susceptible to such mid-season variations in moisture availability such as at the flowering stage in rice. Major crops like rice and maize get seriously affected if monsoonal rains cease early.

The need for modifying and introducing and introducing new technology for increasing and sustaining yield in dry land areas can hardly be overemphasized. Equally urgent is the need to decelerate and ultimately eliminate the process of damage to agricultural assets which are proceeding unbated in dry land areas. Erratic rainfall results in fluctuating production. This in turn leads to frequent scarcities, like the ones experienced in Indonesia and Vietnam in 1977 which created severe food shortages.

Droughts in China in 1972, 1974 and 1985 brought depression of foodgrain production by up to about 25 million tones. Frequent droughts in India during 1966, 1968, 1972, 1974, 1979, 1982 and 1987 seriously affected the food and fodder production in the country. Hence, it is necessary to understand the distribution of South-West monsoon within the season to determine the extent to which the crop productions are likely to be affected by the vagaries of monsoon.

Several attempts have been made to understand the behaviour of South-West monsoon rainfall in different agro-climatic regions on the basis of historical rainfall records.

These studies have brought out that

- There is large variation in dates of commencement of South-West monsoon from year to year in different parts of the country;

- The monsoon rainfall is of sequential nature with long dry spells or breaks extends sometimes to the period of even one month or more;
- There is large year to year variation in dates of withdrawal of South-West monsoon;
- There is variation in quantum of rainfall received from year to year; and
- High intensity rainfall occurs in association with movement of cyclones or depression resulting in sizeable loss of rainwater through run-off and deep drainage. Thus, crop production in dry lands fluctuates widely from year to year due to vagaries of weather.

An aberrant weather can be categorized under three heads i.e.

- Delayed onset of monsoon;
- Long gaps or breaks in rainfall; and
- Early stoppage of rains towards the end of monsoon season. Therefore, to mitigate such weather situations, farmers should make some changes in normal cropping schedule for getting some production in place of total crop failure.

CROP SUBSTITUTION

Alternate crop strategies have been worked out for important regions of the country for *vertisols, alfisols, entisols, submontane* and *sierozemic* soils. Strategy has also been evolved for normal onset of rains, breaks in rains, early withdrawal, its uneven distribution; through selection of uneven crops/varieties which are inefficient utilize of the soil moisture, less responsive to production input and potentially low producers should be substituted by more efficient ones. Appropriate crops, suiting varying rainfall situations, have been identified for most of the dry land regions of India (*See Table 1.2 on next page*).

Crops which do not under normal rainfall years may not do so under abnormal years. Studies conducted in agro climatic conditions of Varanasi (eastern U.P.) revealed that under normal monsoon crops like short duration upland rice, maize, pearl millet, blackgram, greengram, sesame, pigeon pea etc. should be taken up on the basis of needs. These crops should be followed by chickpea, lentil, barley, mustard, safflower, linseed etc. on residual moisture during winter season.

If monsoon sets in as late as second week of july, short duration upland rice (variety—NDR-97 and NDR-118) may be included in place of Akashi and Cauvery is recommended. If the rains are delayed beyond the period but start somewhere in last week of July or first week of August and growing season is reduced to 60-7- days, then cultivation of hybrid pearl millet (NHB 3-4, B.J. 104), blackgram (Type 9), greengram (var-Jagriti and Jyoti) may be included in pace of T-44 and k-851 etc. should be grown. Yet another alternative could be to harvest a fodder of either pearl millet, maize, sorghum or a mixture of cowpea, blackgram and one of the above fodder crops.

In case monsoon rains stop early towards the end of season, normal sowing of short duration upland rice, blackgarm and sesame may be taken up. If the rain stops very early, *i.e.* by the end of August or first week of September, only fodder crops or grain legumes could be harvested. Depending upon the soil moisture condition, relay sowing of crops like chickpea, lentil, mustard, linseed and barley could be done in rabi season.

Table Traditional and Alternate Efficient Crops in Different Dryland Regions of India

S. No	Region Crop	Traditional Efficient	Alternate Crop
1.	Deccan Rabi season	Cotton, wheat	Safflower
2.	Malwa Plateau	wheat	Safflower, Chick pea
3.	Uplands of Bihar Plateau and Orissa	Rice	Ragi, Black gram, Groundnut
4.	South-easy Rajasthan	Maize	Sorghum
5.	North Madhya Pradesh	Maize	Soybean
6.	Eastern UP	Kalitur	Chick pea
7.	Sierozems of North-west India	Wheat	Mustard, Taramira (Eruca sativa)

During the recent drought, it was found that farmers in Karnataka, Andhra Pradesh and Maharashtra who went in for sunflower cultivation were in gainers. Sunflower succeeded where other crops failed. In other dry land regions, alternative efficient crops can profitably substitute the traditional ones (*See Table 1.3 on next page*).

Table Relative Yield of Traditional and Efficient Crops in Dryland Areas

Region	Traditional (q/ha)	Yield Crops	Efficient	Yield (q/ha)
Bellary	Cotton	2.0	Sorghum	26.7
Varanasi	Wheat	8.6	Chickpea	28.5
Ranchi	Upland Rice	28.8	Maize	33.6
Indore	Green gram,	11.8	Soybean	33.3
	Wheat	11.0	Safflower	24.2
Agra	Wheat	10.3	Mustard	20.4
Hisar	Wheat	3.0	Taramira	16.0
Udaipur	Maize	18.0	Hybrid sorghum	29.0

Dry land research has remained confined to important traditional crops such as sorghum, millet, pulse and oilseeds and has not explored the possibility of growing non-traditional crops such as dye-providing crops {*e.g.* Henna (Lawsonia inermis: mehadi) and jaffra(Bixa ovellana) species (*e.g.* cumin), and medicinal value crops (*e.g.* eitronella, lemon grass, senna and isabgol)}. These crops need to find an important place in research aagenda of dry land farming.

Time has come for the relevant researchers to plan a joint integrated research programme for maximizing the profitability, productivity and sustainability of learning systems of rainfed areas. Sericulture offers great promise in rainfed farming strategy, particularly of the watershed approach in peninsular India.

EFFICIENT CROPPING SYSTEM

Besides putting various measures to increase the productivity levels of dry land crops, efforts would also be needed to increase the cropping intensity in dry land areas which was generally 100 per cent, implying that a single crop was taken during the year. Cropping intensities of these areas could be increased by practice of inter cropping and multi cropping (sequential) by way of more efficient utilization of resources.

The cropping intensity would depend on the length of growing season which in turn depends on rainfall pattern and the soil moisture storage capacity of the soil. For example in Indore region, receiving 1000 mm annual rainfall, only single crop can be taken on shallow soils, inter cropping in medium depth soils and double cropping on deep soils. Similar crop combinations have been identified for different regions of the country. In dry land of Varanasi region upland rice-chickpea/lentil sequence can be practices with advantage.

Inter cropping of vegetables with grain crops was pursued vigorously in some centres such as Varanasi and Phulbani. At both the palces long duration pigeon pea was inter cropped with vehetables such as okra, radish and chilli. Such inter cropping systems would be very useful to get maximum returns from rainfall agriculture. Even at solapur, leafy vegetables and some short duration beans were grown as intercrops during the rainy season.

FERTILIZER USE

Soils of dry lands in the country are not only thirsty but hungry also because these soils are severely eroded horizontly as well as vertically. Whenever efforts are made towards bunding and levelling of the fields in dry land areas, it is the surface soil which is removed. The resultant effect is that the fields are rendered shallow in depth and completely deprived of plant nutrients, particularly nitrogen, phosphorus and potassium.

It is, therefore, necessary to apply all the three major nutrients in adequate amounts. Since soil moisture is limiting in dry lands, the availability of nutrients becomes limited, attempt should always be made to apply fertilizers in furrows below the seed. If seed-cum-fertilizer drills drawn by bullocks or tractors are available, this very objective can be fulfilled.

There has been belief among the farmers of dry land areas that use of fertilizer increases the chances of crop failure but recent findings have shown that the use of fertilizer is not only helpful in providing nutrients to crop but also helpful in efficient use of profile soil moisture (*See Table 1.4 on next page*). If dry land farmers are shown such results, they will be convinced to use ore and more fertilizers.

Studies on the management of legumes in crop sequences for their residual effect indicated that in alluvial soils an advantage of 25-30 kg N/ha could be obtained in barley or mustard grown after black gram or green gram. Another possibility for nitrogen management in cropping system is to use legumes as green manures either at flowering stage or after one picking. Studies conducted at Varanasi centres clearly showed that general yield levels of barley and mustard were greater when legumes raised in the previous season was incorporated I soil after first picking as compared to that harvested at normal maturity (*See Table*).

Table Effect of N-levels on Yield and Moisture Use Efficiency (MUE) of Barley and Wheat (Varanasi Centres)

Nitrogen Levels (kg/ha)	Grain Yield (q/ha)	Total Moisture use (mm)	MUE (kg/mm)
Barley			
0	14.05	133.7	10.5
30	20.45	136.3	15.0
60	30.00	142.3	21.0
90	37.20	141.6	26.3
Wheat			
0	9.55	145.5	6.6
30	13.55	144.4	9.3
60	18.35	153.6	11.9
90	24.15	155.1	13.6

In dry land areas, a proper mixing of organic and inorganic would be desirable. Organics have low nutrient content, but help to improve the moisture holding capacity of soils. In addition to yield advantage, nutrients like potassium help to increase drought tolerance by affecting plant-soil relationship. Transpiration losses are reduced and productivity per unit water increases.

Table Nitrogen Economy to Legume-Cereal System (4 years Average)

Nitrogen level (kg/ha)	Incorporated	Crop yield (q/ha) Unicorporated
Green Gram	1.89	2.23
Barley		
0	16.98	13.65
30	21.30	18.64
60	24.43	21.84
90	27.27	25.20

RAINWATER MANAGEMENT

Efficient management of rain water can boost agricultural production from dry lands. The broad bed and furrow system of the Inernational Crop Research Institute for the Semi Arid Tropics (ICRISAT) for managing rain water in vertisols made it possible to increase crop yields four to five times as compared to normal practice. However, this method could not be adopted widely by the farmers in India because it is costly and labour intensive. The vertical mulching developed at Bellary centres increases the infiltration of water in soil profiles and improves *in situ* moisture conservation. The scope for managing profile moisture is limited in alfisols but the surface run off in such soils can be reduced by ridge-and-furrow technique. Alternatively, application of compost and farm yard manure as well as raising legumes will add the organic matter to the soil and increase the water holding capacity.

The winter which is not retained by the soil flows out as surface run-off. The run-off-recycling holds immense prospects in deep black soils where the seepage losses are very much less. This run-off water, if not permitted to drain out safely, causes erosion.

Therefore, safe disposal of excess water from the field drains to the disposal system should be planned properly. This excess run-off water can also be harvested in storing dug out ponds and recycled to donor area in the event of severe moisture stress during rainy season or for raising crops during the winter.

WATER-SHED APPROACH FOR RESOURCE IMPROVEMENT AND UTILIZATION

Watershed management is a holistic approach arrived at optimizing the use of lad, water and vegetation in an area and thus, providing solution to alleviate drought, moderate folds, prevent soil erosion, improve water availability and increase fuel, fodder and agricultural production on a sustained basis. On the basis of the experiences of ICAR Operational research Projects, which attracted the attention of our farmers, State departments, administrators and scientists, 47 model watersheds were established during the year 1983 for development, jointly by the Ministry of Agriculture, ICAR and various State Government Department and Agricultural Universities, in 16 states and then the Department of Agriculture and Co-operation launched the National Watershed Development Project for Rainfall Areas (NWDPRA) covering almost the same states. Out of these 47 model watersheds, the Central research Institute for dryland Agriculture (CRIDA). Hyderabad has been entrusted with 30 watersheds. These activities were in micro and mini-watersheds covering 500-2000 ha.

Major components in these model watersheds are:

- Improvement of water resources;

- *In situ* soil and water conservation: rain water harvesting for safe disposal of surface run-off;
- Increase in cropping intensity; and
- Alternate land use system for efficient use of lands as per land capability to provide stability in productivity.

The model watersheds in operation have provided a fruitful experience of how development can lead to all round improvement in food and fodder production, economic condition of the farmers. Sakho-majori model, where creation of eater source worked as a catalyst and triggered the development process can be repeated under similar situations. Similar experiences have been gained a Tejpura (Jhansi), Ariel (Bareilly District) and Tejpura watersheds which have been awarded the First and Second Prizes respectively by the President of India on 14-11-1988 based on the recommendation of National Productivity Council.

ALTERNATE LAND USE SYSTEM

All dry lands are not suitable for crop production. Some lands may be suitable for range/pasture management, while others for tree farming, ley farming, dry land horticulture, agro-forestry systems including alley cropping. All these systems which are alternatives to crop production are called as alternate land use systems. This system not only helps in generating much needed off-season employment in mono crop dry land but also minimizes risk, utilizes off season rains which may otherwise go waste as run-off, prevents degradation of soils and restores balance in the ecosystem.

Crop production may be disastrous in the years of drought, whereas drought resistant grasses and trees could be remunerative. Scientists of dry land have developed many alternate land use systems which may suit different agro ecological situations. These are alley cropping, agri-horticultural system and silvi-pastoral systems which utilize the resources in better way for increased and stabilized production from dry lands.

- *Alley Cropping:* For imparting stability and providing sustainability to the farming system, a tree-cum-crop system will be one most appropriate for such situations. One such system called 'alley cropping' - a version of agro-forestry system, could meet the multiple requirements of food, fodder, fuel, fertilizer etc. Alley cropping is a system in which food crops are grown in alleys formed by hedge rows of trees or shrubs. The essential feature of the system is that hedge rows are cut back at planting and kept pruned during cropping to prevent shading and to reduce competition with food crops.

For example, fast growing leguminous trees such as *Leucaena leucocephala* or *liliricidia spp.* are planted in rows. During the cropping season, trees are lopped at about 0.5 metre height. These loppings are used as much to reduce moisture loss and improve the nutrient status of soil. Arable crops like maize, rice, pearl millet, legumes, oilseeds etc. are planted in the alleys formed by the two rows of threes. This is also known as agri-silvi culture. Alley cropping is also a form of conservation farming which enhances soil fertility and prevents erosion.

One very strong argument in favour of alley cropping is its ability to produce usable material even in years of severe drought. At Rajkot in 1985, rainfall received during the season was only 30 per cent of the normal. There was total failure of grain production of the three legume crops tried in the system. In sole crop plots production was limited to 5.0 q/ha to 17.0 q/ha of green fodder.

However, in alley cropped plots,- Leucaena hedge-rows produced over 50.0 q/ha of green fodder:

- *Agri-horticultural system:* Agri-horticultural system palys an important role in dry land areas, especially in semi-arid regions where production of annual crops is not only low but also highly unstable. Fruit trees if suitably integrated in dryland farming system could add significantly to overall agricultural production including food, fuel and fodder, conservation of soil and water and stability in production and income. Dry land fruit trees being deep rooted and hardy, can better tolerated monsoonal aberrations than short duration seasonal crops. Hence, in drought year when annual crops usually fail or their production is highly depressed, fruit trees species yield considerable food, fodder and fuel.

A suitable example of agri-horti-system is growing of cow pea/green gram/ horse gram in inter space of *ber (Zizyphus mauritiaria)* at 6 x 6 m spacing at Hyderabad. Phalsa (*Grewia asiatica*) may be planted in between two ber plants in a row with a view to intensify the system.

A well managed dry land orchard of *ber* should give 50 kg fruits per tree/ year. There should be 250 plants/ha for optimized production. The grow income would touch around ₹ 50,000/ha (250 × 50 × 4), assuming that one kg *ber* fetches ₹. 4.

One could get an additional income of ₹. 800-₹. 1000 from green gram/cow pea (2.5-3.0 q/ha):

- *Silvi-Pastoral System*: This system is suited to marginal dry lands and is most preferable where the fodder shortages are experienced frequently. The system essentially consists of a top feed tree species carrying grasses on legumes (preferable perennial) as understorey crops. Dry land farmers having larger holdings and keeping a land follow for a longer period for one reason on the other, should go in for this system which could provide both fodder and fuel. In a survey carried out in Andhra Pradesh, Karnataka and Maharashtra by CRIDA scientists, it was revealed that after food it is the fodder which is of paramount importance for sustaining animal wealth in rural areas. In years to come, fuel will assume greater importance.

In August, 1981 *Leucaena leucocephalla* was planted in contour trenches 7.5 m apart, the plant to plant spacing being maintained at 2.0 m at CRIDA. Four strips at upper reaches of plot (2% slope) were put under *Cenchrus ciliaris,* while lower four strips were seeded with *Stylosanthes hamata.* The system has come up very well.

EFFICIENT IMPLEMENTS

In order to take full advantage of annual precipitation in dry land agriculture, higher doses of energy input is essential. Farmers in dry lands have been using traditional and outdated farm equipments which not only perform poorly but also demand a lot of energy and time and post-harvest operations. Farm implements can help to conserve as much rain water *in situ* as possible and to harvest rain water. Shallow off season tillage with pre-monsoon showers ensures better moisture conservation and lesser weed intensity. It has resulted in 20 per cent yield increase in sorghum in Andhra Pradesh. Deep tillage helps in increasing water in soils having textural profiles and hard pan.

This has resulted in 10 per cent yield increase in sorghum and 9 per cent yield increase in case of caster. For in-situ moisture conservation, land has to be opened so that it can cause hurdle to flow of rain water. Tillage machines of appropriate size and type matching the power sources need to be used. Location specific seeders have been developed for dry land areas and these have shown good prospects and promise. A feature of these machines is that the seeds and fertilizers are placed in the moist zone of the soil resulting in a high percentage of seed germination and good crop vigour. In deciding farm mechanization in dry land areas, where farmers are generally poor, and their socio-economic condition should always be kept in mind.

The foregoing discussions show that technology of crop production in dry land areas have been generated to a great extent. What is important now is to view it in socio-economic context of the farmers. Once the technology is adopted by the farmers, the contribution of dry land areas to the total production can be sizably improved and the living standards of the farmers of these areas can be improved. This has been clearly shown in selected watershed areas and what is needed is to have more watersheds identified, proper technology to be developed and implemented.

CHARACTERISTICS OF DRYLAND AGRICULTURE

Dry land areas may be characterized by the following features:

- Uncertain, ill-.distributed and limited annual rainfall;
- Occurrence of extensive climatic hazards like drought, flood etc;

- Undulating soil surface;
- Occurrence of extensive and large holdings;
- Practice of extensive agriculture *i.e.* prevalence of monocropping etc;
- Relatively large size of fields;
- Similarity in types of crops raised by almost all the farmers of a particular region;
- Very low crop yield;
- Poor market facility for the produce;
- Poor economy of the farmers; and
- Poor health of cattle as well as farmers.

PROBLEMS OF DRY FARMING IN INDIA

The major problem which the farmers have to face very often is to keep the crop plants alive and to get some economic returns from the crop production. But this single problem is influenced by several factors which are briefly described below.

MOISTURE STRESS AND UNCERTAIN RAINFALL

According to definition the dry farming areas receive an annual rainfall of 500 mm or even less. The rains are very erratic, uncertain and unevenly distributed. Therefore, the agriculture in these areas has become a sort of gamble with the nature and very often the crops have to face climatic hazards. The farmers also take up farming halfheartedly as they are not sure of being able to harvest the crops. Thus, water scarcity becomes a serious bottleneck in dry land agriculture.

EFFECTIVE STORAGE OF RAIN WATER

According to characteristics of dry farming, either there will be no rain at all or there will be torrential rain with very high intensity. Thus, in the former case the crops will have to suffer a severe drought and in the latter case they suffer either flood or waterlogging and they will be spoilt In case of very heavy downpour, the excess water gets lost as run-off which goes to the ponds and ditches etc. This water could be stored for providing life saving or protective irrigation to the crops grown in dry land areas. The loss of water takes place in several ways namely run-off, evaporation, uptake through weeds etc. The water could be stored for short period or long period and it can be preserved either in soil, pond or ditches based on situation and utilized for irrigation during dry periods.

DISPOSAL OR DRY FARMING PRODUCTS

In dry farming all the farmers grow similar crops which are drought resistant. These crops mature at the same time and the growers like to dispose off their products soon after the harvest. This results in a glut of products in the market and the situation is badly exploited by the grain traders and middlemen. Therefore, marketing becomes a serious problem in dry farming areas.

SELECTION OR LIMITED CROPS

Only drought resistant crops namely oilseeds, pulses and coarse grains like jowar, bajra, millets etc. can be grown in dryland areas. Thus, the farmers have to purchase other food grains and household commodities that unbalance their economic position.

CAREFUL AND JUDICIOUS MANURIAL SCHEDULING

In case of irrigated farming the farmers are at a liberty to apply [manures and fertilizers according to their availability and facility but in case of dry farming they have to be very careful in fertilizer application. Due to lack of available moisture, broadcasting or top dressing becomes wasteful and meaningless. These can be applied ' by only deep placement and foliar spray for an improved crop production.

UTILIZATION OF PRESERVED MOISTURE

Judicious and purposeful utilization of preserved moisture water depends upon soil type, plant type and other factors. The amount of available water to the plants depends upon the depth of plant roots, their proliferation and density. In case of limited moisture condition, the yield directly depends upon the rooting depth.

The rooting depth can be desirably increased by mechanical manipulation of the soil. If the planting is very dense and all the plants have same kind of rooting then there will be a tough competition among roots for moisture and scarce moisture condition will result in the wilting of plants. Therefore, utilization of preserved moisture is an art in dry farming. The water collected in ponds or brooks may be used to give protective or life saving irrigation.

The widely spaced crops can be intercropped with oilseeds or pulses for increasing the productivity of the land per unit area and per unit time. Therefore, the water., collected during the rainy season need special technique and skill for its efficient utilization.

QUALITY OR THE PRODUCE

The quality of the produce from dry farming areas is often found to be inferior as the grains are not fully developed or they are not filled properly; often mixed with other crop seeds owing to mixed cropping system prevalent in these areas and the fodder become more fibrous. All these factors reduce the market value of produce and the farmers do not get the profit of their labour and Investment.

WORK ON DRY FARMING IN INDIA

As it has already been stated, that crop production is highly risky in arid and semi-arid climates. In such conditions generally two types of agriculture is practised. One is crop production or arable farming and the other is mixed farming *i.e.* animal husbandry together with crop production and pasture management. But this type of agriculture holds true only in those countries where the population is limited and agricultural land is extensive such as Australia, South Africa and some states of the USA. In India, with high population and limited available land for agriculture, we have no other option than adopting arable farming.

The repeated and frequent crop failure in the past, resulting in short food grain supply, attracted the attention of our scientists and administration. Thus the scarcity of food grains in India were made the subject of enquiry in the year 1880 and the first Famine Commission was appointed in the same year. The commission after thorough study of the situation recommended the establishment of protective irrigation projects in South India and formation of department of agriculture in all the states. But nothing could be done till 1923 when the first systematic and scientific approach to the dry farming problem in India was made.

Thus, as a beginning, Bombay research scheme on dry farming was started in 1934 at Solapur and Bijapur after the establishment of Indian Council of Agricultural Research (ICAR) a. New Delhi in 1929. After some time the work on dry farming was started in Punjab, Madras and Hyderabad. Dry farming work in U.P. started in Jhansi and Agra at dry farming centres established—1943-44 and 1948-50, respectively. Since then the work has been in progress. Crop improvement brought out very promising strains during sixties which received our interest in finding out ways and means through which the crop production can be maximized in semi-arid and periodically dry areas of the country. Keeping this in view, the ICAR launched the All India Coordinated Research Project for Dry Land Agriculture in 1970 which was in active collaboration with government of Canada.

The project started with multi disciplinary research units at 23 coordinating research centres located in various typical agro climatic regions of India with Hyderabad as headquarter. The project started with the identification of the constraints responsible for lower yields in different regions: and then to develop a relevant location specific research programme to solve production constraints. Presently a joint team of senior scientists of India and Canada is working at Hyderabad.

To make the programmes more effective it is expanded to 16 agro-economic research centres. These centres have been established with an obvious objective of accelerating the conservation development and efficient, long term use of basic resources of soil and water for a self sustaining production.

The main areas of investigations of these centres are given below:

- Identification of different crops and selection of high yielding varieties for different agro-climatic zones of the country.
- Developing cropping sequences and cropping systems suitable for dry farming.
- Determining the optimal crop population and planting pattern.
- Evaluating tillage implements and practices for water intake and storage in the soil profile, establishment of better crop stand and control of weeds.
- Designing and developing animal drawn implements for speedy and efficient cultural operations.
- Evaluating use of surface mulches, both organic and inorganic for short term moisture conservation.
- Determining ideal fertilizer doses and improving fertilizer use efficiency.
- Testing new planting materials for introduction/substitution after they have proved their superiority over existing ones. -Harvesting and storing inevitable run off and recycling it as life saving or protective irrigation.
- Developing strategies for rneeting the challenges of an aberrant weather like skip or catch cropping etc.

PRINCIPAL DRY FARMING ZONES

Almost all the states have some area under rainfed culture depending upon topography and irrigation facilities, but only the major dry farming areas are discussed here.

THE INDO-GANGETIC PLAINS OF NORTH INDIA

This zone is the youngest in the geological formation. This zone includes districts of Rajasthan, Punjab, Haryana, North- western M.P., and V.P. This zone is characterized by two major soil types namely light loam and heavy loam. The land is nearly levelled with a modest slope of 2 ft/mile length. The soils are very deep and situated at about 700 to 800 ft. above sea level. Because of heavy sand and silt fractions in the soil it has large pore spaces. The soils are rich in essential nutrients like nitrogen, phosphorus, potash, calcium etc. and, therefore, quite good for raising the crop excepting few with high water requirements. The cropping intensity, in this zone, stands around 120 per cent and the major crops which are grown in this zone are millets, cereals, oil seeds and pulses.

As far as rainfall pattern in this zone is concerned, it is observed that about 60 per cent or more of the total rainfall is observed between the end of July to the end of August, and the rainfall in remaining months is quite poor.

Thus, due to very high intensity of rainfall, floods are of frequent occurrence during the first week of September followed by a long spell of drought subsequently.

THE TRAPIAN PLATEAU OF PENINSULAR INDIA

This zone comprises the states of Maharashtra, Karnataka and Andhra Pradesh. The soil of this zone has been derived from the Deccan trap.The tract is undulating and consists of low ridges and valleys due to erosion which results in rapid run-off. About 40 per cent of the land of this zone is not fit for cultivation. This tract is situated; at an elevation of 1400 -2(XX) feet from sea level. The soil may be grouped into three types based on its depth as deep. medium deep and shallow soils.

Leaching of lime has resulted in the formation of lime nodules or kanker on the surface soil. The soil is quite rich in total and available nitrogen. phosphorus and potash which favours production of crops if moisture is efficiently conserved.

In this zone. two high peaks of rain are observed because the area is affected by both south-west monsoon as well as northeast i monsoon. About 40-55 per cent of total annual rainfall is obtained from south-west monsoon and the rest from north-east monsoon. Mostly the millets and some oil seeds like groundnut. are grown in this zone.

PLATEAU OF GRANITE FORMATION

The soils of this zone are grouped as red soils and black cotton soils. Red soils are shallow while black cotton soils are very deep like clayey soils. The topography is of gentle undulations which favour run-off and soil erosion. The high pore space and high swelling of soil obstruct the permeability of rain water in to the lower layers of soil and its shrinkage results in hardening and clod formation on the surface which is unfavourable for plant growth. The red laterite and black cotton soils are deficient in nitrogen and phosphoric acids.

This zone also gets rain from two months namely south-west and north-east and the distribution pattern is more or less like peninsular group. Upland rice, millets, ragi, are the main crops of this zone. However. the yield of these crops is very low.

STEPS FOR RAISING PRODUCTIVITY IN DRY FARMING

To boost the crop production under dry farming, we will have to efficiently manage our soil and water resources in the respective areas as dry land fanning gets more complex and intractable when droughts occur frequently. An efficient soil and water conservation system will play a vital role in boosting the crop yield in dry fanning. The different interdisciplinary approaches which are recommended for dry land farming are categorized in to four major groups namely engineering, physiological, genetic and agronomic approaches.

ENGINEERING APPROACHES

These approaches are aimed at soil and moisture conservation through regulation of run-off, collection of surplus rain water checking evaporation and seepage losses of water. and recycling of collected water as irrigation in times of critical need.

Contouring Across the Slope

Contouring is practiced on the lands with 3-5 per cent slope. This system consists of constructing earthen bunds and the distance between the two bunds ranges from 30-50 m depending on the degree of slope. This is carried out with an object to provide a check to the flow of run-off water which then gets accumulated in the bunded area and is absorbed by the soil. Thus, contour bunding conserves moisture and prevents soil erosion.

Smoothening of Contour Inter-bund Areas

This is practiced only in those areas which have a slope of less than one per cent The smoothening may be achieved by running bullock drawn harrows or cultivators but small undulations are leveled during the process so that impounding of water may take place and maximum water absorption by the soil may be achieved.

Contour Border Strips Method

This method is suitable for areas having a slope of 3-4 per cent In this case parallel strips across the slope ranging from 10-15 m in width are laid down on contours and the soil surface is leveled by scrapping and placing the soil according to the need of the spot It is done to reduce the run-off and to conserve soil and water from the field. It is, however, an expensive method as it requires culling and filling up the soil from higher spots to lower ones.

Scooping or Land

In this practice, the land is generally scooped before the beginning of monsoon showers. By scooping, the soil is exposed for proper absorption and conservation of moisture. However, this is also a tedious as well as an expensive operation.

Opening or Ridges and Furrows

In this practice, the entire land is laid out into ridges and furrows across the slope. The ridges and furrows are opened before onset of monsoon so that the flow of water may be reduced and erosion may be controlled to the minimum. During rainy season, crops like maize, jowar, bajra, etc. may be grown in the furrows and legumes like soybean, arhar, urd, mung, cowpea, etc. may be grown on the ridges. After the monsoon is over the land is again levelled. This way the furrows are used to accumulate maximum water which will supply moisture for winter season crops.

Compartmental Bunding

Areas having a slope of 1% or less are suitable for compartmental bunding. It helps in accumulation of more water and a uniform spread of water in the entire area. Levelling is also done with nominal or no additional expenditure.

Bedding System

In this system, small furrows are opened and the soil from the furrows is uniformly spread in space left between the furrows. Thus, inter furrow spaces form the raised beds of about 4-5 metres width. This method helps in the conservation of soil, moisture and checking the excess run-off of water.

The raised beds, in this practice, are used for growing such crops which need less water like legumes and oil seed crops, while the furrows are used for the crops which need more water.

Broadbased Bunding

This method is especially suitable for heavy black soil. Water is allowed to spread over a vast area by constructing a broadbased bund on a sloppy side. The water stays for a longer time because of high water holding capacity, lower leaching and seepage losses.

The stored water may be used for fish culture and also for providing life saving irrigation grown in surrounding areas of catchment portion. These bunds are also called check dams and are given a regulated drain or outlet for protecting the bunds from breaking.

Deep Summer Ploughing Followed by Surface Tilling

The field is ploughed deep by mould hard plough soon after harvesting rabi season crop with the objectives of:

- Exposing the soil for perfect drying;
- Killing the disease pathogens;
- Destroying eggs of insect pests; and
- Controlling weeds by sun drying. The surface tilling during other seasons forms natural mulch and thereby reduces evaporation loss of water from soil.

Water Harvesting

Water harvesting is a technology of utilizing the collected and conserved water for the purpose of crop production. It includes tillage practices for an efficient use of moisture between and within the crop rows. Frequent stirring of the land by surface tilling provides mulch and prevents the evaporation loss of water from the soil. Besides harvesting moisture from between and within the crop rows, run off losses are considerably reduced. The store water is used for providing life sowing irrigation to the crops grown in the surrounding areas. The water harvesting of this type can be done in areas situated near hill and on greatly undulated lands.

In these cases, check dam tanks, and other reservoirs are constructed. The infiltration or percolation loss of water is prevented by spraying of asphalt compounds or by covering the bottom of the tanks or ponds through thin plastic sheets. The seepage loss may also be checked by providing a plastic lining. The evaporation loss of water is controlled by pouring some burnt crude oil over water surface.

On a highly eroded soil or soils having very high slopes, terraces are made for providing a gentle flow of run off water so that the soil is not further eroded and some crop may be grown on these terraces.

PHYSIOLOGICAL APPROACHES

Hardly one per cent of the water absorbed by the plant roots is used for the growth and development of plants and remaining 99 per cent is wasted through transpiration back to atmosphere. Thus one of the greatest causes of soil water wastage is loss of water through transpiration.

The extent of transpiration can be greatly influenced by using certain chemicals. These chemicals reduce transpiration, encourage root growth and protect the cytoplasmic proteins of the plants. These chemicals bring about more drought resistance in the plants. These compounds, according to their role, are classified as given below.

Anti-transpirants

Any chemical substance, which reduces rate of transpiration on its application to the plant surface, is called anti-transpirant. Any substance which reduces the vapour pressure gradient in the stomatal cavity or increases stomatal resistance to water vapour diffusion, will act as anti-transpirant These substances have been used for arresting water loss from plant body with various degree of success. These are Phenylmercuric Acetate (PMA), Hydroxy Sulphonates (HS), Alkenyl Succinic Acid (ASA), Adol:-52 (a formulation of alcohol), and S-600 (a plastic transplanting spray).

Chemicals for Improved Cell Membrane Permeability of Water

Dry fanning areas are characterized by scarce rainfall and usually the roots have lipid layers which lower the absorption of water from the roots. Some chemicals like Alkenyl Succinic Acid (ASA) and Decenyl Succinic Acid (DSA), when applied, penetrate into the root and increase its water absorption power 8 times. Therefore, these chemicals are applied in the root zone for increased water absorption along with some chemicals to retard the transpiration from foliage.

Use of Plant Hormones and Growth Retardants

Some plant hormones like Indole acetic acid (IAA) and Abscissic acid (ABA) may be used for reducing the frequency and period of stomatal opening thereby minimizing the water loss from the plant body.

There are certain other chemicals known as growth retardants which either modify the plant structure or dwarf the plants by considerably reducing the total water requirement of the plants. The most important chemical of this group is cycocel or CCC (2- chlorocthyl trichloromethyl ammonium chloride). This chemical t\ also induces moisture stress tolerance in plants. Cycocel is presently used in cotton to encourage production of more fruiting branches (sympodial rather than monopodial or vegetative branches) and, Ii thereby even under drought condition it results in higher yield. In case of wheat, the use of Cycocel decreases the cell size and increases the density of the cytoplasm which ultimately results into a drought resistance into the plants.

Use of Chemicals

There are certain chemicals which are used for seed treatment to bring about drought resistance in plants right from seedling stage. Soaking of seeds in calcium chloride solution (0.25 per cent) for 20 hours soaking of seeds with frequent shaking results in better germination and drought resistance in the plants.

Boron solution is also used for soaking seeds. Agrosan is a fungicide but also induces drought resistance in the plants when seeds are treated with this chemical.

GENETIC APPROACHES

Because of scanty and unreliable rains the farmers of dry farming areas are still practicing crop husbandry on the basis of traditional approaches like low intensity cropping, little or no use of fertilizers or manures, raising low value crops. Crop varieties grown till the recent past were generally of long duration and slow growing. They were poor yielders too.

As nearly 70 per cent of our total agricultural land is rainfed and 45 per cent -of rainfed area is dryland, there is no way out but to evolve suitable varieties as well as appropriate technology for getting the most from our rainfed or dryland areas.

As such, the concerted efforts of our plant breeders have resulted in the cultivation of several new plant types which possess all the characters needed for rainfed areas or dry lands. In terms of modem technology, such plant materials are called 'Ideo types'. These are the suitable strains of dry land crops which are characterized by short growth duration, effective and extensive root system, drought tolerance, high yield potential having altered morphology of plants which are conducive to dry lands.

According to breeders, an ideal 'Ideo type" should have following qualities to give desired results in dry farming:

- Early in growth duration and early vigour.
- Deeper root system with maximum branching at deeper zones.
- Dwarf plant types with lesser number of erect leaves.
- Moderate tillering; as profuse tillering causes competition. Very Good expression of ear heads even at higher planting density.
- Resistance to diseases.
- Bolder grains with moderate dormancy in them.
- Effective photosynthetic behaviour with greater sink capacity.

The following are some of the crop varieties recommended for commercial cultivation in different regions.

Black Cotton Soils

Jhansi Region

Sorghum -CSH-5, CSH-6, Spy -370
Pigeonpea -T-21, Pusa Ageti
Groundnut -Chandra \
Green gram -Kopergon
Maize -Satha, Diara
Soyabean -Ankur, J-231
Pearl millet -BJ-I04

Rajkot Region

Sorghum -CSH-6
Black gram -T-9
Green gram -Gujarat -2
Sesamum -Purva -1
Sunflower -EC-68414 f:
Pearl millet -J-1399

Akola Region "

Cotton -DHY -286, H-4, AKH-4,5
Sorghum -CSH-1,5,9, SPV-I02
Pigeon pea -C-ll,T-21
Green gram -Kopergaon, T-44
Black gram -T-9
Groundnut -JL-24
Sunflower -EC -68414
Safflower -N- 7-

Solapur Region

Pearl millet -BJ- 104, BK-560, Rahuri-

Foxtail millet *(Setaria italica)* Arjun, IS-279-
Groundnut -M-13,TMV-I0,SB-ll JIIJ-;:'(Jreengram -S-8,J- 781
Sunflower -EC-69874, EC-68414
Sorghum -M-35-1, SPY-86, CSH-8R
Safflower -Tara, N-628, Bhima (S-4)
Bengal gram -Chafa, N-59

Indore Region

Maize -Ganga-5, Satha
Sorghum -CSH-5, CSH-6
Pigeon pea -No. 148, Khargone-2, HY-4 Soyabean -Bragg,
JS- 72-44, Ankur
Groundnut -AK-12-24, Jyoti
I Sunflower -JSN-l
Wheat -Narmada-4, Narmada-112, Swati
I Bengal gram -Ujjain 21,24

Rewa Region

Rice (uplands) -DR-92, IR-28, Cauvery
Rice (low lands) -Ratna, Jaya
Soyabean -J-231,JS-17, Black soyabean Sorghum -CSH-l, CSH-5, 604,
Swarna Pigeonpea -T-21, BS-l, Prabhat,JA-17
Green gram -ML-5, Jawahar-45
Groundnut -Jawahar, Jyoti, M-13, J-.J 1
Wheat -C-3~,Narmada-4,112,Lok-l,Sujata, Swati
Bengal gram. -BG-200, H-208, Pink-2
Linseed -T-397, R-157

Bijapur Tegion

Green gram -PS-16 Black gram -K-3
Cowpea -C-152
Pigeon pea.C-28, PE-221
Cotton -Suyodhar
Sorghum -M-35-l
Bengal gram -A-I

Udaipur Region

Maize -Ganga -5, Ganga-2
Sorghum -CSH-5, Spy -245
Pigeonpea -Gwaliar-3, Hyderabad-l, Hyderabad-4
Green gram -S-9, Pusa Baisakhi, K-851
Black gram -T-9
Cowpea -C-152

Safflower -N-62-8, JSF-2, JSF-5
Mustard -Durga Mani, T -59, Prakash
Bengal gram -C-235, Dohad, BG-203
Wheat -Narmada-4, Narmada-l 12, MP-175
Linseed -Chambal

Rabi Black Soils

Bellari region
Sorghum -SPV-86, M-35-l I
Safflower -S-144, A-300
Bengal gram -A-I, N-52
Cowpea -CO- 7, CO-8

Alluvial Soils

Agra Region

Pearl millet -BJ-l04
Black gram.T-9
Green gram -T -44, Jawahar -45
Pigeon pea.Pusa Ageti, T -21
Cow pea -C-152
Groundnut -T-64
Safflower -A-300, JSF-5
Barley -RS-6, Ratna I Mustard -T-59, RT-16, Bengal gram - G-24, G-130

Varanasi Region

Rice -Aka5hi, Cauvery, Ratna
Maize -Ganga safed-2, Ganga-5
Pearl millet -Jaunpuri, NHB -3-4, BJ-I04
Black gram -T-9, H-I0, B-76
Green gram -Varsha, K-851, PS-16, T-44 Sesamum -T-13, T-4, T-12
Pigeon pea -T -21
Wheat -C-306, Malviya-12
Barley -DL-3, K-125, Ratna
Bengal Gram -T-l, T-3, T-6, BG-l, BG-2 Mustard -T-59, T-5909
Linseed -T -397, Neelum, Mukta

Semi Arid Red Soils

Anantpur Region

Pearl millet -BJ-I04
Sorghum -CSH-5, SPV-I04
Castor -Aruna

Pigeonpea -PDM-l
Groundnut -TMV-2, Kadiri-l, Kadiri-3

Hyderabad Region

Sorghum -CSH-5, CSH-6
Pigeonpea -Hy-2 and 4

Subhumid Red Soils

Bhubaneswar Region

Upland rice -Subhadra, Parijat, CRM-13-32 41
Green gram -Kopcrgaon, K-8S1, PS-16
Pigeonpea -R-60,Kanka-9,T-21
Cowpea -C-20, C-170, FS-68
Groundnut -M-13,Polachi-1,NG-386
Maize -A-S1-S4, Jawahar, Diara

Ranchi Region I

Rice -Bala, Brown Gora, Kiran
Sorghum -CSH-S, CSH-6
Maize -Ganga safed-2
Arhar -BR-6S, Laxmi, BR-183
Groundnut -AK-12-24
Sesamum -Kanke white
Wheat -C-306, Kalyansona,HD-238S and2402
Barley -BR-1, BR-32, Ratna, K-12S –
Lentil -Pant-209, PL-8, Pant-406
Linseed -T-397, LC-267
Green gram -Sunaina
Black gram -Madhu, BR-10

Sierozemic Soils I

Anand Region

Pearl millet -CJ-104, BJ-104
Sorghum -CSH-S, CSH-6
Green gram -Gujarat-1
Tobacco -Gujarat-4, Anand-2

Hissar Region

Pearl millet -BJ-104 C",
Sorghum -CSH-S, CSH-6 '
Green gram -5-9

Moth -T-2
Castor -Aruna
Bengal gram -H-208, C-214, C-235
Barley -RD-56, Jyoti, C-138
Mustard -RH-30, RL-18

Sub Mountain Soils

Debra Dun Region

Maize -Ganga -2, Ganga -5, Vikram
Rice -RP-79-5,DR-92, CR-142-3-2
Soybean -Bragg, Pb-1, Semmi
Arhar -Prabhat, T-21, Pant A-3
Wheat -.HD-1981, HD-2009, HD -2021
Barley -PL-56, PL-142, PL-133

Hoshiarpur Region

Wheat -WL-410, WL-711, C-306
Bengal gram -C-235 Rai -RL-18

Rakh Dhinsar Region

Maize -GS-2
Bajra -BJ-104
Green gram -R-286-8
Mash -Pant U-26
Wheat -WL-410, IWP-72
Gram -C-235
Mustard -RLM -198,':. Lentil -T-36,";';' Pea -PG-2:i,'-

AGRONOMIC APPROACHES

The major objective of dry farnlingprogramme is to conserve the soil and moisture and to achieve maximum production from the dry farnling areas. In the past two decades, we have been able to' solve many hurdles in the aforesaid areas but there had been no break through as in case of irrigated crop production. Now we have the promising crop varieties and technology available with us about the maximum soil and water conservation.

The agronomic approaches can be dealt with under the following four heads based on land types.

Agronomic Approaches for Highly Undulating Lands

These lands are confined to the hills of the locations which have suffered serious soil erosion problems and have been divided into various gullies. The soils of these areas are more prone to further erosion if they are not properly managed. Therefore, in this category, the crop management practices are entirely different from other areas.

The object of soil and crop management under such situation should be:

- To stabilize the soil by forestry and pasture management with a regulated grazing or no grazing at all.
- To level the land gradually through contour bunding, terracing, etc.
- To practise strip cropping and pitcher farming.

Agronomical Approaches for Marginal Lands

Generally, marginal lands are very poor in fertility. The crop management in these lands is carried out in lines of crop management for leveled lands or flat lands which will be discussed later in this chapter.

Agronomical Approaches for Diara Lands

Diara lands are located on either side of rivers or between two rivers and are often flooded by these rivers. These diara lands are formed due to flood and may have deposition of fine to coarse sands.

These areas often lack irrigation and need a careful crop management. Since the land of this areas is highly susceptible to floods, kharif cropping is practically impossible.

But certain fodder crops can easily be grown soon after the onset of monsoon and harvested depending upon position of floods. The harvesting or cutting of crops is started from close to the river beds and as the water spreads the harvesting is also advanced. The life saving irrigations can be given by lifting water from the river or by drilling cavity wells or bam boo borings. However, in most of the cases these wells go out of order after a flood occurs. Therefore, the cavity wells or bamboo borings are made at a distant location from river stream.

Agronomical Approaches for Plain Lands

Plain lands form the main dry land tracts of the country. There has been major emphasis on finding out ways and means through which the total soil productivity could be increased. Following recommendations should be followed on plain lands for an improved crop productivity and an efficient soil and water conservation.

Tillage Requirements of the Crops

Tillage starts with the seed red preparation and ends with mulching and control of weeds. Deep ploughing during summer helps in destroying weeds and suppressing insect pests and diseases. It also helps in an efficient root penetration very deep into soil Placement of seed at 5 cm and fertilizers at 7.5 cm in the same furrow followed by soil compaction have resulted in better germination, plant vigour, extensive root development and higher crop yields.

Selection or Crops and Varieties

There are a number of improved varieties of different crops which are drought tolerant or resistant to water stress. The most commonly grown crops in dry lands are rice, maize, sorghum, pearl millet. finger millet, wheat, barley, pulses, oilseeds, etc. The improved varieties of these crops have already been described area-wise.

Sowing or Crops

Sowing of crops deals with several associated factors namely sowing time, method of sowing, depth of sowing etc. It is important in the sense that once the ideal plant population is achieved. the crop is bound to give yield.

Sowing time can markedly influence the production and productivity of dry land crops. Early sowing of kharif crops results in early crop maturity and thereby it facilitates early sowing of succeeding rabi crops. Early sowing of rabi crops helps in overcoming the moisture stress at later stages of plant growth, particularly at grain filling stage.

Broadcasting of seeds should be avoided as it involves several losses and seed does not properly come in contact with moisture. Placing the seeds at about 5 cm depth through pora or seed drill is desirable.

To get an ideal plant population it is necessary that about 25 per cent higher than required seed rate should be applied. Care must be taken to reduce plant competition for moisture by removing excess plant population about 2-3 weeks after the sowing depending upon the crops.

Fertilizer Management

Use of fertilizers in dry lands is limited as compared to irrigated areas. Today we use on 'an average only 60kg/ha fertilizers in dry fanning areas as against 60 kg/ ha national average.

Reasons for application of fertilizers in dry fanning are as follows:

- Poor response because of faulty method of application;
- Poor financial condition of fanners to purchase fertilizer;
- Wrong concept of the fanners that fertilizers will burn the seedlings, and harm to the soil; and
- Application of organic manure only, which can not meet the total nutrient requirement of the crop.

There are different Schools of thoughts about the application of fertilizers in the dry lands. Some people think that application of fertilizers in dry lands results in a better crop yield than that in irrigated areas because in the latter case the soil becomes very poor in residual fertility due to high intensity of cropping, whereas, the dry lands still preserve nutrients as they are not depleted badly due to low cropping intensity. Some people think that fertilizer application in dry lands aggravates the moisture problem, but truly speaking deep placement of fertilizers followed by foliar application results in extensive rooting up to deeper soil layers where the plants extract moisture to meet their demands.

Spreading of fertilizers at the surface or applying them at the seed layer is not so beneficial. Therefore, a careful and judicious fertilizer scheduling is a must frr achieving higher and better crop productivity in dry lands.

Use of organic manures is always desirable but they alone are not enough as—they can not supply nutrients at the required speed and dose. Therefore, atleast half of the nutrient requirement of the crop must be met by readily available source of nutrient *i.e.* fertilizers. This also improves water use efficiency.

Following points should be considered to improve the fertility status of dry lands.

- Green manuring should be practised in kharif season.
- Inclusion of a legume crop in rotation adds about 20-25 kg of nitrogen per hectare, reduces cost of fertilization and increases crop productivity.
- Inoculation of legumes through Rhizobium culture and nonlegumes with Azotobactor adds about 30-35 kg of nitrogen per hectare.
- Foliar application of urea having lowest biuret content along with micro-nutrient fertilizers like zinc sulphate will increase grain yields in dry farming.
- Growing forage legumes in rotation with pearl millet in kharif season will provide a better condition for rabi crop.

Therefore, proper fertilizer scheduling will help the farmers to induce drought tolerance/resistance in the crops and provide higher yields.

Cropping Systems

Cropping system refers to an arrangement in which various crops are grown together in the same field. The cropping systems followed in dry lands differ from those followed under normal conditions. Only those crops can be grown under dry land conditions which require less water to complete their life cycle or which can stand or yield under drought conditions. This can include both drought resistant and drought tolerant plants. In addition, plants can be grown only where some water is available to sustain the growth of plants.

Following are a few intercropping systems for dryland areas:

- Moong + Bajra
- Guar + Bajra
- Til + Guar/moth/mung

Mixed cropping is also followed to minimize the effect of unpredictability of rain. Mixed cropping may have low yield potential but it works as a buffer against failure under possible unfavourable conditions. Mixed cropping may be defined as sowing of two or more crops simultaneously on the same piece of land in separate rows. Examples: Guar + Arhar + Moong, Bajra + Arhar + Moong and Maize + Urd etc.

Cropping Pattern

Cropping pattern is defined as sequence of growing crops in a particular field at a particular period. The most common cropping pattern for dry land farming are discussed below:

For North Indian Conditions

- Sorghum -Safflower/mustard
- Sorghum –Mung/urd/cowpea -Gram/wheat -Gram
- Rice -Gram (for low lying areas)
- Bajra -Gram + Linseed
- Bajra + Urd/Mung/soyabean -Wheat/barley +
- Gram/m ustard
- Maize-Gram/safflower

For Central Indian Condition

- Green gram -Rabi sorghum
- Green gram -Safflower

For Bhubaneswar Region

- Rice -Horse gram
- Ragi -Red gram
- Groundnut -Niger
- Maize-Niger

Weed Control

Presence of weeds in the crop field, especially in case of dry lands, cause a severe crop weed competition for water, nutrients and light The reduction in yield due to weeds varies from 30-75 per cent depending upon the crop and nature and extent of weed infestation. Weeds may be controlled by hand weeding, intercultural operations and herbicidal application or by adopting an integrated approach.

Plant Protection Measures

In light textured soils of arid and semi arid regions termites and white grubs cause extensive damage to emerging seedlings and also to grown up plants. Use of BHC 10 per cent dust@ 25-30 kg or Aldrin 5 per cent dust@ 10-15 k/ha, in the soil and incorporating it well into the soil at the time of the last ploughing will control termites. The white grubs may be controlled by drilling of Thimet 200 granules @ 15 k/ha along with seeds. Aphids in mustard are very destructive, therefore, they are controlled by spraying 0.2

per cent Metasystox or Dimecron. Similarly, the pod borers in pulses are controlled by spraying 0.05 per cent Endosulfon.

The viral diseases of pulses should be controlled by seed treatment and spray of some fungicides to kill the insect vectors.

AGRO-FORESTRY AND DRYLAND AGRICULTURE

Agroforestry is the cultivation of trees in association with crops. It has assumed a great importance in order to solve a number of problems of dryland farmers. The twin objectives of Agroforestry are to increase the farmers income and sustain the ecological! Environmental balance. Agroforestry, as it provides fuel wood to the fanners, enables them to save the animal dung and use it as manure.

The following points should be considered while choosing trees for cultivation in association with crops:

- The tree should grow fast and stand repeated prunings.
- Its roots should explore soil layers not tapped by agricultural crops.
- The crown should not be too large to prevent sun light from reaching the crop.
- The peak period of flush and leaf faII should not be detrimental to the crop grown in association.
- As far as possible, the tree species should be a legume, the root nodules of which accommodate nitrogen manufacturing bacteria.
- The branching should be sparse and light.
- The tree should meet the socio-economic and ecological needs of the region.

Some agro-forestry combinations are given for the main dry fanning areas of the country.

Trees suitable for growing in association with crops in different dry land regions are given below:

- *For north-western arid and semi arid zones*: Prosopis cineraria (khejri), Zizyphus mauriliana (jujube), Acacia IOrlilis(israely babool),Leucaena leucocephala (su-babool), Acacia auriculiformis.
- *For Central arid Vindhyan zone*: Acacia nilolica var. cuprissiformis, Punica granalwn (anar).Kinnow (citrus), Psydiwn guajava (guava).
- *South eastern regions*: Acacia albida, Acacia ferruginea, Prosopis cineraria, Leucaena leucocephala.
- *Himalayan regions*: Alnus neplensis (utis), Sehima wallichianum, Citrus species, Sesbania sesban, Prosopsis juliflora

RECOMMENDATIONS FOR DRY FARMING AREAS

The research programmes of all India coordinated research projects for dry land agriculture have concluded into certain recommendations to the farmers of dry land areas which are described below:

- Bunding across the slope and levelling the land should be done before onset of monsoon.
- Deep summer ploughing should be followed by surface tillage during monsoon months and also rest of the year.
- Application of organic manures like FYM compost. etc. @ 15-20 tonnes/ha or green manuring should be done. These manures should be applied about 20-25 days before sowing and should be well mixed in the soil.
- Fertilizers should be basal placed at a depth of 7.5 to 10cm in the soil and the seeds should be sown in the same furrows about 3 cm. above the fertilizers. This is important especially during winter season. The nitrogen (20-50% of total) should be top dressed by side or band placement method at about 10- 15 cm apart. The crop rows should be done soon after the rains but if there is not sufficient moisture in the soil, the nitrogen should betrayed over the foliage with urea solution containing 3-5 per cent nitrogen. Zinc and sulphur should be applied as basal if needed.
- Soil application of BHC (10%) dust @ 25-30 kg/ha for termites and Thimet 20 G @ 15 kg/ha for white grub should be done. These chemicals must be mixed with soil properly while ploughing or at the time of sowing.
- Selection of suitable crops and their varieties should be done according to their suitability to a particular region/micro climate.
- Seeds must be treated with a suitable fungicide and that of legume with Rhizobium culture before sowing. Soaking seeds in plain water for rabi sowing helps in getting higher germination, better seedling vigour and an early maturity within weeks time.
- Proper crop rotation should be followed which should preferably have at least one legume every year.
- For better seed soil moisture contact through soil compaction should be done by running a plank or roller especially for rabi crop.
- At the event of total crop failure during kharif season a suitable catch crop like urd (T-9) or toria etc should be sown.
- Intercropping of oil seeds and pulses should be done with jowar, bajra and maize crops for the purpose of making best use of soil and inter row moisture harvesting.
- Line sowing by drilling the seed at a depth of 7.5 to 10cm or even more depending upon the situation should be practiced because it helps in better seed germination. This also helps in stabilizing the required plant population and thereby in getting better yield.
- Proper weed management practices should be followed by adopting integrated weed control measures.

- Mulching should be done by providing frequent interculture and pulverizing the soil. If intercultural operations are not possible then use of artificial mulches like covering the surface with tree leaves, uprooted weeds, sugarcane leaves, saw dust or polythene sheets are used to check the evaporation of water from the soil.
- Water harvesting between the rows should be done by growing some pulse crops and run off water should be collected in some nearby located ponds and used as life saving irrigation.
- An efficient plant protection measure should be adopted to protect the crop from insect pests and disease damage.
- The crop should be harvested at proper physiological maturity so that the following or succeeding crop may be sown slightly earlier than the scheduled time and best use of rain water or residual moisture may be made for crop production.
- Crops like cotton, chilies, etc. should be sprayed with CCC or cycocel and groundnut should be sprayed with planofix for modified growth, higher drought resistance and better yield.

2

Technologies of Mitigating Risk in Drought Prone Rainfed Area

BACKGROUND

The vulnerability of Indian agriculture to risk and uncertainty has increased rapidly due to changes in farming conditions, pressure on natural resources and climate variability, as also the changes in policy environment due to global market integration.

The climatic aberrations such as incessant rains, temperature swings, droughts, cyclone and degradation of natural resources have exposed the farmers to risk at all stages of the production chain. Unfortunately, the existing responses to mitigate risks are inadequate to provide safety net for the poor and vulnerable farmers. Hence, there is need for ensuring livelihood safety and income insurance to the farmers through using innovative insurance products including weather based derivatives.

Agricultural insurance is an important instrument for management of production risks. But the available options and insurance products are limited to mitigate risks that farmers are likely to be exposed to. The situation becomes worse because of the currently limited coverage and inadequate access to information to the farmers and other stakeholders.

The designing and developing demand-driven agricultural insurance products requires evolution of efficient tools and refinement in methodology of accurate risk profiling. The novelty of linking quantitative risk to agricultural insurance products is that it takes care of variety of risk regimes protecting millions of small farmers against risks. This is a major challenge to agricultural R&D system and policy makers. The implications of climate change for the agriculture sector are incorporated in the National Policy for Farmers, 2007 which was approved by Government of India basing on the reports of the National Commission on Farmers.

Apart from conservation and development of bio-resources required for sustainable development of agriculture sector, the Policy provides for preparation of contingency plans, alternative land use and water use strategies, training of experienced farmers as 'climate managers' in the art of managing drought, floods and aberrant monsoons. The policy also provides for preparation of Drought Code, Flood Code and Good weather Code for drought prone, flood prone and arid areas respectively, so that the required corrective/mitigation measures can be taken well in time.

PRIORITY AREAS FOR ACTION

For improving the risk management in agriculture sector, the following priority areas have been identified in the National Action Plan for Climate Change (NAPCC):

- Strengthening of current agricultural and weather insurance mechanisms.
- Development and validation of weather derivative models (by insurance providers ensuring their access to archival and current weather data).
- Creation of web-enabled, regional language based services for facilitation of weather-based insurance.
- Development of GIS and remote-sensing methodologies for detailed soil resource mapping and land use planning at the level of watershed or a river basin.
- Mapping vulnerable eco-regions and pest and disease hotspots.
- Developing and implementing region-specific contingency plans based on vulnerability and risk scenarios.

STRATEGY

RESEARCH AND DEVELOPMENT

Following are the strategies to implement the priority areas of action:

- Development of the models of risk assessment under various risk regimes:
  - Magnitude of risk exposure and the availability of the supportive infrastructure including resources and relevant data depending on risk measures vary differently depending on the risk mitigation measures. While the impact of risk increases from national to individual farmers' level, the resources, on the contrary diminishes at the farmer level. Therefore, Developing differentiated strategies for risk management and mitigation, particularly for the small and marginal farmers is important.
  - Development of dynamic models and methods for risk assessment considering multiplicity of risks.

   — Availability of appropriate technologies and their back-stopping support system that has long term effect on reduction of risk mitigation.
- Linking the model parameters to develop innovative insurance products and address the issues of existing calamity mitigation measures:
   — Weather index based insurance measures are new generation agricultural insurance products, which need effective promotional strategies and vali-dation at the grass root level. This has the advantage of speed and accuracy of loss assessment.
   — There is also need to evolve strategies to design, develop, disseminate the products to ensure farmers' acceptance. The products need to be designed to suit the different risk regimes and to capture cross sectional variability. This will include development of blended and integrated farming system insurance for different agro-ecological zones as well as for different Farmers' Groups.
- Gravity of emergence of newer sources of risk due to climate change:
   — Strategies are also required to deal with the emerging newer types of risk due to climate change These include high intensity rain, depletion of ground water and water contamination, increasing global warming, hailstorm, frost etc.
- Developing good governance and risk mitigation strategies:
   — The challenge for evolving governance structure and institutional framework for sustainability of risk mitigation measures requires more in-depth attention in order to make the insurance products more farmer-friendly.
- User-friendly decision support systems (DSS) for risk assessment and alternative insurance products:
   — Appropriate decision support system (DSS) is needed, which require more synergistic development of scientific information for assessing risk and risk profiling at farm level, regional level as well as at national levelincluding appropriate advisories for risk mitigation. Relevant information need to be converted to knowledge before it is transferred to the grass-root for wider impact and dissemination.

STRENGTHENING THE CURRENT AGRICULTURAL AND WEATHER INSURANCE

The following strategies would be adopted for strengthening the existing agricultural and weather insurance mechanisms.

- It is important that the financial support from the Government is available for the agricultural insurance since it is difficult to make these insurance schemes financially self-sustaining. The existing arrangement is to share the financial burden on the government between the Central and State Government in the ratio of 50:50. Hence continued financial support from the Government would be necessary for modifying or strengthening agricultural insurance to make it more effective and farmer friendly.

- The emphasis would be on preventing the risk in addition to mitigation. Capacity building of the farmers to manage risks more effectively would be a necessary element of the strategy.
- The climate change along with other factors impinge significantly on the agricultural bio-security of the country. Threat of new pests and diseases apart from preventing and controlling the existing pests would be a priority. As provided in National Policy for Farmers, the National Agricultural Bio-security system would be put in place to effectively deal with this problem.
- The plan of action to strengthen the existing agricultural insurance products should focus on increasing the coverage of farmers from the existing level and reducing the response time between detection and mitigation measures.

PLAN OF ACTION FOR STRENGTHENING INSURANCE SYSTEM

Taking into account the current state of development in the crop insurance sector, following plan of action for strengthening the current agricultural insurance mechanism would be undertaken:

Strengthening Area Yield Crop Insurance (NAIS)

Though a number of operational limitations have been observed in area yield insurance, however its conceptual strengths hold substantial relevance for Indian agriculture based on its dependence on actual yields for insurance payout. Due to the large diversity in agro climatic parameters (soil profiles, terrains, microclimates etc) and intra-farm differences (nature of inputs used, staggered sowing, irrigation facilities, intercropping, susceptibility to environmental risks), area yield crop insurance that factors in such variability should continue to be promoted both independently and also in conjunction with other emerging crop insurance product types. Area yield crop insurance should continue to be the mainstay of the Indian crop insurance programme.

The following improvements in traditional crop insurance have to be pursued vigorously for enabling it to meet the expectations and requirements of Indian farmers:

- *Scaling down of insurance unit to the village/village Panchayat level for major crops*: For area yield insurance to be effective, the yield variability within the area (insurance unit) should ideally be very low if not zero. However, considering that the present insurance units are largely administrative and political boundaries, yields within the unit are hardly uniform. It is desirable that the insurance unit should be as small as possible.

- *Improvements in computation of threshold yield (Guaranteed Yield)*: Presently Guaranteed Yield, based on which indemnities are calculated, is the moving average yield of the preceding three years for rice and wheat, and five years for other crops, multiplied by the level of indemnity. The present method does not provide adequate protection to farmers, especially in areas with a perpetual high risk regime which pulls down the average yield. Such average guaranteed yields may represent only a segment of the overall farmer population in an insurance unit. Use of long period average with appropriate de-trending method would be effective particularly in the context of climate change.
- *On-account payment of claims*: To offset the delays in claim settlement, it would be of great value to introduce on-account payment of claims based on indices like weather, satellite imagery based crop health, etc. The on-account payment could be adjusted against the final payment based on yield estimates.
- *Individual assessment of losses in case of localized risks*: NAIS presently provides for individual assessment of losses in case of localized disaster events *viz.* hailstorm, landslide and flooding, on an experimental basis. It is felt that the experiment is not adequate, and it should be implemented on a full scale, covering all areas. Earlier reviews have supported the view that the localized calamities should be assessed on an 'individual' basis in all the areas. Action in this direction needs to be expedited.
- *Coverage of pre-sowing and post harvest losses*: In some states, crops like rice, wheat etc. is left in the field for drying after harvest. Quite often, this 'cut and spread' crop is damaged, by rain, cyclones and floods. Since, the yields are estimated on the basis of crop cutting experiments, post-harvest risks are outside the purview of the present programme. There is a scope to pay indemnity for such losses on a re-sampling basis, or on 'individual' plot basis. Similarly, pre-sowing risks could be covered based on weather index.
- *Review and improvement of yield estimation methods*: On account of the procedural limitations and perceptual biases associated with the existing method of yield estimation based on Crop Cutting Experiment, there is a need to identify administratively robust and more reliable alternatives for yield estimation. With rapid

improvements in computation of production estimates for major crops through remote sensing technologies, it is quite possible to provide solution in the long term not only as a substitute for the expensive method of crop cutting experiments, but also in minimizing the moral hazard (of under reporting of yield estimates). Therefore, greater use of remote sensing technology needs to be promoted and used such assessments.

- *Actuarial Regime*: An actuarial premium rate supported by up-front subsidy in premium is most likely to inject the much needed professionalism and financial discipline to the programme, besides minimizing the delays in settlement of claims. However, keeping in mind the catastrophic nature of claims, it would be appropriate if in the initial years, the government acts as the 'reinsurer of last resort' or integrating relief administration with insurance in order to encourage smooth transition to an actuarial regime for agricultural crop insurance.
- *Risk due to Pests/diseases*: Potential threat due to altered biotic stress out of the novel organisms, mutants or variants of the existing pest-species as well as those that come up due to ecosystem and population displacements is perceived under the influence of climate change in agriculture. The quick response shall be towards mobilization of mitigation measures like activated and dynamic surveillance (through ground-truth surveys with digitization and e-reporting system), remote sensing-based database as well as by futuristic reconnaissance research on anticipated risky organisms in agricultural pestilence, mobilization of pest suppression measures including adequate expertise, appliances and pesticide for destruction of primary inoculums source and reconnaissance efforts to suppress multiplication of the organism. In order to anticipate and prevent the spread of pests/diseases, it is necessary to develop a system for reducing response time between detection and actionable decisions to manage/contain pests/plant diseases. The National Agricultural Bio-Security System that is proposed to be established by the Ministry of Agriculture would initiate appropriate action in this regard.
- *Application of Information Technology*: Information and Communication Technology (ICT) would be utilized for collating information relating various weather, soil, water and pest related risks. Converting the information to knowledge and transforming into action required to prevent/manage the risk would be ensured through application of technology. Synergy in the existing efforts of various Ministries/ Agencies to create a data base with advisory for farmers to effectively manage the risks would be emphasized.

Strengthening Weather Index-based Insurance

Weather insurance has emerged as a potent instrument for managing risks of farmers arising from weather vagaries. Its strengths of objectivity, transparency and faster settlement have been well-established during the five years of its usage in India. It also can virtually obviate the possibilities of moral hazard making it an attractive proposition for insurers. However, the two biggest limitations of the present weather-based crop insurance programme are: designing a proxy weather index with predictive capability to realistically measure crop losses taking into account the inter-farm variability; and the large basis risk inherent in the rainfall index which is the most preferred and widely-adopted weather index in India.

However, it can substantially contribute to improve the risk management in agriculture through following action points:

- *Weather index insurance products for crops where no historical yield estimates exist*: There are still crops in India which do not have adequate historical yield data or where the yield data is unviable/infeasible to collect. Many of these crops do not lend themselves to 'traditional insurance' due to either low value or high complexity. Weather insurance could be the answer for these crops and areas.
- *Use of weather index to design double trigger insurance products*: For major crops of India grown on a large scale, it can complement traditional crop insurance by acting as the basis for indemnifying catastrophic losses on account of weather events. This provides a scope to base a portion of the total crop insurance coverage of the farmer on weather index. The insurance product can be developed on two independent parameters (triggers)—1st trigger being weather index and would operate early; and 2nd trigger being area yield estimate and operate after harvesting of the crop.
- *Design of macro level insurance products using weather index*: Weather index based insurance could be an ideal tool for limiting state liability at District/Regional/State level against drought or floods. The macro level weather index could be constructed using the network of weather stations at District/ Regional/ State level.
- *Infrastructure for collating weather data*: Weather data are critical for weather insurance to generate credible results in terms of payouts. The higher the quality of the data, the stronger would be the forecasting capability of the weather insurance models. There are about six lakh villages, about 2.7 lakh gram Panchayat and about 5000 blocks in the country. It would be difficult to set up weather stations/ rain gauge stations at the level of gram Panchayat/village level. Assuming that a weather station can be representative in about 5 km radius, the country needs about 20000 automatic weather stations

(AWS). If one automatic rain gauge (ARG) can be installed in a radius of about 2.5 km, then about 80000 ARGs would be required. This infrastructure can effectively cover the data at Panchayat level. At present, there are 550 weather stations and 3500 rain gauges functional in the country. One AWS can be set up in each block by IMD for crosschecking and validating the data. Hence about 5000 AWS cab be installed by IMD with an investment of about ₹ 50 crore, which can be shared equally by Central and State Governments. Rest of the AWSs and ARGs can be installed by private sector for which an appropriate revenue model would be worked out.

Blended Crop Insurance Products

During the recent years, the agriculture risk management sector has witnessed the introduction of a number of products which blend the features of the three major basis of indemnification namely area yield, weather index, and remote-sensing based indicators (like Normalized Difference Vegetative Index, Leaf Area Index, etc). Blended products, by their very nature, would be introduced as these products incorporate the respective strengths of indemnification parameters while limiting the undue dependence on any one of them.

Catastrophe Protection

Non-loanee farmers account for more than 50 per cent of the total farmer base in the context of institutional/formal sources of credit. Such a huge segment of farmers comprises mostly the non-loanee farmers, who are already devoid of cheaper institutional credit; virtually pay the penalty as they are largely left out of a majority of governmental programmes including the crop insurance programme. At present, there are provisions to provide relief to such farmers in case of catastrophic weather events or natural disasters, but the quantum of such relief is limited. In order to protect the non-borrowing farmers from extreme financial distress and provide basic economic security, 'Catastrophe Protection' for farmers as a safety net needs to be examined. This protection would operate in circumstances that manifest into large scale crop losses on account of extreme weather conditions.

Linking with Agricultural Relief Measures

Operation of Calamity Relief funds with objective of assisting the farmers affected by natural calamity needs further strengthening. Crop insurance can be used as a conduit for channelizing calamity and disaster relief funds from central and state governments. By linking relief funds to Crop Insurance or Catastrophe Insurance, the benefit of such relief can be passed on to the targeted groups with greater efficiency and transparency.

Integrated Farming System Insurance

Despite huge subsidy on the current crop insurance, its penetration has not been growing at desired pace. Steps would be taken for developing insurance products to address the needs of different farming systems, transition towards insurance of mixed crops and integrated farming systems with crop, livestock and fisheries having much lower risk perception compared to mono crop systems and with lower risk premium as a consequence.

Crop Insurance Under Contract Farming

With an increasing focus and participation of private sector entities across the entire agricultural value chain, the role of quality-oriented agricultural production is also gaining impetus through an increasing number of contract farming initiatives. It is a known fact that the economic exposure to uncontrollable risks is significantly higher for a farmer participating in contract farming initiative than his peers on account of the higher investments by the former for crop inputs, technology and quality control. In order to safeguard the interest of farmers participating in contract farming and to promote trials/ adoption by other farmers through demonstration effect, crop insurance needs to be given the status of a mandatory input under contract farming initiatives. The responsibility of arranging crop insurance from suitable insurers may be with the contract farming sponsor or aggregator. Taking into account the diverse nature of crops covered under contract farming, it is essential to give thrust to new product development by insurers to cater to the demand by contract farming sponsors.

SHGs and other Farmers' Group-based Models of Crop Insurance

Self-help groups (SHGs) for rural women and farmers are one of those few programmes that have endured and given good results in terms of improving income and improving access to credit and marketing institutions. Their achievements have been impressive in mobilising the potential for savings and thrift even among the poorest of the poor. They have helped in delivering bank credit to the poor and in inculcating the habit of timely repayment of bank loans. With the outreach and penetration of self-help groups (SHGs) and other Farmers' Groups spreading deep into the rural hinterlands of India, there are enormous opportunities to leverage these SHGs for increasing the patronage and reach of crop insurance in India. In stead of covering individual farmers, farmers as a group can be covered under insurance products. SHGs and Farmers' Groups can also be utilized as a vehicle for change. Distribution and post-sales service delivery which is going to be a win-win proposition as it can reduce the typical insurance problems of moral hazard, high administrative and transaction costs, and lack of customer feedback and poor post sales service delivery.

Public-Private Partnerships in Agricultural Risk Management

The agricultural risk management sector in India can take cues from successful models of public-private partnership (PPP) in other countries. PPP would be encouraged under Area Yield Insurance in a phased manner. To begin with a 'co-insurance pool' would be created with scope for participation of private sector.

Capacity Building and Training

Self Help Groups (SHG) is found to be effective in empowering the farmers. SHGs will be strengthened for delivering bank credit and insurance facility. Capacity building and training of farmers through SHGs will be given high priority. SHGs would be provided with revolving funds. Farmers and elected Panchayat members would be trained to advise farmers for better management of floods, drought and aberrant monsoons would be accorded high priority.

PLAN OF ACTION

Priority Areas of Action	Further Action to beTaken
(i) Strengthening existing agricultural and weather insurance mechanisms	(i) Testing the efficacy of the severalexisting products under different production environments (ii) Develop models and methods of risk assessment under different risk regimes (iii) Strengthening and enforcement of insurance system and develop innovative products (iv) Strengthen SHGs and capacity building of farmers about risk prevention and mitigation (v) Implement proposed modified NAIS and widen scope of weather index based insurance
(ii) Development and validation of weather derivative models (by insurance providers ensuring their access to archival and current weather data)	(i) Derive demand-driven innovative products suitable for heterogeneous production systems (ii) Validation and piloting of different products (iii) Develop business models for insurance products (iv) Develop insurance pricing mechanisms including actuarial methodology
(iii) Creation of web-enabled, regional language based services for facilitation of weather-based insurance	(i) Development of regional and sub-regional hub for identifying and assessing location specific requirement of insurance products to mitigate specific risk

(iv)	Development of GIS and remotesensing methodologies for detailed soil resource mapping and land use planning at the level of a watershed or a river basis	(i)	Creation of on-line data base and analysis using state of art tools.
(v)	Mapping vulnerable eco-regions and pest and disease hotspots	(i)	Identify the sources of risk (conventional and newer sources)
		(ii)	Map the risk hotspots
(vi)	Developing and implementation of region-specific contingency plans based on vulnerability and risk scenario	(i)	Develop user-friendly decision support system to help assessing risk and develop region specific contingency plans.

COLLABORATING AGENCIES

Following are the collaborating agencies for above plan of action for strengthening agriculture risk management:

- *Research and Policy: National*: NCAP, NDRI, ICAR, IARI, IMD, CAZRI, CRIDA, SAUs, IFPRI, ICRISAT and India based CGIAR centres as well as the Insurance Companies in the public and private sector would be associated in the research and development for risk management.
- *Development and dissemination*: AIC, private insurance companies, SAUs. State Agriculture Departments, NGOs, civil society organizations and Farmers' groups.
- Develop location and situation specific insurance products, which require real time data on disaggregated level and be orchestrated in collaboration with the Insurance Companies and the Economic Statistics wing of the Ministry of Agriculture as well as States, NIC and IMD.

FINANCIAL OUTLAY

DEVELOPMENT COMPONENT

It has been assumed that the proposed Modified NAIS is to be implemented on pilot basis in 100 districts during the remaining three years (2009 to 2012) of the 11th Five Year Plan. The penetration of the scheme has also been assumed at 25 per cent. The estimated financial implications to the Government would be about ₹.1, 839 crore (₹.613 crore per year). In case the Modified NAIS is to be implemented in all the 500 districts of the country at 25 per cent penetration the financial implications works out to ₹.3,065 crore approximately per annum. With penetration level of 50 per cent likely by start of the XII Plan, financial implication would be about ₹. 5,000 crore per annum for entire country and financial implication may be higher by about ₹.10, 000 crore for XII plan period. With increase in the risk pooling because of greater penetration the liability is not likely increase proportionately because of law large numbers and better risk management.

The outlay for strengthening of existing insurance products under development component is as per details in Annexure—V for total of about ₹. 17,214 crore (to be shared between Central Government and State Government at the ratio of 50:50) for XI and XII Plan period, assuming a penetration level (coverage) of 25 per cent. For higher level of penetration the financial implication would be about ₹. 5000 crore per annum assuming extension of Modified NAIS to the entire country and accordingly the financial implication would be higher. Above estimate of ₹. 17214 crore includes the cost of infrastructure required for expanding weather index based insurance products and most of the infrastructure is envisaged through private sector with an appropriate revenue model that will be worked out by Agricultural Insurance Corporation.

RESEARCH COMPONENT

	Groups	**Coverage**	**Budget (₹. in Crore)**
A	Risk and Insurance modelling. At least four groups will be identified covering the critical ecosystems to develop ecosystem based risk assessment methods and models to create appropriate insurance products including blended products farming system approach.	Strategic institutions/organizations	32.18 (details as in Annexure - VI)
B	Requirement analysis, Constraints Analysis, village survey and Pilot testing. A representative set of selected blocks will be studied.	Selected sampling of desirable size with proper representation	Included in A
C	Capacity building, training, advocacy and Dissemination	Implementation and dissemination	10.00
	Total		**₹. 42.18 Say 42.00 Crore**

GENERAL SYSTEMS CLASSIFICATION

Discussion and analysis of systems can be of them as *actual systems* (*e.g.*, of constituent physical processes in the case of natural physical systems) or as *representational systems.* Common representations or models of actual systems take such forms as written descriptions, physical models, mathematical models, flowcharts, tables of data and computer programmes. In the following discussion, reference is to representational systems.

NATURAL, SOCIAL AND ARTIFICIAL SYSTEMS

Systems can be classified into three broad families or divisions as either natural, social or artificial systems (See Figure on page 71).

- *Natural systems*: Those that exist in Nature - consist of all the materials (both physical and biological) and interrelated processes occurring to these materials which constitute the world and, *inter alia,* provide the physical basis for life. They exist independent of mankind. Our role in relation to natural systems is to try to understand them and, as need be, make use of them. We also (increasingly) attempt to duplicate them, in part or whole; but at this point they become, by definition, man-made or artificial systems. These fundamental natural systems remain unaffected by attempts at imitation. Those natural physical and biological systems (shown in their totality as the division of natural systems in Figure) which are relevant to agriculture will be self-apparent: rock weathering to form soil; plants sustained by such soil; animals sustained by such plants... are examples of the outward forms of agriculturally relevant natural systems in operation.
- *Social systems* are more difficult to define. Essentially they consist of the entities forming animate populations, the institutions or social mechanisms created by such entities, and the interrelationships among/ between individuals, groups, communities, expressed directly or through the medium of institutions. Social systems involve relationships between animate populations (individuals, groups, communities), not between things. Concern here is with human social systems as they relate to or impinge upon farming, and the term social system is used broadly to include institutions and relationships of an economic, social, religious or political nature. There is a certain degree of ambiguity in defining social systems. As an example, the law of property is in its essence a social system. Insofar as it is viewed as consisting of concepts, principles and rules, it is a pure social system, independent of natural systems. But its existence also presupposes the existence of property, including natural physical things, some of which exist as systems. To this extent, as a social system the law of property is dependent on or subordinate to natural systems.
- *Artificial systems* do not exist in Nature. They are of human creation to serve human purposes. All artificial systems, including agricultural systems, are constructed from either or both of two kinds of elements:

— Elements taken from either or both of the other two higher-level orders of systems at division level, *i.e.*, from natural and social systems, and

— From elements which are constructed or Proposed for specific use by each respective artificial system as the need for this arises.

The upper part of Figure depicts the dependence relationship between natural and social systems on the one hand and between these and artificial systems on the other.

The relevant relationships are:

- Natural systems are independent of systems of the other divisions;
- Social systems could also be viewed as being independent, but generally a more legitimate view would be that they depend immediately or eventually on natural systems for the essentials of their material existence; and
- Artificial systems are directly dependent on either or both natural and social systems, or indirectly on natural systems (through the dependence of social systems themselves on natural systems).

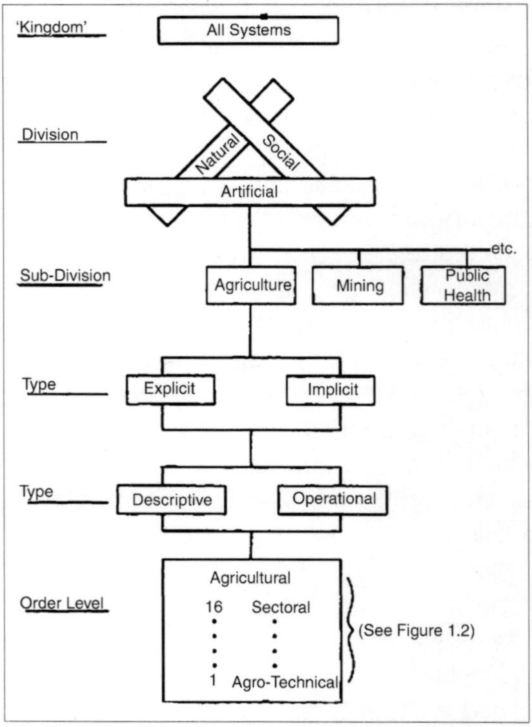

In the Figure, agriculture is shown as comprising one of a very large number of actual or potential artificial systems at the sub-division level. Others are those relating to mining, transport, public health, education etc. What such systems at this sub-divisional level have in common is that each is artificial:

each is based upon or draws elements from higher-level natural and social systems; and each also contains elements which are purposefully created by some human agency in order to meet its needs.

FURTHER SUB-CLASSIFICATION OF SYSTEMS

As shown in Figure, systems within the three broad divisions or their multitudinous subdivisions can be further classified according to system 'type', a loose term but one which might be used to differentiate among agricultural systems according to a number of factors of which only two are shown in the sketch. As outlined below, first, the system might be either an explicit or implicit one; second, its purpose might be either descriptive or operational.

Other 'type' designations could be added; e.g., operational systems could be further classified according to whether or not they are amenable to optimization:

- *Explicit systems* are those in which the constituent elements are more or less closely identified and defined, and the relationships among these elements are stated formally in quantitative, usually mathematical, terms. Agricultural scientists and economists who work with farmers are concerned mainly with explicit systems of Order Levels 1 to 10 as specified in Figure. But farmers themselves will seldom be concerned with explicit systems - only with systems of a simpler kind, or only with selected parts of such systems.
- *Implicit systems* are systems in which only the main or critical elements are acknowledged and only the major or immediately relevant interrelationships are considered. However, these elements and relationships are not formally recorded, analysed or evaluated. Farmers themselves deal primarily with implicit systems. In both traditional and more modem societies particular agricultural systems of Order Levels 1 to 10 are implied in what farmers do, or deliberately do not do. In more 'advanced' societies, farmers might formalize and work with a few explicit systems or parts of systems (farm record books, simple crop budgets, household expenditure accounts) but here also most agro-management systems will exist by implication.

The purpose in here distinguishing between explicit and implicit systems is to discourage the view that, because farmers (especially small traditional farmers) do not deal with explicit formal systems, these farmers are backward, ignorant, unsophisticated and generally inferior as resource managers. If anything, the facts generally point to a contrary conclusion. While bad farmers can be found anywhere, any close study of small traditional farmers and farming villages in the developing world will, with patience, identify implicit systems at agro-technical, enterprise, farm, farm-household and village levels which are far more complex, sophisticated, sustainable and socially efficient than most agricultural systems found in developed countries.

- *Descriptive systems* are usually intended to facilitate an understanding of the organization, structure or operation of a productive process. This might be their sole purpose; *e.g.*, a farmer might construct a simple input-output budget table in order to learn the structural configurations of some potential new crop. Depending on the results of this, he or she might then proceed to construct a more detailed budget (an operational system) to find how best to fit this new crop into his or her farm plan. At higher Order Levels an organogram describing the administrative structure of a ministry of agriculture or of an extension service might be constructed or the flowchart of a commodity from farm to consumer might be drawn—these also are descriptive systems.
- *Operational systems* are constructed (by an analyst or manager or research worker) as a basis for taking or recommending action aimed at improving the performance of the system. Such systems are often elaborate (as exemplified in Chapters). However, increased precision is not infrequently achieved at the cost of decreased practical usefulness. Thus farm managers themselves work primarily with simple operational systems, although the actual physical systems which these represent may be very complex.

As outlined by Dillon (1992), it is also sometimes useful to recognize that, like other systems, agricultural systems may be categorized as:

- *Purposeful* or *non-purposeful* depending on whether or not they can select goals and the means by which to achieve them.
- *Static* or *dynamic* depending on whether or not they change over time in response to internal or external influences.
- *Open* or *closed* depending on whether or not they interact with their environment.
- *Abstract* or *concrete* depending on whether or not they are conceptual or physical in nature.
- *Deterministic* or *stochastic* depending on whether or not their behaviour exhibits randomness over time, *i.e.*, their future behaviour is uncertain.

AGRICULTURAL SYSTEMS CLASSIFICATION AND ORDER HIERARCHY

Agricultural and particularly farming systems exhibit great diversity as shown by, *e.g.*, Duckham and Masefield, Grigg, Kostrowicki and Ruthenberg. They have been classified in various ways as reviewed by Fresco and Westphal who also present an ecologically-based classification and typology of farm systems. The hierarchical classification of farm systems presented here is distinctly different.

It is specifically oriented

- To a farm management and farm-household perspective; and
- To use as a framework for analysis of what are proposed as the six basic types of farms found in Asia (and elsewhere in the developing world).

Figure 2.1 is an elaboration of the lower part of figure and relates specifically to agricultural systems. These are listed in largely hierarchical order encompassing 16 Order Levels. Alternatively, with a few minor exceptions, the Order Levels 1 to 16 could have been depicted, reflecting their nested character, as a set of concentric circles with Order Level 1 as the innermost and Order Level 16 as the outermost circle.

In Figure 2.1, the sectoral system, 'all agriculture', is specified as being of the highest order rank, *i.e.*, Order Level 16. Any national or regional agricultural sector, however, consists of such subordinate sub-sectors or subsystems as agricultural credit, education, research, production, transport etc. Each of these constitutes and would be analysed, administered and managed as a system of Order Level 15.

Each such (sub)system may then be further disaggregated into commodity-based industry systems of Order Level 14 such as for coconuts, rubber, wheat, coffee, fish etc. If that flow-path relating to production is being followed, as depicted in Figure, this would then lead to villages or other community units where such production occurs (systems of Order Level 13); these would in turn consist of and could be disaggregated into the individual farm-household systems of Order Level 12 which comprise such villages.

Further lower Order Level systems relate to the agro-economic structure of individual farms and, in turn, their component crop and livestock enterprises and to the activities and individual agro-technical processes which underlie such enterprises.

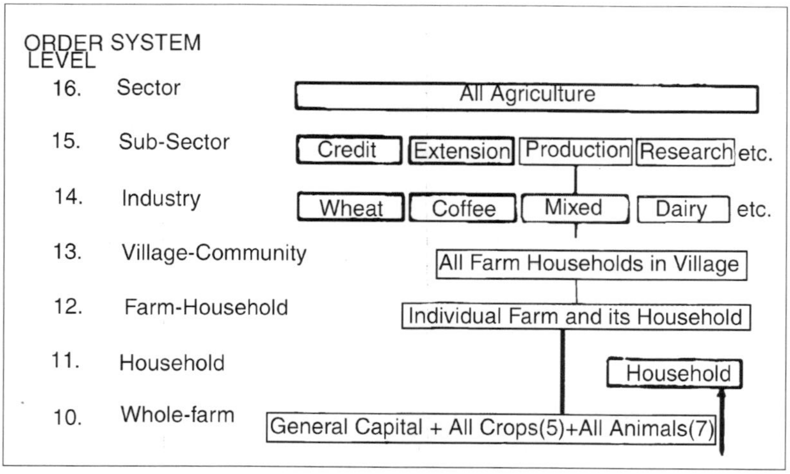

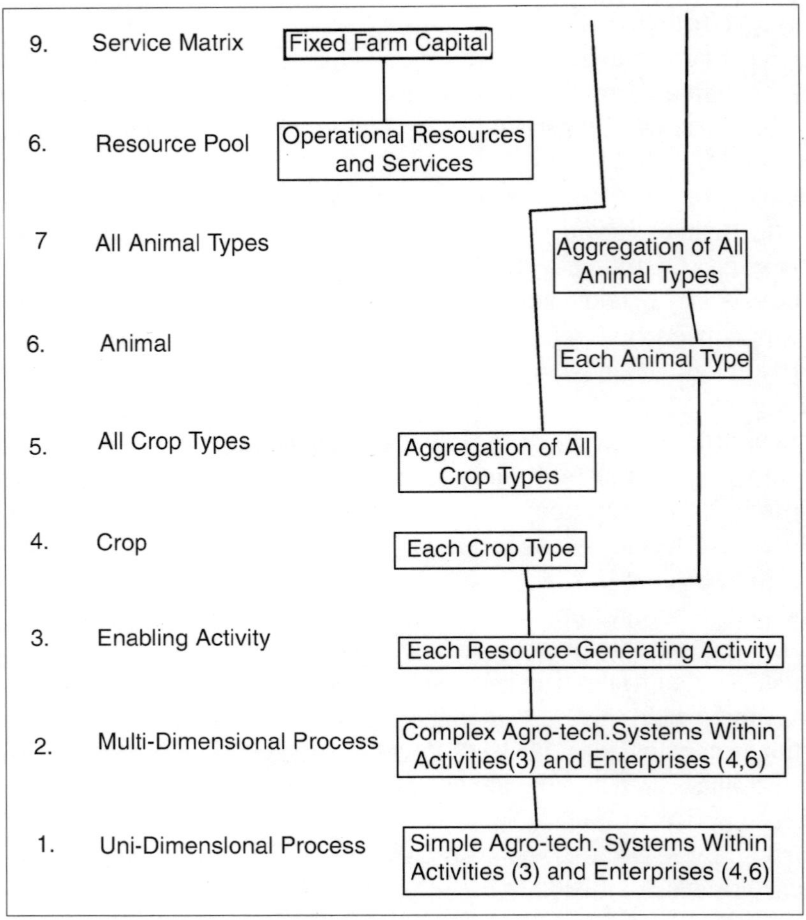

Fig. The Hierarchy of Agricultural Systems

Systems of Order Levels 1 to 12 comprise the field of farm management. But systems of Order Level 1 and 2 are also, indeed primarily, the domain of the applied agricultural sciences. A further proviso is that the 'household' components of farm-household systems of Order Level 12 remain as yet not very well understood. This component is primarily the province of workers in such fields as household economics, rural sociology and social anthropology.

While these various farm family-related fields are fairly well established, they have yet to be brought together in a comprehensive and cohesive way at farm-family level to provide verified models of how rural families in the developing world think about, plan and operate the 'farm' component of their farm-household systems.

Figure 2.1 depicts the direction of hierarchical status as proceeding downward from sector to industry to village to farm to crop etc. But whether this direction of subordination is valid will depend on circumstances and analytical purpose. Agricultural scientists would probably reverse the order-ranking shown for the systems on the grounds that, unless the basic agro-technical processes (Order Level 1 and 2 systems) are well developed, the production of individual crops will be inefficient, total farm production will be low and the agricultural sector itself will in consequence be an impoverished one. Similarly extension workers might be inclined to place household systems at the top of the systems hierarchy on the basis that good farming practices (Order Level 1 and 2 systems) will not be adopted unless the household systems are working well, nor consequently will the 'higher'-order systems at industry and sector level operate at their full potential.

NATURE OF FARM-LEVEL SYSTEMS

The nature of each farm-level system (i.e., Order Levels 1 to 12) of the hierarchy presented in Figure 2.1 may be specified from a management point of view as follows:

- *Order Level 1: Uni-dimensional process systems.* Systems of this lowest order are of an agro-technical nature. They involve an issue or problem which for purposes of analysis or management is abstracted from the context in which it naturally or normally occurs. One example is the application of a single fertilizer element, say nitrogen (N), to a crop and consequent plant response to N in terms of crop yield Y. As noted previously, systems of this order are primarily the domain of physical scientists, but those systems which have practical relevance for farmers thereby also have an economic dimension and so fall within the scope of farm economics. Such simple single-dimensional systems are later examined as processes and as input-output response relationships.
- *Order Level 2: Multi-dimensional process systems.* Systems of this second order are also concerned with limited agro-technical relationships and again they are primarily the domain of physical scientists. They differ from Order Level 1 systems in that they take - or are defined to take—a wider and more realistic view of a subject or problem. To use the same example of fertilizer response: at Order Level 2 an agro-technical system might involve the response of plant growth or yield Y to not one but to several or a large number of input factors such as nitrogen, phosphorous, irrigation water, crop hygiene, soil tilth etc. These multi-dimensional systems also are later examined as processes and as response relationships. Order Level 2 systems can be viewed as aggregations (often interactive) of constituent Order Level 1 systems.
- *Order Level 3: Enabling-activity systems.* Systems of this order are certain enabling activities which generate an intermediate product

intended for use as an input/resource by enterprises which do produce a final product. An example is offered by a legume crop turned under to provide fertility for a following (final product-generating) paddy crop. There will often be alternative ways of obtaining this resource: *e.g.*, stripping leaves off leguminous trees, keeping cattle for their manure, or buying a bag of fertilizer. These are all enabling, resource-generating activities but only some of them, the complex ones, warrant designation as systems. They are intended to supply resources to systems of Order Levels 4 and 6.

- *Order Level 4: Crop systems.* Systems of this order relate to the production of individual crops; but if these are primarily intended to produce inputs for other crops or livestock, they are regarded as systems of Order Level 3. On many small farms, crop and livestock enterprises produce both final products and resources.
- *Order Level 5: All crop systems.* Systems of this order, known also as *cropping systems,* refer to the combined system of all the individual crops on a farm. On a farm with a single mono-crop, this Order Level 5 system will obviously be equivalent to an Order Level 3 system; but on small mixed farms there will usually be four, five, six or more different crops (of Order Levels 3 and 4) grown in some degree of combination and as many as 20 or more on the highly diversified forest-garden farms of South Asia.
- *Order Level 6: Animal systems.* These systems relate to single-species animal enterprises or activities - *e.g.*, dairy cows, camels, fish, ducks. They are the animal equivalent of Order Level 4 (*i.e.*, individual crop) systems.
- *Order Level 7: All animal systems.* These systems are the aggregation of all Order Level 6 (sub)systems on a farm. Known as *livestock systems*, they are the animal equivalent of Order Level 5 (*i.e.*, all crop) systems.
- *Order Level 8: Resource pool.* This subsystem is a conceptual device for farm-system planning in which resources and fixed-capital services required by other subsystems are 'stored' in a 'resource pool' from which they are allocated to the other subsystems (of Order Levels 1, 2, 3, 4 and 6). The resource pool is central to operation of the whole farm-household system. It is discussed in Chapter 3.
- *Order Level 9: Farm service matrix.* A system of this Order Level consists of all the fixed capital resources of a farm which are pertinent to the operation of the farm as a whole but are not assigned to the exclusive use of any particular enterprise or activity: land, fences, barns, irrigation channels and work oxen are common examples. Some of these capital items are true (sub)systems, having interdependence

among their component parts (as in an irrigation storage/delivery/ distribution network, a grain drying facility, an integrated network of soil conservation structures etc.). Some are only things (*e.g.*, fences, a plough, a barn). But, in its totality, such capital is managed and manipulated as a system for the purpose of providing general services which, while not specific to them, enable the functioning of lower Order Level systems of the farm.

- *Order Level 10: Whole-farm systems.* Systems of this Order Level consist of all the lower Order Level (sub)systems which go to make up a farm. They consolidate in a single entity all the farm fixed capital, all the operating capital, all the final-product enterprises, all the activities and all the agro-technical processes which underlie such enterprises and activities. Structuring and managing systems of this Order Level are the main tasks or focus of farm management as carried out, on the one hand, by farmers and as investigated, on the other hand, by farm management economists in their professional capacity of providing advice to farm managers, development agencies and governments.

  The terms farm *system* and *farming system* are often used interchangeably. Here the practice is to use farm system to refer to the structure of an individual farm, and farming system to refer to broadly similar farm types in specific geographical areas or recommendation domains, *e.g.*, the wet paddy farming system of West Java or the grain-livestock fanning systems of Sind.
- *Order Level 11: Household systems.* On small farms the household itself is the most dynamic and complex of all farm-level systems, although it is a social system not an agricultural one. It dominates the agricultural systems which comprise the farm component. It has two functions: as *household* it provides purpose and management to the farm component, and as major system *beneficiary* it receives and allocates system outputs to itself and other beneficiaries.
- *Order Level 12: Farm-household Systems.* These consist of two components or (sub)systems of Order Levels 10 and 11, *i.e.*, the whole-farm system and its associated household system, respectively. The term is a very useful if not mandatory one when used to refer to the small farms of Asia. It carries an insistence that the technical analysis discussed in following chapters will amount to nothing at all unless it is applied to achieving the real needs and aspirations of the household—which, as discussed in Chapter 6, might be quite a different thing from evaluating the performance of a farm system according to the subjective or preconceived ideas of agricultural

technicians and economists. As the peak farm-level system, the farm-household system may be described in system terms as a goal-setting (*i.e.*, purposeful) open stochastic dynamic system with a major aim of production from agricultural resources. These attributes are sufficient to make it also a complex system. The purposefulness of a farm-household system is ensured by its human and social involvement which enables the system to vary its goals and their means of achievement under a given environment. The openness of the farm-household system is obvious from its physical, economic and social interaction with its environment. The non-deterministic or stochastic nature of the farm-household system is guaranteed both by the free-choice capacity of its human (and, if present, animal) elements and by the stochastic nature of the environment with which it (and all its subsystems) interacts. Necessarily, a farm-household system is also dynamic by virtue of its purposefulness, openness and stochasticity which ensure that the system changes over time. Too, any farm-household system is a mixture of abstract and concrete elements or subsystems. The concrete elements are associated with the physical activities and processes that occur in the system. The abstract elements relate to the managerial and social aspects of the system.

VILLAGE-LEVEL FARMING SYSTEMS

Not infrequently in parts of Asia, as also elsewhere in the developing world, the village may replace the farm-household in whole or part as the focal entity for agricultural production.

Systems of Order Level 13, i.e., village or community systems, are thus often relevant to the performance of farming systems.

- *Order Level 13: Village-community Systems.* Village-level systems or community systems in some situations replace all or part of individual farm-household systems. Three situations are common. *First*, some production activity in its entirety, including the operation of whole farms as production units, may be on a formal cooperative or group basis. *Second*, only part of an activity might be carried on by individual farmers while critical parts of it (such as land preparation, the supply of inputs, harvesting and/or marketing) are the responsibility of a formal farmers' club or cooperative. *Third*, and most difficult to analyse, is the situation found in many Indonesian villages where informal and temporary groups form to perform certain production tasks in common (such as land preparation, irrigation and/or harvesting) then disband and re-form to do different tasks on different crops, with membership continuously changing as individuals drop in and out of groups according to their interests, needs and mutual obligations. In a village there might be 10, 20 or 30 such 'cooperatives', though none might exist officially. Other examples are offered by the semi-nomadic livestock farmers of West Asia who sometimes operate as individual households and sometimes as members of a collective. In all these situations the boundaries of individual units are often so fluid and obscure that the focus for productive analysis has to be the group or village community. (Nevertheless, much externally sponsored farm-development planning remains locked into the mythology of agricultural individualism; perhaps that is why on the small farms of Asia it has borne so little and often poisonous fruit.)

Before proceeding, however, it will be useful to examine those constituent structural elements of a farm-household system which are relevant to its organization and management.

STRUCTURAL ELEMENTS OF THE FARM-HOUSEHOLD SYSTEM

The definition of an agricultural system given in Section 1.1 is a general one and applies broadly to systems of all the Order Levels.

When applied specifically to a farm-household system of Order Level 12 it implies the system involves ten structural elements or components:

- Boundaries
- Household
- Operating plan
- Production-enabling resources: the resource pool
- Final product-generating enterprises
- Resource-generating activities
- Agro-technical processes
- Whole-farm service matrix
- Structural (interdependence) coefficients
- Time dimension.

Those elements marked by an asterisk have been considered above as subsystems of the farm-household system. The ten elements are briefly discussed below and, except for structural coefficients and the time dimension, their interrelationships as components of a farm-household system of Order Level 12 are sketched in the example of Figure where they are denoted E1, E2... E8.

- *Boundaries:* This first element, the boundaries of the farm-household system, set it apart from other systems and from the world at large. These boundaries are provided partly by the structural characteristics of the particular type of farm, and partly by the purpose of analysis, *i.e.*, to some extent they are subjective and relate to more than the simple physical boundary of the farm. Boundaries are discussed in Chapter.

- *Household:* As previously noted, the household plays two roles: first, it provides purpose and management to its associated farm system and, second, it is the major beneficiary of its associated farm system. Its role as beneficiary is discussed. In its first role it provides purpose, operating objectives and management to the farm component of the farm-household system according to its broad domestic and social goals. Obviously these goals vary widely with culture, tradition and the degree of commercialisation and external influences to which the household is exposed. However, one would probably be not too far wrong in offering a generalization that the primary economic goal on most small farms is security and the primary non-economic goal is social acceptance. If this is correct, the primary objectives for the farm are, first, production of a low-risk sustainable subsistence for primary system beneficiaries; second, generation of a cash income to meet needs not directly met in the form of food and other farm-produced materials; and third, pursuit of both of these in ways which are not in conflict with local culture and tradition. Goals, objectives and planning criteria are discussed.
- *Operating plan:* The above objectives are pursued through preparation and execution of a farm operating plan. The core of this may be taken as selection of the best possible mix of agro-technical processes, activities, enterprises and fixed capital (systems of Order Levels 1, 2, 3, 4, 6 and 8). Formulation of operating plans is discussed.
- *Resource pool:* This element was noted above as a system of Order Level 8 central to the management of other subsystems within the farm system. It is discussed in Chapter.
- *Final product-generating enterprises:* These were noted as systems of Order Levels 5 and 7 in the previous section and are discussed.
- *Resource-generating activities:* These also were previously discussed as systems of Order Level 3. They are intended to supplement or entirely supply the resource pool as discussed.
- *Agro-technical processes:* These were defined above as systems of Order Levels 1 and 2. Processes may be of a biological or mechanical kind. They are a shorthand designation of all the potentially complex and interrelated physical and biological factors underlying production from crop or livestock species, only some of which may be economically relevant.
- *Whole-farm service matrix:* This was discussed previously as a system of Order Level 9. It is further examined.
- *System structural coefficients:* These coefficients identify and quantify linkage relationships

— Among the various parts or elements within each sub-system; and

— Between subsystems. From the general system definition, an essential property of any system is that there be interrelatedness between its parts. In farm-household systems (and in subordinate subsystems of lesser Order Level, particularly Order Levels 4 and 6) such interrelatedness is specified by these coefficients.

- *Time dimension:* Unlike mechanical systems which stamp out buttons or TV sets, agricultural systems rest on biological processes which occur over considerable periods of time - from, *e.g.*, a few days in the case of quick-response agricides to 70 or more years in the case of growth and decline of a coconut palm. Agricultural systems are thus inherently stochastic: being dependent on the passage of time, *ex ante,* their outcomes are uncertain. Moreover, because agriculture is also a set of economic activities, the old adage applies: time is money. Other things being equal, a system which yields its product or ties up resources over a short time is better than one which yields its output or occupies resources over a long time. Strictly speaking, time is not a system component; rather it is a dimension in which the system operates. The time dimension in relation to resource use is discussed. The evaluation of activities which occur over long time periods is examined. The latter chapter also considers uncertainty as it occurs in farm planning and decision making. Also important from a time perspective are the sustainability and environmental compatibility of the farm system being used. If, over time, the farm system is not biologically and economically sustainable or causes resource degradation, as discussed, this is to the disadvantage of both the farm household and society at large.

STRUCTURAL MODEL OF A FARM-HOUSEHOLD SYSTEM

Before examining the elements of a farm-household system in more detail in later chapters it is useful to consider where they lie in relation to each other in the structure of a small mixed farm as exemplified in Figure 2.2.

Element 1, system boundaries: Depending on the purpose of analysis, the farm-household system may be specified with different boundaries. In Figure, these are suggested by the shaded circle around the system which sets it apart from other neighbouring systems and from the larger community or environment in which it is imbedded.

Element 2, household: As noted at the top of Figure, the household provides objectives and management of the farm-household system and, at the bottom, it exists as the primary internal beneficiary of the system, while distributing some of the system output to external beneficiaries. *Element 3, Operating Plan:* As shown in Figure, this is determined largely by the household but it might also be influenced by the requirements of external individuals, agencies or other influences, some of whom might be (external) beneficiaries of the system as outlined below.

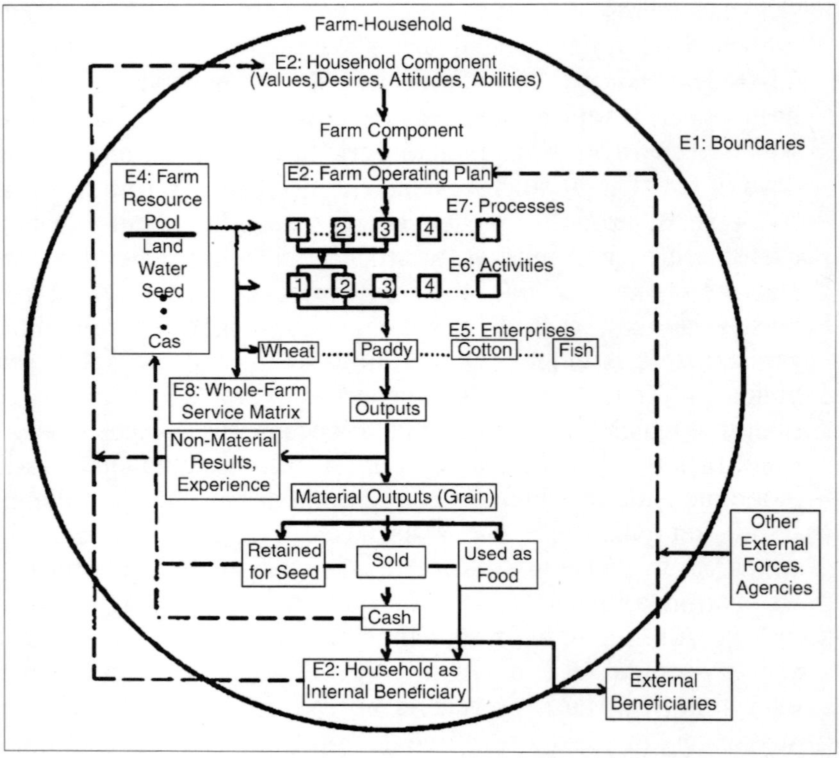

Fig. Interrelationships of Elements in a Simple Farm-household System

Element 4, Resource Pool: This element consists of resources which are initially present at the time of planning or commencing operation of the system—some pool or stock of land, water, seed, cash etc. which the other elements of the farm system may draw upon. Once the system begins operating, certain components of it (the resource-generating activities and by-products of the enterprises) will replenish the pool.

In the schematic sketch of Figure, the arrows from the farm resource pool indicate that items from the resource pool flow to processes as well as to activities and to enterprises (as well as possibly to maintenance of the whole-farm service matrix).

Strictly speaking, resources should be shown as flowing directly only to processes, since this is the level (subsystems of Order Levels 1 and 2) at which they are actually used. But from a practical viewpoint and because most of the potential processes are actually ignored in planning the operation of a farm system, resources may also be viewed as flowing directly to activities and enterprises as indicated.

Element 5, final-product Enterprises: Only four enterprises are shown in the system of Figure: wheat, paddy (rice), cotton and fish. Only the flow lines of inputs to and output from the paddy crop are shown.

Element 6, Resource-generating Activities: In the example of Figure, there are two of these supplying some resources to paddy (*e.g.*, a prior fertility-generating legume crop and possibly a cattle activity providing oxpower).

Element 7, Agro-technical Processes: These underlie the activities and enterprises. Only three are indicated as relevant to paddy in Figure but there are a very large number of biological and mechanical processes actually present in any form of agricultural production.

Element 8, Whole-farm Service Matrix: This was defined previously in relation to Figure as a system of Order Level 9. It consists of fixed farm capital which provides a flow of services (not shown in Figure) to all other elements of the system, particularly to Elements 5, 6 and 7 but it is not specific to any one of them.

Element 9, Structural Coefficients: These are not depicted in Figure.

Element 10, Time: In the schematic example of Figure, the time dimension is not specified explicitly but the model would probably refer to a single operating phase with a duration equal to the life of the longest-term enterprise subsystem, here cotton with a term of six to seven months, or, if climatic seasons are constraining, to a full seasonal cycle of one year. If the system proves to be a 'good' system in terms of household objectives, it might be reactivated in successive phases and continue indefinitely; if a 'very good' system it might permit further farm intensification and development; if a 'bad' system it might be restructured; if a 'very bad' system it will, in the absence of restructuring, prove to be non-sustainable and eventually collapse.

Figure 2.2 is intended only as a schematic example to indicate the broad relationships which the elements of a farm-household and its associated whole-farm system bear to each other. Real small-farm systems are much more complex than Figure suggests, particularly in their internal cycling of resources. The following chapters are essentially an elaboration of Figure 2.2 in terms of managerial considerations.

Outputs of the farm component of the farm-household system depicted in Figure are, as an example, shown as flowing from the paddy enterprise. They do not comprise a separate element but are part of Element 5 (final-product enterprises). Outputs are allocated to the farm component and to system beneficiaries. Thus, to enable continuation of the system in subsequent phases (seasons or years), some paddy grain output is cycled back to the resource pool to replenish the seed stock. Similarly, to replenish the cash resource which was used up in this phase, some rice grain is sold.

Whatever grain is left might also be sold to generate cash income or be used as food. These latter outputs will be distributed among system beneficiaries who might be internal to the system, *i.e.*, the household, or external to it. External primary beneficiaries may consist of needy relatives and friends, landless neighbours, a landlord receiving cash or part of the crop as rent etc. External secondary beneficiaries, as discussed, might also be present - usually the tax collector. External beneficiaries often also play another role: they can exercise a direct influence on how the system is planned, constructed and operated. This influence is indicated in Figure by the broken line indicating feedback from external beneficiaries to Element 3, formulation of the farm plan. Returning to the paddy flow column of Figure, the system will also generate a second type of output apart from the material one of grain, namely *non-material output.*

This consists of the knowledge and experience gained from operating the system over any phase. Farm-household systems are dynamic: the results of one operating phase flow back not only as products giving sustenance and cash income to the household but also as knowledge and experience to influence the formulation of plans for future phases.

3

Drought Areas and Farm Management

INTRODUCTION

SCOPE

To a layman 'farm management' probably means just that— a body of activities and procedures carried out by a farmer in the ongoing management of his or her farm and for which advice may be available from professional specialists in farm management. To an extent this is correct (as per farm management in Field A) but, more broadly, farm management as considered here is a professional discipline which relates to the description, construction, analysis and evaluation of farm systems of Order Level 10 (Figure). In this wider sense, farm management is the discipline within whose ambit farm-level systems analysis most clearly falls. (This does not exclude from farm systems analysis other disciplines of a technical or special-purpose nature.) Farm management system analysis can have several operating *objectives*; there are several alternative *bases* on which analysis can proceed; and it can operate in four *fields* and in four *modes* within these fields. These several aspects of farm management as a systems-related discipline are now briefly discussed in turn.

DEFINITION

Except when it serves a descriptive purpose, farm management is the science (and art) of optimizing the use of resources in the farm component of farm-households, *i.e.*, in systems of Order Level 10, and of achieving the optimal functioning of these systems in relation to household-specified objectives; and since Order Level 10 systems consist structurally of subsystems, farm management is also concerned with the operation of subservient subsystems of Order Levels 1 to 9 in such fashion as to optimize the whole-farm system. However, for reasons discussed in Chapter, it is often essential, especially when dealing with small farms, that farm management extends also to the family or household component, thus its true scope extends to Order Level 12 systems. A second consideration is that the village is sometimes a more relevant unit for analysis than the farm, and where this is so the scope of 'farm' management extends to systems of Order Levels 1 to 13.

OPTIMIZATION

Optimization of the planning objective is defined as achieving the farm household's goals as efficiently as possible in the face of whatever constraints of a physical, environ-mental, legal or socio-cultural nature may be relevant. This implies obtaining maximum possible net benefit over time from the operation of the farm system. Net benefit is measured, as appropriate, in terms of output or profit or, more broadly, as satisfaction or utility. Maximization of net benefit implies efficient use of available resources and opportunities. For the achievement of a given level of net benefit, it implies the minimization of costs. This reflects a theoretical view. In the real world, as discussed in Chapter, the general objective is often constrained by household and social factors other than availability of physical inputs and their costs. Thus many small-farm households place a high value on the long-term sustainability of their farm system. Also, in the real world, uncertainty will generally prevail about yields, prices and other relevant influences so that the farmer's choice will lie not between sure alternatives but between alternative (subjective) probability distributions of net benefits..

Optimization can occur at two levels: local or global. When operating in Field A, farm management will seek optimization at the global level of the Order Level 12 farm-household system. This sets it apart from other farm-related agricultural sciences which are usually (though not always) concerned primarily with optimization of lower order subsystems, *i.e.*, local optimization. Two examples will clarify this point. First, a farm might involve only two irrigated crops, cotton and sugarcane. If only the cotton is considered, the local optimum might be to use all of the water supply on cotton, but if the farm as a whole is considered, *i.e.*, a global optimum sought, this might well require that the water be shared between both crops.

Second, a farm-household system itself might be only a subsystem within some larger system. For example, the optimal irrigation water supply to a farm might, from the viewpoint of the farm, be 1 000 m^3, but if such water is to be provided only as a minor by-product by a large multipurpose dam project (the chief purposes of which are power generation and flood control), these purposes will determine what discharge rate/farm supply is optimal from an overall project or global viewpoint and this would override whatever supply rate might be optimal from a farm perspective.

OBJECTIVES

Optimization of farm-household systems takes the form of conditional maximization over time of the socioeconomic welfare of farm families. The term 'welfare' is used broadly to include money income, sustenance food, farm-produced consumption goods and factors of production, non-material benefits such as those enabling the attainment of education and health standards, and satisfactions derived from work well done as well as from cultural and religious sources. Whichever of these system outputs/family benefits are relevant in a particular farm situation will depend on the farm type and on the values held by the particular family-values which will normally reflect the society and cultural context in which the farm-household exists. Welfare maximization is conditional because it is constrained by resource availability and, as relevant, legal constraints and socio-cultural mores.

Typically the farm plays only an enabling role towards achieving broad family goals. Thus farm management is concerned with conditional optimization of only part of a farm-household system—but usually the most important material part. The specific objective might be to maximize money profit or, recognizing the presence of uncertainty, to maximize the expected utility of risky profit (farms of Type 4, 5 and 6 and possibly Type 3), or such money profit might be only incidental to other objectives (Type 2 farms), or hardly relevant at all (Type 1 farms).

ECONOMICS AS THE FRAMEWORK FOR FARM-SYSTEM ANALYSIS

Economics or *economic analysis* is the science of making choices so as to best achieve desired objectives given that only limited (physical and other) resources and opportunities are available and that the future is uncertain. There are no choices to which the science of economics cannot be applied. It is just as pertinent, *e.g.*, to the choice of a spouse as to the choice of which crops to grow or to the choice between using an insecticide or using environmentally friendly integrated pest management. In contrast to this wide applicability of economic analysis, *financial analysis* is restricted to matters that are naturally of a financial or monetary nature.

Financial analysis is thus a subset of economic analysis and, in circumstances where everything is valued in money terms, may be the natural way in which to conduct economic analysis. In other cases, it may be feasible to facilitate economic analysis of possible choices by imputing money values to possible gains and losses. And in yet other cases, such as assessing the resource sustainability and environmental compatibility of alternative farm systems, it may often be infeasible to impute money values to the gains and losses of alternative choices. Decisions must then be made using economic analysis based on non-money values, intuition and judgement.

Farm management economics (*i.e.*, economic analysis applied to the choices confronting farmers) provides the general disciplinary basis for farm-level systems analysis. Obviously other farm and family-related disciplines will be involved in systems' construction: agronomy, animal husbandry, soil and water conservation/management, human nutrition etc. However, except in the case of special-purpose technical systems (*e.g.*, when the farm-household unit is analysed in terms of nutritional or energy flows among components as discussed below), these other disciplines should play subordinate contributing roles coordinated by farm management economics as the lead discipline. That in fact this often does not happen and the lead is taken instead by workers in other disciplines is really not important.

It might just reflect the fact that many agriculturists are aware of the necessity for a systems approach if application of their expertise is to be effective; or that many agricultural economists are content in the more modest role of economics apparachnik.

Nevertheless, the disciplinary basis of farm management remains economics - but economics of a special wide-ranging kind, the core of which is production economics supported by other branches of economics of which marketing, resource economics, agricultural credit and data analysis (including operations research, econometrics and risk analysis) are probably the most important. When working with the household component, especially of small traditional farms, the most important supporting disciplines are sociology and social anthropology.

ALTERNATIVE BASES FOR FARM-SYSTEM ANALYSIS

There are several reasons why farm economics provides a good conceptual framework for most farm-household systems analysis. The most important of these is the necessity to bring the many relationships of a system and between systems to some common unit or basis of comparison. Unless this is done, systems analysis and the comparison of alternatives will not be possible. The base usually most convenient—and in the case of commercial farm systems most relevant and which has the highest degree of universality—is money or financial value. But several other bases for systems analysis are possible and in certain circumstances they might well be more relevant than money value.

The four most important bases of comparison are as follows:

- *Money Value:* The convenience of using money or financial values as the basis of commercial farm systems analysis will be obvious: it permits the various system inputs (*e.g.*, seed, fertilizer, power, labour etc.) to be standardized as money costs and the various system outputs to be standardized as money returns so that net revenue, *i.e.*, money returns minus money costs, can be used as the basis of comparison between alternatives. In commercial farming, all or most of these inputs/costs and outputs/revenues can be stated in explicit quantitative terms. On the other hand, when dealing with less commercialized systems where there are no actual price-setting markets for farm inputs and/or outputs, one is often obliged to base the analysis on imputed values.

However, this is possible only up to a point; beyond this point, as one moves further from a commercial environment towards a traditional one, the attempted use of money value as the basis or numéraire for analysis becomes too abstract to be useful and one has to search for some other base.

- *Family Labour Effort:* Probably the best alternative to money value on small family farms of a subsistence or semi-subsistence nature is labour input, both as a measure of inputs and as a yardstick to judge the worth of outputs. At least this is so in the eyes of the majority of Asian (and African) small-farm families for two reasons. First, on these farms most production activities involve few if any commercial inputs and most outputs are also not disposed of through commercial channels. Money hardly enters into the matter at all. What such activities do have as their common factor is family labour—often very hard labour—from hand-preparation of fields, to carrying all inputs/outputs perhaps long distances, to hand-pounding the harvested grain. Not unnaturally then, these families plan, compare and evaluate their several different farming activities and alternatives (*i.e.*, analyse their systems) in terms of labour content. To conduct such analysis on any other basis such as money value would be an incomprehensible abstraction. However, 'labour' is not a simple quantity. It can have several dimensions: quantity when labour is measured in terms of standardized units (*e.g.*, labour-days or task-days on estates); quality where the relevant factor is the actual effort required or the degree of skill or unpleasantness associated with separate tasks; and agency where the labour measurement reflects the social position or status of the person performing the task. Thus, in different societies, patriarchal or matriarchal, women's labour will be valued less or more highly than the labour of men regardless of the actual effort expended, while the labour performed by children might also be valued according to their (usually inferior) social status rather than to the actual work they perform. These dimensions of labour and the implied difficulties of measurement often limit the use of this factor as an alternative to money value. Nevertheless labour often provides a more relevant basis for systems analysis of a very large number of small traditional farms than does money.
- *Bio-mechanical Energy:* A factor which all farm-household systems and their subsystems have in common is their explicit or implicit energy content. Farm-system models have sometimes been structured on the basis of such energy content and inter-component energy flows—see, *e.g.*, Axinn and Axinn. Use of energy-based farm systems analysis rests on the view that, in a world of declining energy resources and materials

that can be represented by their energy content, the energy generation and consumption of farm-household systems is a more valid basis for systems analysis than is money profit, and usually also that energy flows which are directly or indirectly involved in all economic activities (including agriculture) are not properly represented—indeed they are often severely distorted—by commercial pricing mechanisms. However, these views involve issues and require solutions at much higher than farm level. Farm systems analysis based on energy flow is more appropriate for some aspects of macro/industry/sector strategic planning than for farm-level operational planning where the immediate interest of farm families is in income (in whatever form it takes) and the effort required to achieve it.

- *Water Consumption:* A fourth possible basis for analysis of farm systems is offered by water with systems analysis conducted in terms of the relative water consumption of different crops and animal populations and the implicit water content of products and by-products. Water is obviously the critical common factor in all the farming systems of that great belt of lands stretching from North Africa to India, so much so that even the very wealthy Gulf States, while they have been able to import or create all other agricultural resources, including soils, micro-environments and farmers, remain constrained by water. Moreover, in the 'wet' tropics, the critical nature of this input common to all parts of all farming systems is not yet widely recognized; *e.g.*, even 'well-watered' Java will probably exhaust its water supplies before its soils. However, as important as water is, like bio-mechanical energy it is more appropriate as a basis for some aspects of macro-level systems analysis than for operational-oriented systems analysis at farm level.

In summary, except when used in connection with special-purpose systems, such bases of analysis as energy, water, ecological balance etc. lack the universality and the value orientation required of a general systems base. Money value and labour will probably continue to be used as such a base, either separately in the case of commercial and near-subsistence farms respectively, or jointly in the case of the bulk of small traditional partly commercialized farms.

FARM MANAGEMENT FIELDS

Farm management analysis and advisory activities can be categorized in terms of four fields defined in terms of the purpose of the analysis as follows:

Field A consists of those problems and analyses which are only or primarily of direct interest to the farmer subjects of the analysis and where solutions to problems are offered on the basis of their beneficial effect on the welfare of these farmers and their families. The great bulk of farm management systems analysis occurs within this field. Field A is the conventional area in which farm management operates, directed to solving the on-farm problems of individuals and groups. Except where otherwise noted, this book is concerned with farm management within Field A; it needs no further discussion at this point except to note that such analysis should, whenever possible, involve farmer participation so as to ensure that the farmer's felt needs are considered.

Field B consists of those problems and analyses which should not really fall within Field A (*i.e.*, they do not properly constitute farm-level problems) but which for convenience or purposes of analysis can be defined, regarded and treated as if they do. Examples of the scope of Field B farm management analysis are offered by the agricultural industries and sectors of some of the mini-states. For example, the agricultural sector of the island nation Kiribati is equivalent to not much more than a single good-sized coconut estate with a few supplementary enterprises added.

This sector (a system of Order Level 16) could easily and probably most effectively be analysed, of course with the necessary modifications, as if it were a system of Order Level 10 or 12. An example at industry level is offered by the banana industry of Western Samoa which, although it consists of a large number of individual farms, has been centralized (through the government) in fruit collection/inspection/transport/export and other important aspects. The industry could justifiably be analysed as a single large 'farm system' even though in fact (and in respect of banana-growing activities) it really consists of many farm-household systems.

Obviously, since this type of higher-than-farm-level analysis will be concerned with a range of subject matter in addition to farm economics—processing, marketing, transport, research, extension etc.—farm management can operate successfully in Field B only if the analyst can ignore artificial divisions which are conventionally imposed between the various disciplines. Another condition is that the analysis could not be better performed by a systems analyst working within the conceptual framework of some other discipline. (If this is the case then farm management analysis would operate in a subservient role in Field C.)

Field C consists of problems or issues arising within or in relation to higher systems of Order Levels 13 to 16, towards the resolution of which farm management plays only a secondary contributing or partial role, *e.g.*, the lead discipline might be water resource engineering if the problem is planning of a public irrigation project, or agronomy if it consists of planning for the introduction of new crops, or agricultural credit if it is to plan the establishment of a farmers' bank. In this type of supporting role, farm management can operate in any or successively all of Modes 2, 3 and 4, *i.e.*, description, diagnosis and prescription, respectively, as defined below. However, any 'prescription' that is offered will be of a limited kind and fall short of being a plan for the overall project or programme. Analysis will be directed towards the achievement of some global optimum which is not defined in terms of farm management itself.

A few of the very large number of situations in which farm management operates in Field C are:

- *Descriptive* studies of farm-household systems to provide background for local or multi/bilateral investment programmes in agriculture and/or agricultural infrastructure (*e.g.*, the Country Background Reports of the World Bank). This type of analysis is in Mode 2.
- *Diagnostic* studies of farm-households to determine just what developmental or investment assistance is needed (*e.g.*, roads, health, transport, extension, credit etc.), and the priority ordering of specific projects to provide such assistance (Mode 3).
- *Prescriptive* analysis (*i.e.*, Mode 4) aimed at providing the farm-related part of some uni- or multi-purpose project or plan: *e.g.*, farm-level demand schedules for irrigation water in a multi-purpose water storage project (where irrigation is only one planned activity in addition to power generation, flood control, fish production etc.); scheduling of produce supply as part of a feasibility study for the establishment of a cannery.

Field D consists of farm management in the role of generating data for the guidance or support of agricultural policy making. Provision of such data might not require special studies or systems analysis for this particular purpose; often such data will be an incidental output of analysis undertaken for some other purpose, *e.g.*, in Field A. Field D analysis is also of a supportive kind and operates in Modes 2 and 3. The aim is usually to generate knowledge about farm-households or their component subsystems which is to be used by governments, public agencies etc. as a basis for structuring agricultural or broader economic policies—setting farm-input prices or consumer food prices, establishing transport services or credit programmes etc.These policies might imply either enhancing farmer welfare or reducing it (*e.g.*, if their thrust is to minimize urban living costs). This is a very important and wide-ranging field: it is difficult to think of any policy which is to affect farmers which should not be based at least in part on farm-level analysis, despite the fact that such farm-level analysis is in fact frequently not carried out, much to the detriment of sound policy making.

FARM MANAGEMENT MODES

Farm management operates in four modes within the above fields.

Mode 1 encompasses *routine operational and control* activities. It is concerned with the day-to-day operation and management of an actual farm, estate, cooperative or other farm-based producing/marketing entity. This may be thought of as practical or 'muddy-boots' farm management. Management in this mode is largely outside the scope of the present discussion, except that the systems concepts discussed here will, it is hoped, provide principles to guide practical (*i.e.*, Mode 1) management.

Mode 2 refers to *descriptive* activities whereby farm management provides a conceptual framework for the study, understanding and description of farm systems or farm-related problems. This might be an end in itself; or more likely it will be a necessary stage in the logical-event sequence towards action, as suggested in Figure. The chief function of descriptive farm management studies is to provide a basis of understanding before problem diagnosis is attempted. There are still many societies in the world with farm-household systems of which we are in nearly complete ignorance; understanding and description of these systems must precede problem diagnosis and, if need be, prescription of solutions.

Mode 3 refers to *diagnostic* activities concerned with the identification of problems and weaknesses in farm-level systems of all Order Levels 1 to 10 and those parts of Order Level 11 household systems relating to the farm. Such problem diagnosis includes the identification of potential opportunities. Problem diagnosis is usually carried out as a separate mode, but on some commercial farms it might be built into their routine monitoring and management mechanisms (as also on more sophisticated estates).

Mode 4 refers to *prescriptive* activities in which farm management is aimed at the prescription of action plans for both (*a*) the overcoming of problems or weaknesses and (*b*) the seizing of opportunities uncovered in Mode 3 (diagnostic) analysis.

Analytical Situations Within Modes

In Modes 3 and 4, three analytical situations will arise, viz.:

- *Diagnose and Prescribe:* First, the problem might require that a diagnostic analysis be made of a system of Order Level from 1 to 10 (or 1 to 12) leading to the identification of some specific weakness or opportunity to be investigated by research on the farm or experiment station - see Norman *et al.* If the problem falls within the competence of the investigator, the analysis would at this point go into prescriptive Mode 4 to develop and offer solutions.
- *Diagnose and Refer:* This second situation arises when the diagnosed problem lies beyond the competence of the analyst: *e.g.*, low milk production on a dairy farm might be due to animal disease or a genetic factor or to the household itself (such as a low educational level leading to product adulteration). In such situations the role of the farm analyst is - or should be - to refer the problem to some relevant agency or specialist, *i.e.*, to diagnose but not to prescribe.
- *Prescribe Only:* Often only a prescriptive analysis is called for: *e.g.*, if the problem is to generate land-use plans intended to serve as the

agro-economic basis of new settlement projects or transmigration schemes.

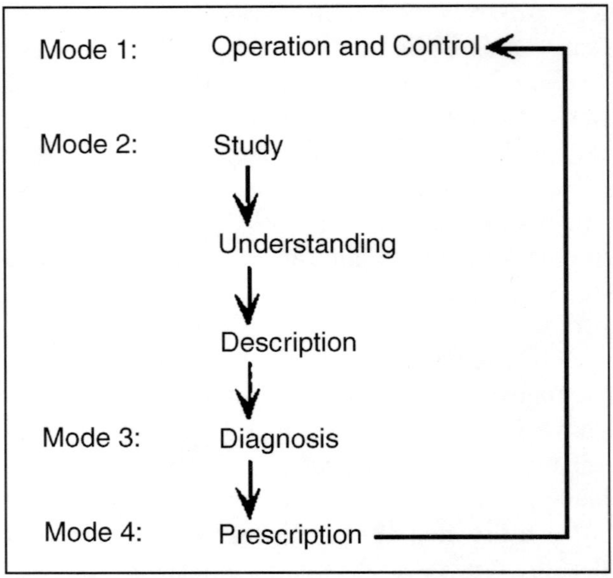

Fig. Relationship between the Four Modes of Farm Management Activity

FARM TYPES AND STRUCTURE

To date, farms have most often been classified on the basis of agro-ecological factors (such as climate, soil, slope, altitude and, not unrelated to these factors, the crop and livestock systems used) overlaid, to a lesser extent, with socio-economic criteria (Fresco and Westphal). Inevitably such an approach leads to a plethora of farm types. A different approach is taken here.

Emphasis is on farm-system structure from a farm management and farm-household perspective with classification based on:

- The main purpose of the farm;
- Its degree of independence; and
- Its 'size'. From such a structural viewpoint there are basically six major types of farm system to be found in Asia and elsewhere around the developing world with dozens of subtypes constituting a continuum of farm types between the extremes of a totally subsistence to a totally commercial orientation.

FARM TYPES

The six basic farm types are:

- *Type 1*: *Small subsistence-oriented family farms.*
- *Type 2*: *Small semi-subsistence or part-commercial family farms*, usually of one half to two hectares, but area is not a good criterion: the same

basic structure can be found on much larger 20- to 30-hectare farms as in the Punjab, Sind, and North West Frontier Provinces of Pakistan.

- *Type 3*: *Small independent specialized family farms.*
- *Type 4*: *Small dependent specialized family farms*, often with the family as tenants.
- *Type 5*: *Large commercial family farms*, usually specialized and operated along modified estate lines.
- *Type 6*: *Commercial estates*, usually mono-crop and with hired management and absentee ownership.

Each of the six farm types is now discussed in turn.

Type 1 Small Subsistence-oriented Family Farms

There are two main subtypes. First, and of lesser numerical importance, are those based on only one or two crops or livestock types (*e.g.*, on maize or cassava or coconuts; or on yaks or camels). Some farms of this subtype are based more on exploitation or management of a local natural resource—in the extreme case, by use of shifting cultivation or by nomadism—than on deliberate choice of their main farm enterprise (*e.g.*, on indigenous sago palm, palmyrah, coconut or nipah).

However, the main group of Asian subsistence-oriented farms is based on a wide range of crops and animal types. This second subtype is of necessity more highly mixed than are Type 2 part-commercial farms. Farms which are completely self-sufficient are rare, but self-sufficiency remains the operating objective and, if forced by circumstances, farms of this type could exist in isolation from the outside world. The structure of a Type 1 farm is exemplified in Figure.

The focus for evaluation and analysis of Type 1 farms is the household rather than the farm component of the system. However, Type 1 farms have most of the characteristics of Type 2 farms and these are discussed below in relation to this latter type.

Type 2 Small Semi-subsistence or Part-commercial Family Farms

This type is predominant throughout South and South East Asia in terms of the number of such units, the large number of people supported by them and the total volume of their production—especially of basic foodstuffs.

- *Operating Objective:* The general operating objective of this farm type is family sustenance, pursued first by production of foodstuffs for consumption and of produce/materials for use on the farm, and second by generation of some cash income for the purchase of
  - — Non-farm produced food essentials (salt, tea etc.);
  - — Other essentials such as clothing, medicines, transistor radio, batteries etc.; and

— Some farm inputs (such as agricides and fertilizer). Such cash is obtained primarily by sale of commodities which are surplus to family requirements, and secondarily—where this is possible - by production and sale of some cash crop raised specifically for this purpose.

- *Production Activities:* Type 2 farms can be further classified according to geographical occurrence (*e.g.*, wet tropics; sub-tropics of India/ Pakistan; temperate zone of North India, Nepal, Bhutan), and by whether these farms are dryland (as most are) or part irrigated. However, they are all basically similar in their crop activities which consist essentially of one or more staple food crops plus a leguminous protein source plus an oil crop. Some examples of geographically typical crop mixes are:
  — *Himalayan Hills*: Barley or buckwheat; beans or peas; mustard.
  — *Sub-tropics*: Wheat; Soybeans; Sesame.
  — *Wet tropics*: Cassava or rice; groundnuts; coconut or sesame.

In general, land is cropped to its maximum intensity, but the number of crop species grown in each of the energy/protein/oil crop subgroups, as well as the area of each, is limited by length of growing season (dependent upon temperature), rainfall occurrence and/or irrigation water supply.

Livestock, whether fish, poultry or larger animals, are typically important on Type 2 farms. They are closely integrated with the crop activities, and here—unlike the situation on farms in developed countries—they are kept for a range of purposes: direct production, draught power (except on the smallest farms), transport, manure production to sustain field and pond fertility levels, and as a store of wealth. The combination of livestock with crops results in a large number of activities, and an even larger number of different farm products.

A special subtype of this highly-mixed farm type consists of the forest-garden farms of the wet tropics as found in Kerala, Sri Lanka, Malaysia and Indonesia. These consist of both whole farms, *e.g.*, the forest-garden farms of Kandy in Sri Lanka—see McConnell—or the house-yard parts of farms forested with a more or less dense mix of economic species as in the Pekarangan lands of Java. Except for poultry, livestock are relatively unimportant on this subtype.

Farm System Boundaries: Discussion of system boundaries in Chapter mainly relates to farms of this type. Briefly, boundaries of Type 2 farm systems (and of Types 1, 3 and 4) segregate them distinctly from the external world, but the boundaries between individual farms are relatively weak. In contrast with farms in developed countries, they often have much stronger links to and interdependence with other farms in the local community than they do with the outside world, *i.e.*, with commercial input suppliers and markets for their outputs. Through such practices as exchange of labour and animal services among farms, group farming, community work ('gotong royong' in Indonesia) to develop irrigation channels, village roads etc., barter of food grains for animal products, and village-level savings' mobilization ('arisan' in Indonesia), each farm-household unit is a link in an often highly developed agro-socioeconomic network within the local community. Whatever the basis for such informal integration - culture, religion, isolation—its effect is to provide strong structural boundaries around groups of farms, hamlets and villages rather than around individual farms. Each Type 2 farm is very much a part of the community and often could not function effectively if divorced from it. It might well be said that 'No such farm is an Island, entire unto itself.'

Activity and Product Diversity: Diversity, or the degree to which farm income (however measured) is derived from a range of activities and products rather than from a single. Type 2 farms are typically the most diverse of all farms. Diversity has three elements: the number of crop/livestock activities present; the number of products obtained from those activities; and the number of ways in which each product can be used or disposed of.

The mixed farms of the Punjab commonly consist of four to six crop activities and three to six livestock activities; those of Bhutan somewhat fewer. In Sri Lanka the forest-garden farms commonly grow up to 16 or so tree and vine species producing 20 to 30 different products; and since each can be disposed of in up to four different ways (sold/bartered, consumed, processed, stored), such a system will possibly generate some 60 or so end products. This contrasts sharply with the situation on farms of Type 6, the estates producing a single product (tea, rubber etc.) with a single end use (sale).

Even a common field crop such as maize may be managed so as to yield four or five primary products (green pick, dry grain, fodder leaves and stalks, fuel, live stripped stalks as supports for a companion bean crop), and two or three subsequent processed products (maize cakes - an important kitchen industry in parts of Bhutan, alcohol etc.).

Diversification of Type 1 and 2 farms has several bases. Broadly it follows from their sustenance orientation. In remote tracts of Nepal and Bhutan it is a necessity. In the Punjab it results largely from the possibility of growing a wide range of summer and winter crops and combining these with livestock. On the closely integrated vegetable-poultry-pig-fish farms of West Malaysia and Sarawak it results from a business-like approach to profit maximization. On the forest-garden farms of Kandy in Sri Lanka it results partly from historical circumstance (the wide botanical base provided by Indian, Arab, Portuguese, Dutch and British immigrants and colonizers) and partly from a tendency of the Kandyans to plant a tree/vine/shrub in any vacant space. (If they did not, the space would soon be filled anyway through natural seed fall and germination.)

Sources and Uses of farm Resources: An important characteristic of Type 2 farms (and of farms of Type 1) is the high proportion of farm and household resources generated on the farm and, correspondingly, the low level of dependence on purchased inputs. Further, where purchased resources are used, it is common practice to restrict their use to cash crops (cotton, sugarcane, tobacco etc.) with non-cash crops receiving no purchased inputs or being grown on the residual fertilizer (and often soil tilth and soil moisture) from some previous commercial crop. Those farms which do use purchased inputs often operate at dual levels of technology—'advanced' for some main crop, 'traditional' for the rest.

Farm-generated resources including food supply (as distinct from purchased resources) are obtained in a wide variety of ways as follows:

- By operating separate specific-purpose resource-generating activities. These, as distinct from cash-generating activities, are relatively important on farms of Types 1, 2 and 3. The most common example is livestock kept primarily for manure production (as well as for other purposes). Growing a green manure crop serves a similar purpose. Growing and lopping the leaves from leguminous trees for paddy fertilizer is still common in Java. Such activities need not be elaborate: in Bali and Sri Lanka the most common 'resource-generating' activity is simply growing a clump of bamboo in the house-yard (for construction material, produce containers, fences, water pipes).
- Through simple apportionment of part of a commercial crop for household use as food or livestock feed.
- By carrying on parallel crop activities by growing one variety/type for the market and another for the family's own use. The first, typically a high-yielding improved variety, might be deficient in taste and storability but will generate cash. The second might be capable of long storage and possess other qualities valuable in rural but not in sophisticated urban markets.
- Through extensive use of all by-products: stalks of maize, tobacco, pigeon pea, cotton etc. as household fuel; wheat straw for mud brick making; etc. With some crops—especially tree crops—the 'by-products' may take on such relative importance in the range of their uses as to make unclear just what the 'main' crop is.
- By growing/keeping generally low-yielding but multi-purpose types of crops and livestock rather than high-yielding specific-purpose types. Maize, wheat etc. might be grown nearly as much for green/dry animal fodder as for grain, or—in the case of maize—as a standing trellis for some following climbing crop, *e.g.*, beans or cucumbers. (Thus the not uncommon observation that farmers are 'backward' because they do not adopt 'improved' varieties is often based on ignorance as to the real reasons why the 'old' varieties are grown.)
- Finally, resources are also generated by the multiple use of farm capital. A common example is provided by farm boundary and roadside

fences. In the Matale district of Sri Lanka most of the fences consist of kapok trees planted at very close spacing. They also support pepper vines and thus yield four 'products': kapok floss and seed (for oil) and black pepper, as well as field security. Farm fences in the Yogyakarta-Boyolali area of Central Java are used to generate a wider range of resources (or to directly produce a marketable commodity). There are four main types:

i Bamboo-lattice fences, invariably used also as supports for long-beans;

ii Napier grass fences consisting of a single row of grass, laced together into an upright position by a strip of bamboo about a metre above ground level which permits the growing top of the fence to be regularly cut for cattle feed;

iii Live leguminous trees whose leaves are harvested periodically for cattle feed or seasonally as field green manure; and

iv Cassava fences, formed by planting cassava very close (15 to 20 cm) and weaving one or two bamboo strips through the line of cassava stems at about one metre from ground level. The cassava stems are then used also as a bean trellis.

Following is a partial list of the farm and household resources/inputs/capital equipment commonly generated on farms of Types 1 and 2.

The list suggests the high level of self-sufficiency that characterizes these farm-system types, especially in isolated areas.

- *Labour and power:* All labour (except at peak periods, then by labour exchange or mutual help); all ox/buffalo/camel draught power, grain grinding power and transport; ox/buffalo treading power for grain threshing (mainly of paddy).
- *Crop inputs:* Most seed, animal manure (with a chemical fertilizer supplement on some cash crops); lopped high-nitrogen tree leaves for paddy fields (wet tropics); packing materials for market (woven bamboo baskets, teak and plantain leaf wrappers).
- *Capital equipment:* All ploughs, harrows, rakes and levellers from farm or village timber; all animal harness and repairs; fences (live kapok, areca palm, napier grass, cassava, woven bamboo); sugarcane roller crushers; oil extractors; irrigation water delivery systems (bamboo pipes in parts of Bali and the Madiun Valley of Indonesia).
- *Buildings and household:* Building panels/roofing/flooring (woven bamboo and sago/nipah/coconut leaves); buckets, containers (areca palm spathe and woven bamboo); cordage, twine, ropes; granary containers (woven, wood, packed earth); stoves and jaggery sugar boilers (packed earth); household fuel (crop residues, tree prunings); domestic light (coconut oil, butter lamps).

Type 3 Small Independent Specialized Family Farms

The key characteristics of Type 3 farms are:

- Their specialization in some particular crop or livestock activity which distinguishes them from the mixed farms of Types 1 and 2; and
- Their management independence which distinguis-hes them from Type 4 farms.

Type 3 farms fall into three subgroups according to their management orientation/purpose and type of income:

- Commercially-oriented farms, and family sustenance-oriented farms which achieve this objective through either
- Sale of part of their production (which makes them of necessity part-commercial farms) or
- Multiple-use of produce from their single specialized activity and/or barter of some of this produce for necessary commodities/goods which cannot be produced or purchased. In this latter situation such farms are also a subtype of subsistence farms (Type 1), but differ from the main body of near-subsistence farms in that only one main production activity is pursued. A sub-classification of Type 3 farms is shown in Figure. Some examples of these Type 3 farm subtypes are noted below. Probably the most important are the Subtype B near-continuous paddy farms of the wet tropics.

Subtype A (commercial):

- Small farms specializing in poultry, pig, dairy or vegetable production around metropolitan areas.
- Orchid and horticulture farms.
- Vegetable farms in upland areas throughout Malaysia, North Sumatra and Java.
- Smallholder rubber, oil palm or pepper holdings in Malaysia and Indonesia.
- Citronella and cinnamon farms in southern Sri Lanka.

Subtype B (part-commercial):

- Continuous and near-continuous paddy farms of the monsoon lands.
- Upland/dryland maize and cassava farms.
- Smallholder coffee or cacao farms.

Subtype C (near-subsistence):

- Near-subsistence maize farms of East Bhutan, Nepalese hills and Sarawak.
- Cassava-based farms on poor soil in South Java.
- Sago farms of South East Asia and New Guinea.
- Yak/sheep migratory farms of the high Himalayan valleys.

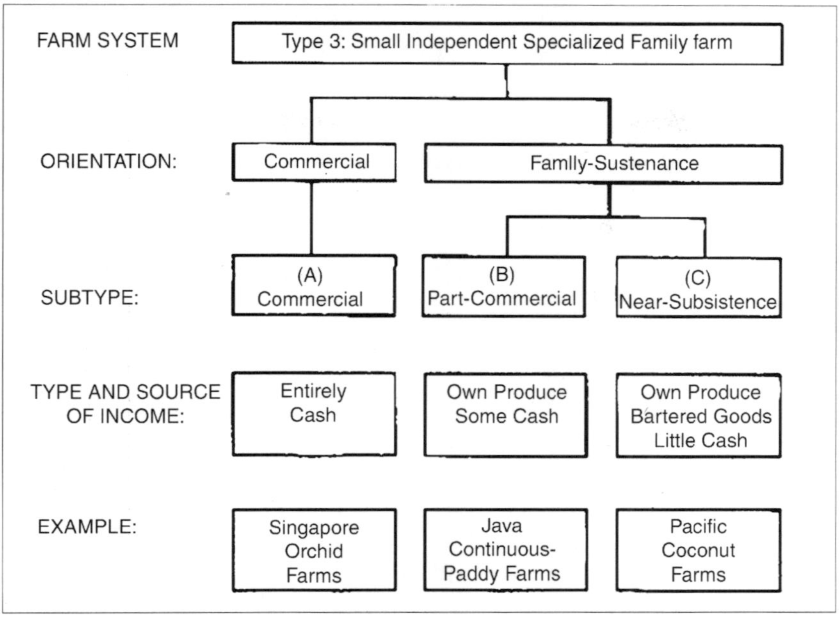

Fig. Sub-classification of Type 3 Fanning Systems.

The specialization of Type 3 farming systems is based on a wide range of factors as follows:

- *Subtype A farms*: On commercial/profit opportunity and proximity to urban markets (poultry, pig, dairy and vegetable farms). The development of such profit-oriented peri-urban farm activities is a reflection of economic growth with its demands for intensively produced products with a high income elasticity of demand.
- *Subtype B farms*: On the presence of specific physical/geographical factors (water and good soils for continuous paddy farms; favourable temperature and rainfall regimes for coffee or cacao farms).
- *Subtype C farms*: On necessity (cassava on the poor soils of South Java; yaks and sheep in the high valleys of Nepal and Bhutan).

Yet other bases for specialization are historical accident (*e.g.*, smallholder tea in Sri Lanka on lands acquired from previous tea estates); or prior presence of some natural resource (*e.g.*, the sago and nipah farms in the coastal swamps of the Philippines and New Guinea).

Type 4 Small Dependent Specialized Family Farms

Structurally, except for their lack of independence, Type 4 farms are quite akin to Type 3 farms and contain the same three:

- Commercial
- Part-commercial and
- Near-subsistence subtypes; however, they are sufficiently important to be examined as a separate type. The characteristics which set them

apart from farms of Types 1, 2 and 3 are their high degree of activity specialization and the lack of real decision-making power possessed by the farm family. The specialization characteristic may be based on the same factors noted above for Type 3 (independent specialized) farms. The dependence characteristic arises from the fact that on Type 4 farms the family is not free to decide what to produce, nor frequently the conditions under which some obligatory activity is to be carried on. This lack of independence can be due to several factors, *viz.*:

- *Terms of Tenancy:* Tenant farmers are often obliged to produce one or more specific crop or livestock products, as dictated in a landlord-tenant agreement. The tenant-operated vegetable farms of Qatar are an example.
- *Structural Integration:* In this situation small family farms are integrated more or less closely as the production arm of some larger farming cum processing system. Small tenant-operated farms supplying sugarcane to a mill or leaf to a tobacco-processing factory are common examples of such vertically integrated farms. Not only is the crop which is to be grown specified, but the conditions of production—timing of planting and harvesting, amounts of fertilizers to be used, spraying programmes etc.—are also dictated by the controlling authority.
- *Debt:* Some agro-industrial units (such as milk processing plants) often provide farmers with input factors (such as cattle, feed and technical assistance) in order to achieve a regular or higher quality supply of their needed raw material (*e.g.*, milk). These advances are usually made in the form of a loan at attractive terms, but often the only way farmers can liquidate this loan (and perhaps eventually regain their independence) is to continue to produce the particular commodity—usually under conditions set by and to the relative advantage of the lender.
- A second kind of debt, that entered into for consumption rather than production purposes, can also provide the basis for farmer dependence. Thus for generations the small cardamom farmers of the southern Bhutan hills have been indebted to the cardamom traders/money lenders of the towns along the West Bengal border. The only hope these farmers have of liquidating such debt—usually used for food, clothing and household items—is to continue to grow this specialist crop and sell it at whatever terms may be offered by the traders.
- *Government Policy Directives:* In some countries, farmers' lack of independence in production decision making is the result of government power to issue production directives. In Indonesia, *e.g.*, the Government

has the broad power to direct that some percentage of those village lands which lie within the command area of each sugar factory be planted to sugarcane. Typically each hectare of land, owned by individuals of the village, might be under sugar for one year during which time it is farmed by the company as part of a larger estate. It then reverts to its owner for three years during which period he or she will operate it as a complete and independent farm, until it is again taken for sugar. During this three-year period the farmer has all normal decision-making powers (crop selection and how each is grown). During the one-year cane phase, for which the farmer receives payment as a 'landlord', he or she has no decision-making power whatsoever. This system thus involves the alternating of two distinctly different farming systems (as shown diagrammatically in Figure).

- *Lack of Alternative Market Outlets:* Absence of any real independence in management can also be due to lack of alternative market outlets, especially when the product is too bulky or fragile to be transported far from the farm. For example, most of the small cassava farms of Perak in West Malaysia are located on poor soils which would grow little else except cassava (many are located on tailings or spoil from tin mines). This accounts for their specialization. The second factor, their lack of management independence, is due to the high bulk/low value of their product which must be disposed of to chipping factories in the immediate vicinity. There is little practical possibility of seeking higher prices by transporting the raw cassava further afield. Similar situations face the citronella grass and cinnamon leaf farmers of the Galle-Matara district in southern Sri Lanka. Here again the high bulk/low value of these farm outputs deny the growers any real choice in disposing of their crops to other than the local oil mills under price/quality conditions set by the mills.
- *Source of farm Resources:* Farms of Type 4 (and Type 3) are usually not self-sufficient in resource-generation; *e.g.*, the continuous cropping of specialized paddy farms (Subtype B) is usually possible only because it is based on some purchased package of 'high technology' inputs-HYV seed, artificial fertilizer and agricides. Dependence on commercial inputs is even greater on farms of Subtype A, *e.g.*, purchased feed and veterinary supplies for specialist poultry and pig farms. However, Subtype C farms might exist with only minimal purchased inputs; *e.g.*, the upland near-subsistence maize farms of Nepal, Bhutan and Sarawak are based on use of retained 'local' seed, no artificial fertilizer and no agricides.
- *System Boundaries:* The boundaries of the specialized farms also vary with subtype. Those of the commercially-oriented farms of Subtype

A will interface more to the outside world (*i.e.*, to suppliers of inputs and product markets) than to other farms; however, the boundaries of farm-system Subtypes B and C will tend to be stronger around groups of contiguous farms or all the farms of a hamlet or village in much the same way as the communal boundaries of Type 1 and 2 farming systems set these apart from the outside world.

***Type 5* Large Commercial Family Farms**

Type 5 farms are similar in most respects to estates except that usually the primary beneficiaries are members of an (often extended) family rather than absentee owners or shareholders. They fall into two subtypes. The first consists of mono-crop farms which are at the fringe of the estate sector proper and which are usually dependent on this estate sector for research, availability of new crop varieties and often for processing and marketing facilities. The 10- to 20-hectare coconut farms of Sri Lanka which exist side-by-side with the large (now nationalized) coconut estates are examples.

The second subtype consists of either mono-product or mixed farms which are not part of any estate sector but are organized along commercial lines, *e.g.*, using hired labour, being dependent on purchased rather than farm-produced inputs and, except in the case of tree-crop farms, adjusting the activity or activity mix according to commercial opportunity. The larger cinnamon farms of Galle-Matara and the mixed coconut-dairy farms of Sri Lanka are examples of this subtype. So also are the large 30- to 50-hectare mixed grain-livestock farms of Sind and Punjab.

The operating objective of Type 5 farms is profit or utility maximization through market sales. As a group and in pursuit of that objective, they are the most dynamic of the six farm types discussed here.

***Type 6* Commercial Estates**

Commercial estates are generally mono-crop in nature. They are largely a colonial legacy, first established to provide cheap raw materials (and later some food and beverage products) to the industries of Europe and North America. This role continues except that they now also serve national industrialization.

The Chief Characteristics of this farm Type are as Follows:

- *Crops:* The main crops on which Type 6 farms were initially based are rubber, sugar, cinchona, cacao, tea, coffee, cinnamon, cloves, nutmeg, coconut and the coarse fibres. Some of the old traditional crops have become uneconomic (sisal and to some extent cinchona); some have become primarily smallholder crops (the spices and coffee); and new estate crops (such as flowers, oil palm and citronella) or improved varieties of old crops have emerged. Recent years have also seen the emergence (usually close to metropolitan areas) of livestock-based estates, particularly for pork and broiler production.

- *On-estate Processing:* Primary processing is an integral part of the operation of most estates (*e.g.*, tea manufacture, sheet and crepe rubber production, copra curing). This requires a high level of capital investment which, to be fully utilized, requires a flow-type of operation rather than a batch-type. This has two effects. On the one hand it tends to restrict estate production to those crops which yield a fairly uniform year-round flow of produce (tea, rubber, coconut, cocoa etc.). On the other hand it gives estates certain advantages, *e.g.*, quality control, relative to smallholders producing these same products. Some crops which naturally give an intermittent or irregular product flow are also made amenable to continuous estate-type production by relay-planting or chemical control of growth time-patterns (*e.g.*, sugar, sisal and pineapple).
- *Size:* Estate size is commonly from 200 to 2 000 hectares but area itself is not an important criterion: a 40-hectare orchid estate will generate about as much income and employment as will a 200-hectare tea estate or a 400-hectare coconut estate.
- *Marketing:* Marketing plays a very important role in estate operations. Most estates are jealous of their product reputation or 'mark' and make deliberate attempts at product differentiation. They also maintain close contact with buyers and monitor demand trends. Thus the larger cacao estates of Malaysia might be in daily telex or e-mail contact with buyers in Hamburg and Amsterdam. This contrasts sharply with the situation on smallholder farms growing the same crops: most smallholders have little interest in their product once it leaves the farm gate and, not infrequently, have no knowledge of its use after export.
- *System Beneficiaries and Operating Objectives:* Previously, the primary beneficiaries of estates were usually absentee shareholders who employed professional expatriate management and often also a docile expatriate labour force (as was the case in Malaysia, Sri Lanka, Fiji and Mauritius). Thus, before their nationalization, the estates of Sri Lanka were referred to accurately, if somewhat emotively, as 'islands of privilege and prosperity in a sea of poverty'. With exceptions, this situation has changed markedly; consideration of the interests of secondary beneficiaries now receives far greater attention than formerly and these are more widely defined to include the host government, the estate labour force and their dependants, local communities and councils. Profit remains the main operating objective but this is increasingly tempered by the condition that worker retirement schemes, schools, clinics, roads, village welfare centres etc. be provided at estate cost. In short, increasing proportions of

operating profit are being diverted from the primary to the secondary beneficiaries of this system type.

- *Management:* A mono-product estate system is at once more simple and more complex than the systems found on mixed family farms. Since only one product is usually involved, only one production activity exists, and there is no need to allocate resources among five, six, seven or more competing production enterprises, as on a typical mixed family farm. Also, very little if any of an estate's resources have to be generated within the system's boundaries. (On a typical tea estate usually only fuelwood and hydro power might be produced as inputs to tea production, and even the use of these is declining.) Thus, again in contrast with family farms, there are no resource-generating activities to divert attention from the main production task. However, although only one production enterprise subsystem rather than a multiplicity exists, it is carried on at a sophisticated level. Volume production usually means that per unit profit margins are thin; the wrong decision at some critical time, especially with long-term tree crops, can have serious and long-lasting consequences.

Specialization means that the advantages of crop diversification are not available; there is no possibility of making up on the swings what might be lost on the roundabouts. If a Bhutanese farm with one pig suffers an outbreak of swine fever the farmer would probably shrug his shoulders and go off to the paddy field or do something else. If it happened on a 500-sow estate it could spell disaster.

Moreover, insofar as most estates are based on one or other of the tree crops, the effects of some sub-optimal decisions (*e.g.*, regarding variety/strain of crop to be planted, spacing, initial fertilizer etc.) might well have long-lasting if not permanent adverse effects, possibly over the 30-year life of a rubber stand, the 65-year life of a coconut stand, or even longer in the case of tea.

While not requiring the allocation of resources among enterprises, planning and management of a mono-product estate system requires the explicit recognition, organization and optimization of a large number of agro-technical processes. An example is given in Figure which shows the sequential steps in establishing and operating a tea crop. For each step, several alternatives are possible.

If this were only one of several crops to be grown (*e.g.*, as on a mixed smallholding), most of the questions listed in Figure would not be asked; each operation would proceed on the basis of village tradition, farmer experience or local lore.

But on an estate they have to be explicitly asked and answered if the optimal level of long-term sustainable production and profit is to be achieved. In the management planning of estates,

Three kinds of management analysis can be particularly important:

- Evaluation of some single production enterprise (crop or livestock) over a long time period;
- The optimization of processes because even small marginal reductions in inputs/costs will become important when spread over many hundreds of hectares or thousands of tonnes of produce; and
- Simulation of estate operations as a whole system under uncertainty.

Having defined the six main farm types and outlined their chief structural characteristics, it is now possible to turn in following chapters to a consideration of the field of farm management analysis as this would be applied to these farm types, especially the small farms, *i.e.*, Types 1 to 4. First, however, two contrasting examples of small-farm systems are presented in the following section.

Table. Alternative Processes in Producing Tea on an Estate

Sequential operations		Alternative processes for each operation	
(1)	Clear land	Method:	Labour? elephants? tractor?
		Level:	What season? depth? tilth?
(2)	Establish cover crop	Method:	Which crop?
		Level:	for how long? 15,18 or 24 months?
(3)	Plant tea	Method:	What kind? seedling or vegetatively propagated?
		Level:	What population density? 3-4-5 000 plants/acre?
(4)	Weed	Method:	How? hand? chemical? men? women?
		Level:	Every 4, 6, 8... weeks?
(5)	Fertilize	Method:	What type(s)?
		Level:	What levels of application? frequency? timing
(6)	Pick	Method:	How? machine? hand? male or female?
		Level:	Frequency? every 25, 30, 35... days?
(7)	Cure/pack	Method:	How? for which of many markets?
		Level:	Mix grades? in what proportions?
(8)	Etc.		

STRUCTURE OF SMALL-FARM SYSTEMS

A useful way of introducing the discussion of following chapters is to look briefly via examples at the structure of two of the small-farm types, the partly commercialized farms (Type 2) and the near-subsistence farms (Type 1).

Model of a Type 2 Farm

Based on McConnell, Figure presents a model of the annual operation of a 'representative' Pathan farm in the Peshawar district of North West Frontier Province, Pakistan (the data are actually means of a group of 11 similar farms). The central core of the farm system consists of two livestock, seven crop and two on-farm processing activities: dairy and draught cattle, berseem (clover), a mixed orchard, sugar beet, sugarcane, maize, millet and wheat. The processing activities consist of converting some of the milk to ghee for sale or consumption (in this particular year it was all consumed), and crushing/ boiling some of the sugarcane to make gur (unrefined 'country' sugar), some of which is consumed, some sold.

These 11 activities are represented by bar columns in the middle part of Figure. Input and output values are in rupee (Rs) terms. The levels of the various activities, livestock population and other relevant structural data are summarized below.

Crops		Level
Berseem (cattle feed)		0.6 Acres
Orchard (use + sale)		1.1 Acres
Sugar beet (sale)		0.7 Acres
Sugarcane (sale + gur)		1.3 Acres
Maize (use)		1.3 Acres
Millet (use)		0.2 Acres
Wheat (use)		2.0 Acres
Sugarcane:		
	Produced	542.0 Maunds[2] plus 15.5 Maunds of gur
	Sold as cane	542.0 Maunds
Livestock		
Bullocks		2.0 Head
Milk animals:		1.7 Head
	Producing	1.1 Head
	Dry	0.6 Head
Young Stock (Dairy + Draught)		1.2 Head
ox traction available (pair)		365 Days
	Actually used	74 Days
Milk produced:		22.0 Maunds
	Used/sold as milk	18.4 Maunds
	Converted to ghee	3.6 Maunds

Note: [2] Maund (abbreviated to mds in Figure 2.4) is a volumetric measure corresponding to about 90 pounds (40 kg) of sugarcane; ghee is measured by the seer (about 14 pounds or 6 kg).

Figure consists of two sections: the *household component*, circumscribed by a boundary line in the top right section of the diagram, and the *farm component* of the farm-household system which constitutes the remainder of the diagram.

Referring to the *household component* of Figure, the farm family consists of seven members of all ages. Together these members are capable of supplying 1 053 labour days annually. In fact there is only enough work on the farm to occupy 443 labour days, and only 21 days of off-farm work can be found, thus 589 days are either occupied in farm maintenance or development work not connected with any particular crop, or are occupied in social/religious activities, or are idle. (Here they are shown as 'idle'.)

The second general input by the family into the farm component is cash for meeting the direct costs of each of the production activities. This cash is obtained by the household as ₹ 2 848 from sale of farm produce plus ₹ 65 from 21 days of off-farm work. (Of course the family component also supplies other vital inputs to the system—management, direction and purpose — but these cannot be measured.) These family-provided inputs into each of the activities, cash and labour days, are shown in Figure in the two top rows of the farm component.

Consider now the *farm component* as depicted in Figure. *Activities:* Referring to the activity columns in the body of Figure, each of these is an abbreviated activity budget showing first the inputs to and then the outputs from the activity. For example, the inputs to 0.7 acres of sugar beet are cash ₹ 79, labour 48 days, bullocks 8.5 days, manure 66.5 maunds; and the outputs are 32 maunds of leaves (by-product) and 175 maunds of beets.

Similarly, the inputs to sugarcane are cash ₹ 250, labour 82 days, bullocks 14.4 days, manure 80.6 maunds; and the outputs are 185 maunds of cane tops (for bullock feed) and 542 maunds of sale cane, plus a small but unknown amount of cane diverted to home processing for gur which as a separate activity uses ₹ 77 cash, 25 labour days and 2.2 bullock days, and yields 15.5 maunds of such 'country' sugar of which 6.8 maunds is consumed and 8.7 maunds is sold.

The two livestock activities—dairy and draught oxen—are shown at the left side of the model. Inputs are cash costs, labour and livestock feed.

This latter is somewhat complex.

- *Livestock Feed:* Feed is shown in two units of measurement: amount (*i.e.*, maunds of around 40 kg) of actual material, and the equivalent in maunds of total digestible nutrients (TDN). This conversion is desirable in order to standardize each of the several different feedstuffs produced on the farm, each having a different nutritional value, into a common basis of units of TDN. The total amount of feed fed to the livestock is shown at the top of the livestock columns, 101 maunds of TDN, coming from the 'total feed pool'. All feed entering this common pool comes from one of three sources:

- — Grass (cut from the orchard) equivalent to 5.9 maunds of TDN;
- — 613 maunds of green feed, equivalent to 63.8 maunds of TDN, which comes from some of the crop activities (berseem 246 maunds, beet leaves 32 maunds, cane tops 185 maunds, maize green chop 150 maunds) and

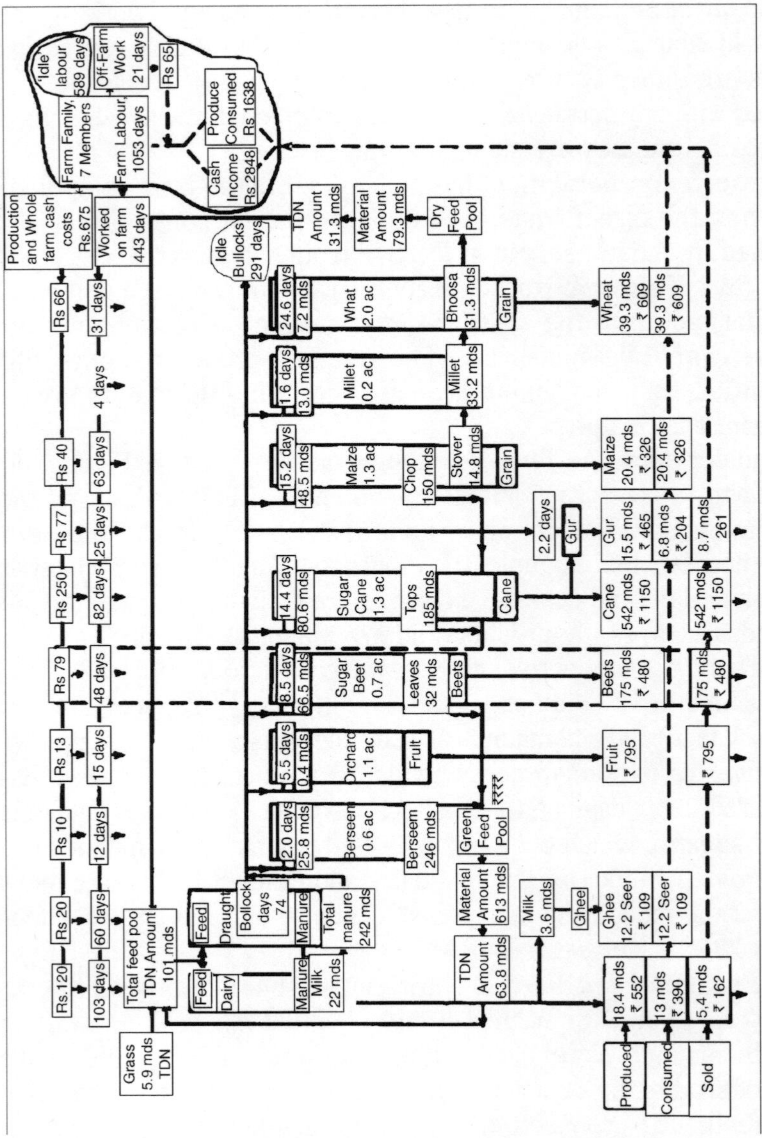

Fig. Structural Model of a Pathan Farm Exemplifying a Type 2 Farm

- — 79.3 maunds of dry feed, equivalent to 31.3 maunds of TDN, from some of the crops (maize stover 14.8 maunds, millet 33.2 maunds, bhoosa/wheat straw 31.3 maunds).

The green feed is shown as cycling to the left and being accumulated in a 'green feed pool' totalling 613 maunds of material, equivalent to 63.8 maunds of TDN; the dry feed items are accumulated to the right into a 'dry feed pool' totalling 79.3 maunds of material or 31.3 maunds of TDN. Then, as the arrows indicate, both these green and dry feed pools are accumulated above the livestock activities into a 'total feed pool' which, when supplemented by cut grass, totals 101 maunds of TDN flowing to all the dairy and draught animals (which include young and dry stock as previously listed).

These feed flows refer only to feed produced on the farm. In addition, stock are grazed on village common lands when grass is available there (the amounts of such grazing could not be recorded).

In summary, the following widely diversified feedstuffs are obtained on this type of farm: grass from the orchard, some rough common-lands' and roadside grazing, berseem clover, beet tops, sugarcane tops, green maize chop, dry maize stalks, millet and wheat bhoosa (straw).

Only two of these items are specially grown for the cattle, namely berseem and millet.

- *Livestock Outputs:* The cattle activities generate three outputs: bullock power, manure for the crops, and milk. The number of bullock days flowing to each of the crops are shown, being 2.0 for the clover, 5.5 for the orchard, 8.5 for the sugar beet etc. Crushing of sugarcane for gur also uses 2.2 days of bullock power. Bullock power not used is shown as 291 'idle' bullock days. Below the livestock activities, a total of 242 maunds of manure are accumulated from all the livestock. This also is shown flowing to the crops: 25.8 maunds to berseem. 0.4 for the orchard, 66.5 for the sugar beet etc.
- *Final Activity Outputs:* The lower section of the model shows the final products flowing from each activity and the amount of each product consumed by the household or sold, each in quantity and value terms.
- *Household Income:* Farm income consists first of the value of produce consumed. This is accumulated to the right in Figure and enters the household component of the system as a total value of ₹ 1,638. Second, cash from farm sales is similarly accumulated and has a total value of ₹ 2,848. Total income, real plus imputed, is ₹ 4,551 which includes the small income from non-farm work. Thus, for this year, income in kind from home-consumed production constitutes 1,638/4,551 or 36 per cent of total gross family income. On this basis, it might be said that the farm is about one third subsistence oriented and two-thirds commercially oriented.

As shown, total cash inputs into all the activities amount to ₹ 675. Thus, in this particular year, the household would have a cash 'surplus' of ₹ 2 848

+ 65 - 675 or ₹ 2 238. This amount would be available to meet any cash costs in farm maintenance (which were not considered as a cost in the model), and to meet cash living expenses for purchased clothing, food, medical expenses etc. Any final surplus after meeting these latter expenses would be available as savings.

In summary, this Pathan fanning system from the North West Frontier Province of Pakistan is a highly diversified one. It has 11 major production and processing activities and it produces 15 separate products and by-products (excluding bullock power, young livestock and manure for the fields). Cash inputs are low, mainly for fertilizer for some of the crops and a minimal amount of agricides; most seed is retained. Although a significant degree of self-sufficiency is present, it is not a true subsistence farm.

Model of a Type 1 Farm

Most farms of Type 1 (*i.e.*, small subsistence-oriented family farms) in Asia now have at least some element of commercialisation and generate at least some small amount of cash for the purchase of essential items. At the top end of the structural scale this type merges into the small mixed Type 2 farms; at the bottom end it includes the locally-shifting cultivators of Sarawak-Kalimantan (and these merge into the hunter-gatherers and forest dwellers of New Guinea, Kalimantan, Sarawak and Sumatra).

Subsistence or near-subsistence is a condition more often imposed than voluntary: one sub-classification could be on the basis of external causal factors; *e.g.*, the near-subsistence farms of India, the hills of Nepal and parts of Java exist because of shortage of land; those of Bhutan (where land is seldom limiting) because of isolation and the lack of roads and markets; and those of the new settlement areas of Sri Lanka because of the lack of family labour and oxpower to till more than a minimal subsistence area.

When examined from the viewpoint of their range of activity, variation of this farm type ranges all the way from being highly mixed to almost mono-crop. In the first of these conditions, this type merges into Type 2 farms. In the second extreme condition these farms are structured around production of a single bulk staple - usually maize, dry paddy, cassava, palm sago or coconut. Secondary foodstuffs and non-food subsistence items are obtained by supplementary activities: fishing; hunting or collecting in nearby forest areas for food or items for sale (birds, monkeys, butterflies, orchids, beeswax, rattan etc.); or by sending a family member off to work somewhere outside the subsistence environment.

Although they can generally be described as resource-poor, poverty is not necessarily a characteristic of Type 1 farm families. At one end of the scale the economic condition might be poverty verging on destitution, even starvation. At the other extreme it might be prosperity when that condition is judged by an availability of resources in excess of those needed to maintain a reasonable physical existence.

Again the best way of illustrating systems of this subsistence type is with the aid of a model. Such a model is shown in Figure which describes the structure and operation of a near-subsistence farm located at about 1 700 m (5 500 feet) above the town of Wangdiprdan in Central Bhutan. The chief features of this farm are its highly diversified activities and its very high level of self-sufficiency. In this example the farm is a prosperous one (as that term was defined above) and its subsistence nature is based on isolation, poor roads, lack of markets and therefore of incentive—indeed opportunity—to enter the commercial world.

The model refers to an operating period of one year:

- Data from a 1985 farm survey by Nim Dorji and the senior author. The monetary unit is Ngultrum (Nu) = US 8.7 cents in 1985.

The farm's land resources consist of 1.75 langdo[4] (0.25 hectares) of dry paddy fields, 1.25 langdo (0.18 hectares) of dry fields, and 4.00 langdo (0.4 hectares) of wetland rented from a local monastery. However, the effective size of this farm is only 5.75 langdo: the 1.25 langdo of dryland is too far away to be easily worked and, since more accessible land can be rented from the local monastery, the dryland portion is not used.

(If it were cultivated there would be no market for the extra produce, which would also be surplus to family requirements.)

- [4]A langdo is the area a pair of oxen can plough in a day: a dry langdo is about one seventh of a hectare and a wet paddy-field langdo is about one tenth of a hectare.

The farm family consists of five adults, all able to work full-time if necessary, *i.e.*, a population density and potential workforce of six persons per hectare. It is assumed that this family could provide a potential supply of 1 200 labour-days annually. Livestock resources are also high relative to farm size: two oxen, two milkcows, three young cattle, three pigs, three hens. Cattle are grazed off the farm on common lands for more than half the year.

The farm structural model of Figure consists of six parts as indicated by the circled numbers 1 to 6 in the diagram. Part 1 shows human, livestock and land resources, as noted above. Part 3 shows the farm resource pool. All resources except rented land are owned or are generated by the system itself (all seed, manure, bran, labour etc.).

There are no purchased inputs; even the rented land is paid for by barter with the monks. In Part 2 of the structural model, all productive activities (subsystems) are listed in separate activity columns. There are nine of these (plus one external resource-generating activity): tending cattle, pigs and poultry; growing paddy, wheat, buckwheat, mustard, vegetables/chillies and fruit. The external resource-generating activity consists of one family member working part-time off the farm (for local government, clearing paths and roads after landslides).

The coefficients within each upper column of Part 2 are the resources used by the respective subsystems: *e.g.*, the paddy crop uses 5.25 langdo of land, 115 labour days, 29 kg of seed, 14 tonnes of manure and 23 draught ox days. Of the used total area of 5.75 langdo, two langdo are doublecropped. Part 4 shows all intermediate products (bran, grain, straw, draught days, manure and seed) which are produced by the nine farm activities. These are generated in the activity columns, accumulated to the left in the 'intermediate outputs' section (Part 4), then cycled back to the resources pool of Part 3 and from there to the activities which use each such resource/input. As shown by the left-side arrows from Part 4 to Part 3 and thence to Part 2 of Figure, resources used up by the activities (Part 2) in any year are replenished by the activities producing intermediate products, but these need not exactly balance because some resources may be held over in storage: *e.g.*, in this year 21.5 tonnes of manure are used on the crops but only 15 tonnes were produced; 6.5 tonnes came from storage not recorded in Part 3 of Figure.

Part 5 of Figure lists and aggregates final outputs from the nine activities: *e.g.*, for the paddy activity the intermediate products from paddy (bran, straw, seed) cycle to the left in Part 4 and then up to the resource pool. But the final paddy products consist of 934 kg of grain used for family food, 340 kg converted to alcohol (consumed not sold), 410 kg bartered to other families for other types of food not produced on this farm and 112 kg of paddy paid as rent to the monks for the four langdo of wetland. The various food items produced and consumed on the farm are shown in the 'food' line of Part 5: 13 kg of butter and 50 kg cheese from the cattle, a 50 kg pig, 10 kg eggs, 934 kg of paddy, 20 kg of wheat etc. Alcohol was made from a total of 366 kg of grain (paddy and wheat).

The bottom of Part 5 shows those outputs which were sold. In this particular year the only marketed items were some citrus fruit (76 kg) and vegetables (70 kg) which were sold for Nu 16 and Nu 50 respectively at the Wangdiprdan weekly 'hat' (street market).

Clearly this farm system is one very close to complete subsistence. There are no purchased inputs into the crop/livestock activities and all farm capital items such as ploughs, harrows and ox gear are home-made, as are the woven storage bins for grain storage. The mustard seed oil for home use is extracted using a kitchen press and used for both cooking and in the lamps before the family's Buddhist altar. Parts 1 to 5 of the model refer to the farm components of the farm-household system. Part 6 refers to the household component: this consists of data relating to the use of family labour, and to family income (cash plus food) and non-farm family expenditure. Of the 1 200 days of family labour available, 444 days are used in farm activities and off-farm work, leaving 756 days designated as 'idle'. (In fact some of these would be used in general maintenance around the farm in jobs not directly related to any of the nine production activities.)

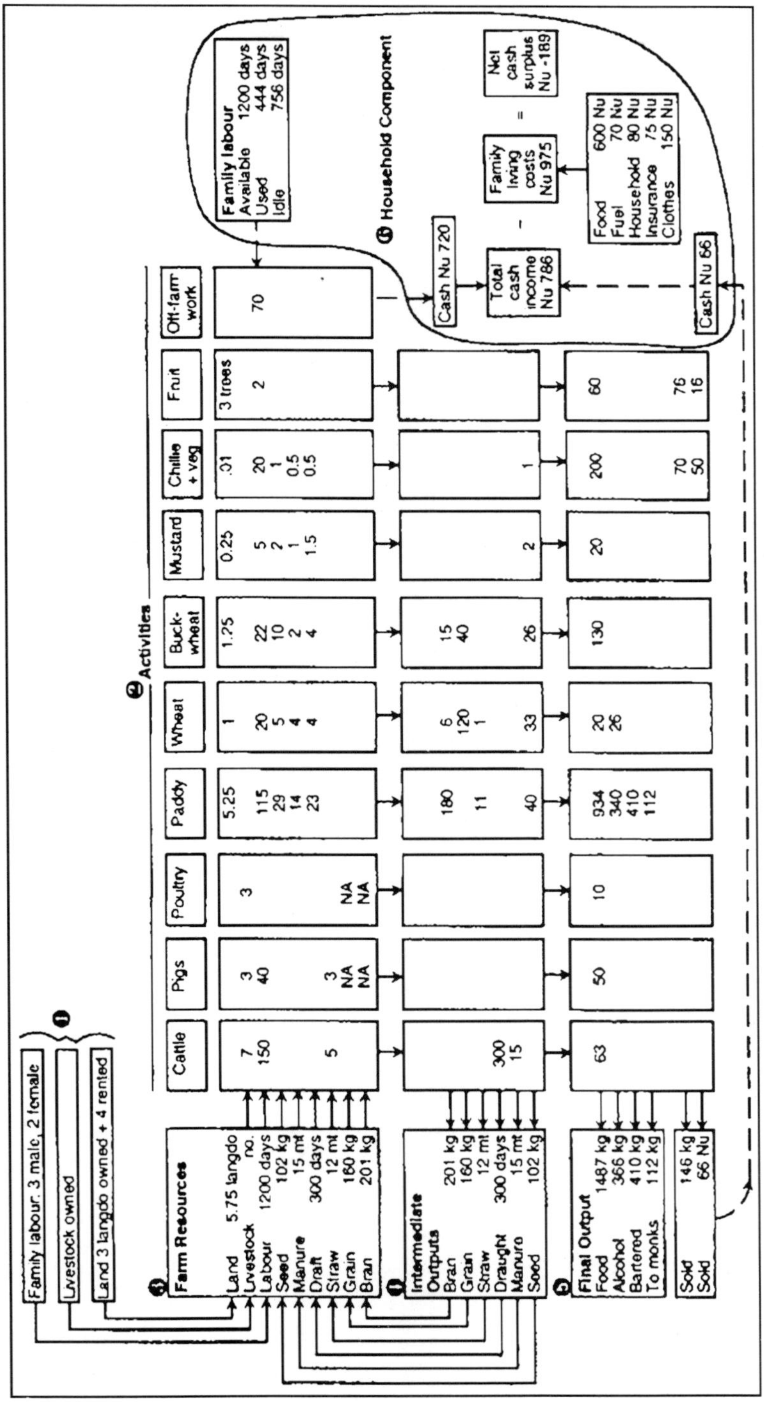

Total cash family income as shown in Part 6 amounts to Nu 786: Nu 720 is from off-farm work; only Nu 66 is from sale of farm produce. From this cash income, family cash (non-farm) living costs are deducted, leaving an apparent net deficit this particular operating year of Nu 189. The items comprising family cash expenditure are shown: Nu 600 for purchased food, Nu 70 for purchased fuel (kerosene), Nu 80 for household items, Nu 75 for insurance and Nu 150 for clothing. The apparent negative cash balance of Nu 189 would be made up from savings or by obtaining credit for purchases.

Due to off-farm work and cash expenditures for the items shown, the farm-household system at this point has ceased to be a purely subsistence one. However, if the family's economic conditions changed for the worse, the expenditure pattern could be easily adjusted to reduce or eliminate some of the cash expenditure items (especially food which consists mainly of 'luxury' items), and the remaining needs for cash could be met by sale of a pig or a little mustard oil.

It is now possible to turn in following chapters to an examination of the individual structural elements of this and other types of farm systems.

FARM HOUSEHOLDSYSTEM BUDGETING

ENTERPRISES *VERSUS* ACTIVITIES

In everyday language, the terms 'enterprise' and 'activity' are often used interchangeably. In technical usage, however, these terms have quite distinct meanings. There are two reasons for this.

First, in systems analysis, many 'enterprises', if they are to be analysed as systems, must be broken down into subsystems. 'Coconut enterprise' is a good enough description if it refers to growing and selling coconuts; but if it includes selling some nuts, making coir from the husks of others, making and selling yam from this coir, and making and selling charcoal from the coconut shells etc., it will obviously be necessary to differentiate among these various subsystems of the coconut enterprise.

This is best done by referring to all coconut-based subsystems in aggregate as an enterprise, and to each respective subsystem as a separate activity. Clearly, selling fresh coconuts will involve different resource inputs, product outputs and management problems than spinning coconut-husk yam. Thus a particular farm enterprise may involve one or more activities.

Second, some planning methods in farm-system analysis and construction (*e.g.*, budgeting and linear programming) require that the alternative tactics or technologies which can be used in the production of some resource or final product be specified.

To take a very simple example, production of one hectare of paddy might require 100 kg of cattle manure or its equivalent as fertilizer. If the farmer has no manure, possible alternative tactics for obtaining it might be for him or her to buy NPK fertilizer, or to exchange labour with a neighbour for the needed manure, or to grow a green manure crop in the future paddy field, or to buy a cow. These alternative tactics (or any particular mixture of them) are each different activities which might be used to the same end of producing paddy. An important aspect of farm planning is thus to determine which technological activity or activities might best be used within each enterprise.

There are three ways in which 'activity' may be used as a technical term relative to the hierarchy of agricultural systems of Figure.

These are:

- To refer to a particular technology or process used at Order Level 1 or 2 in the farm system;
- To refer to a resource-generating subsystem of Order Level 3 in the farm system; and
- To distinguish at Order Levels 4 and 6
  - — A particular method of producing the product of an enterprise from other methods of producing the same product or
  - — The production of a particular product in an enterprise which has a variety of possible products. In general, which meaning should be given to the term 'activity' will be apparent from the context. Most often it will have the enterprise-related meaning pertinent to systems of Order Levels 4 and 6. Fuller consideration of the various types of activities relevant to the planning of farm systems is given.

ENTERPRISES

As noted above, an enterprise consists of a farm subsystem aimed at the output of final product. It may involve one or more activities in terms of the technologies used and the form of the final product.

ENTERPRISE BOUNDARIES

For farm management systems analysis in all Modes, an essential property of enterprises is that they be possible of identification and disaggregation from the whole-farm system context in which they occur, *i.e.* that their boundaries be defined and that their input-output relationships be measurable.

Where the enterprises already exist as part of a mixed farm system this proceeds by the three sequential steps of:

- Examining the farm system to identify the main commodities being produced;
- Identifying the resources used in relation to each commodity; and
- Identifying and quantifying enterprise input-output relationships in the form of an enterprise budget table as outlined.

ENTERPRISE STRUCTURAL TYPES

In terms of their structure, enterprises may be broadly categorized as simple, composite or complex. A *simple enterprise* is one which can be readily identified within and disaggregated from a whole-farm system. The extreme case is found on mono-crop estates and single-enterprise farms (*e.g.*, Sri Lankan tea estates, Singaporean pig farms) where the enterprise subsystem is practically equivalent to the whole-farm system. Only slightly more difficult to identify/disaggregate/quantify are the buckwheat and apple enterprises on small Himalayan hill farms; but the disaggregation of, *e.g.*, cotton/wheat/paddy/livestock enterprises on a mixed Sind farm is usually more difficult because of the structural interrelationships among enterprises.

A *composite enterprise* is one which aggregates what structurally or logically should be considered as two or more different enterprise subsystems into a single composite enterprise for one of two reasons—the practical difficulties of disaggregation, or the fact that the work involved in disaggregation might not be warranted for the purpose at hand. An example would be the 'livestock' component of a typical Peshawar mixed farm where the livestock could consist of two cows (for milk, butter, ghee, cheese sale and/or consumption), two oxen for ploughing (but sometimes rented out), three young sale cattle, one camel and three donkeys for transport, six sheep for wool (to be sold or spun) and five goats for milk and meat.

All these classes of stock would usually be run/pastured together most of the year, none receiving any special treatment. While the different classes of stock can be readily identified, it would be very difficult indeed to disaggregate them into seven separate livestock enterprises, *i.e.*, to define meaningful boundaries for each livestock species subsystem. For most planning purposes they could be regarded as a single composite 'livestock' enterprise.

A similar situation arises on the intensive vegetable farms in the mountain zones of Java, where five, six, seven... vegetable species occupy the same field simultaneously, some directly dependent on others for shade, wind protection or live trellis support, and where each relay of each crop is partly dependent on previous relays for residual fertilizer and pest reduction. It is very difficult to disaggregate the species into separate bean, maize, sweet potato... enterprises. Possibly the most difficult of all systems to disaggregate are the highly mixed forest-gardens of the wet tropics, partly because the mix of 15 or more species is continuously changing.

A *complex enterprise* is one in which there is more than one important product and where there is some considerable degree of cycling of resources within the same enterprise, usually via the farm resource pool. This is common in traditional agriculture as exemplified in Figures. By comparison, most enterprises on modem commercial farms are structurally simple. Using wheat production as an example, the situations are compared in Figure.

As shown on the righthand side of Figure, on modem commercial farms most resources are typically purchased, wheat is often grown as a sole crop for grain which is sold, and that is the end of the matter. On the other hand, in the traditional Asian situation, wheat is usually combined with several other enterprises and most resources are farm-generated. Thus, in the lefthand-side example of Figure, wheat both uses and produces some of its resources (retained seed and stockfeed cycled as oxpower and manure fertilizer). The enterprise has several products: grain (for family sustenance, sale and farm use), retained seed, bhoosa (straw, some of which might be sold for use in brickmaking and some retained for use as livestock feed/bedding), and stubble which will be used or sold to other villagers as grazing. In addition, the enterprise might provide the basis for kitchen-scale food processing/marketing activities. Figure clearly illustrates the complexity of what at first glance might seem a fairly simple enterprise.

ENTERPRISE AND ACTIVITY BUDGETS

An enterprise or activity is defined and quantified in terms of a budget table which, relative to some specific time span, defines the boundaries of the subsystem.

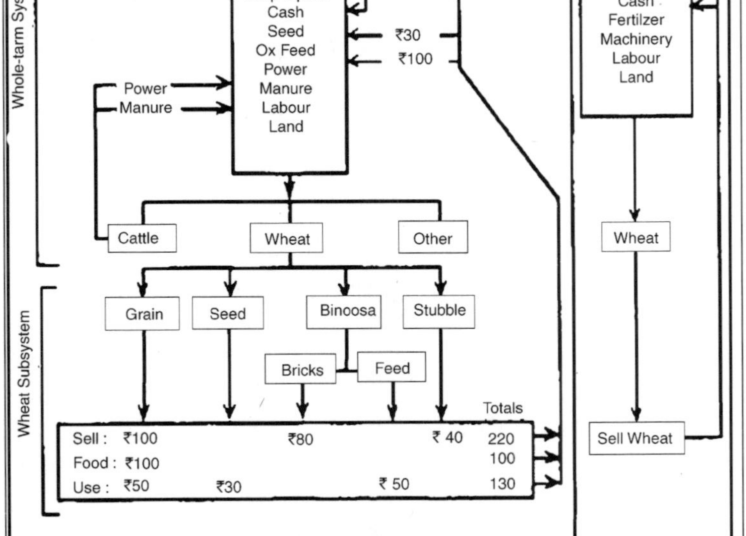

Fig. Comparative Structure of Traditional and Modern Wheat Enterprises

A *budget* is essentially a listing of all resource inputs to an enterprise or activity and their costs, and all outputs and their values, both inputs and outputs being measured over some specified time period.

As appropriate, a budget can also show the difference between total costs and returns which is*enterprise net return* or, if no allowance is made for fixed costs, *enterprise gross margin*. The time span to which the budget refers needs always to be specified and borne in mind. This period of time may be the production period of the output involved or some other period such as an annual cycle.

BUDGET TYPES AND PURPOSE

From a time perspective there are three kinds of budgets pertinent to enterprises and activities:

- *Planning budgets* are forward-looking projections of the resources which will be required to obtain some anticipated outcome. They are prepared as a basis for formulating an activity, enterprise or whole-farm production plan, usually for the next crop or seasonal or annual phase (if it is a long-term activity). They are concerned with what should happen.
- *Control budgets* are used to maintain a current check on and adjust resource supplies to an enterprise or activity once it is in operation, *i.e.*, once the planning budget has been activated. They are not used on small farms but are an important management tool on estates. Usually they take only a financial form and are designed to control fiscal expenditure in the activity or enterprise. The degree of control can be very high: *e.g.*, on Malaysian and Sri Lankan rubber, tea, oil-palm and coconut estates the daily-prepared control budget can show on any day of the operating year the amount of money spent on and the amount and value of product harvested from the enterprise, down to practically the last cent and kilogram. Control budgets are used for these and other continuous activities (such as on orchid, dairy, pig and poultry farms). Obviously, the shorter the production phase, the less need there is for budget control.
- *Evaluation budgets* are backward-looking summations of what did happen. They are essentially accounting documents intended to measure the past performance of an activity or enterprise over some period, usually the prior phase. They are better referred to as *operating statements* because they state with certitude the facts they contain (inputs, outputs etc.). These might be intended only to offer an accounting of past results or, more analytically, to allow diagnosis of weaknesses within the system (or subsystem) and prescription of remedial action.

Table. Example of an Enterprise Planning Budget: Inputs, Costs and Returns for 2.5 Acres of Dryland Ginger in the Wet Zone of Sri Lanka[a]

	Real level (per 2.5 acres)				Per acre or unit level
Labour[b]					
Operation	**Timing**		**Labour days**	**Family or hired**	**Labour days**
Clear land	Mar		25	F	10
Clean drains	Mar		38	F	15
1st fork	Mar		125	H	50
2nd fork	Mar		88	H	35
3rd fork, smooth	Apr		63	H	25
Line for planting	Apr		5	F	2
Hole, plant, mulch	Apr		38	F	15
Fertilize	Apr		5	F	2
Weed once	May		25	F	10
Fertilize	Jul		5	F	2
Weed twice	Jul		40	F	16
Guard	Dec-Jan		75	F	30
Harvest	Jan		40	H	16
Total family labour			256		102
Total hired labour			316	₹ 3 160	₹ 1 264
					Materials
Item		**Amount**	**Price**	**Cost**	**Cost**
Seed	Mar-Apr	1 635 kg	₹ 5.90/kg	₹ 9 647	₹ 3 859
Tools	Mar-Apr			63	25
Watcher's hut	Mar-Apr			25	10
Fertilizer	Jul	340 kg	₹ 1.60/kg	544	218
Straw mulch	Jul	3 750 bundles	₹0.10/bundle	375	150
Crop storage	Jan	(already exists on farm)		0	0
Transport	Jan			63	25
Market sacks	Jan			250	100
Total materials				₹ 10 967	₹ 4 387
Total all costs[c]				₹ 14 127	₹ 5 651
Output					
Clean ginger		6 825 kg	₹ 4.50/kg	₹ 30 713	₹ 12 285
Gross margin				₹ 16 586	₹ 6 634

Note: [a]For purposes of later analysis related to Figure, note that these total costs are all variable costs. There are no fixed costs pertinent to this particular budget formulation.

Feedback

The use of evaluation budgets for diagnostic purposes implies feedback from evaluation to planning budgets: adjustments to the system made on the basis of the former will occur via the planning budget prepared for the next operating phase.

Even if there are no weaknesses to correct, the actual enterprise outcome will seldom be exactly as predicted in the planning budget. Referring to Table, hired labour actually used might be 270 rather than 316 days and actual achieved yield might be 6 270 rather than 6 825 kg. These results would now flow back as guides to hopefully more accurate updated estimates in the next planning budget.

Data Content

In addition to summarizing likely enterprise or activity results, planning budgets are primarily concerned with identifying those resources and other factors which might limit or constrain production. Accordingly, in constructing them, it should be kept in mind that what might be apparently unimportant outputs (by-products) of one system might be critical inputs to another.

In control budgets the most important and often the sole data recorded might relate to flows of finance to the activity or enterprise; alternatively, the critical factor to control might be labour, or in an irrigated desert environment it might be water. Control budgets are not further discussed.

The basic data content of an evaluation budget depends on analytical circumstances, specifically the operating objectives of the enterprise or farm. If this is profit maximization, financial data alone will enable the evaluation; but if the objective is subsistence food production, the data will relate to resource inputs (mainly labour) in comparison with food outputs. But while either of these might be sufficient for only an accounting of what did happen, they would in themselves be practically useless if the analysis was in diagnostic mode. Evaluation budgets in this mode have the most extensive and detailed data requirements.

These are discussed in general terms in the remainder of this chapter and are applied in examples of systems' comparative analysis.

Hazards

The different types of budgets and their purposes will be clear enough. But budgets are not always what they seem. On one group of commercial farms it was routine office practice, until recently, to propose planning budgets for each enterprise in the approved way but then, at the operational stage, as the need arose, to allocate cash which had been budgeted for the wheat to the sheep, fertilizer budgeted for the pyrethrum to the wheat etc. In consequence, at the end-of-year evaluation stage, all that could be said was that some total amount of cash, fertilizer, labour etc. had disappeared somewhere into the farm, but as to the economics of the individual subsystems, or whether uneconomic enterprises should be curtailed or replaced by more efficient ones.

BUDGET STANDARDIZATION UNITS OF MEASUREMENT

For some purposes and modes of analysis (*e.g.*, description), the budget might be specified at *real level* (*i.e.*, at the actual levels of the input and output variables) and refer to the enterprise as it actually exists. But for most planning and evaluation purposes, since - *e.g.* - 2.5 acres of ginger cannot be directly compared with 1.9 hectares of paddy, it will be necessary to standardize the various enterprise or activity budgets by bringing them to a per acre or other *unit level* as in the righthand column of Table 5.1. Further, for purposes of comparison between enterprises or activities, these unit-level budgets must also refer to a common time basis such as, *e.g.*, per hectare per year.

Use of land area as the basis for standardizing crop and livestock budgets is not always appropriate or possible. The most appropriate standard unit to use will depend on the category to which the enterprise or activity belongs and the particular farm type/situation. Most field-crop and tree-crop budgets will in fact usually most appropriately be on a land-unit basis. So will budgets for the horticultural crops on large farms. But for small farms growing tree or vine crops and some horticultural crops (anthurium flowers in Sri Lanka, vanilla in Java), a more appropriate budget basis might be costs and returns per 100 plants or even per single tree (as for the houseyard farms of Java growing three or four high-value clove trees). Further, in the wet tropics the tree crops in particular are often grown in highly mixed stands: a forest-garden farm in Kerala or in Java might consist of six coconut palms, two breadfruit, three jackfruit, four coffee trees, three pepper vines, etc. These species-enterprises would be best budgeted/evaluated on a per tree or per vine basis (or for some purposes these various species might be consolidated into a single composite enterprise budget).

In other situations, even though a species might be present in large numbers as part of the whole of a farm system, it might be grown/managed/exploited without any regard to the land area it occupies—as in the case of nipah palms along the rivers of Trengganu, sago palms on village lands in Irian Jaya and palmyrah palms in the dry zone of Sri Lanka. Perhaps the extreme case is found in Kordofan where the baobab trees, each of which is the property of some family or clan and an important basis of their semi-nomadic existence, might be scattered along the clan's seasonal migration routes over a distance of 600 kilometres or so. Budgets for these and similar tree-crop enterprises could obviously not be expressed on a unit of land area basis; more appropriate would be inputs/outputs per family, or, since labour is a common factor in their control or exploitation, per labour day of effort expended in maintaining or exploiting some specified number of trees.

Livestock enterprises can present special problems in preparing standardized budgets for purposes of comparison. In some cases it will be possible to construct budgets for dairy cows, sheep etc. on a 'per hectare of land use' basis; but the yak herders of Haa and the camel people of Wajir would not have the slightest idea of the number of hectares over which they range.

Highly-mixed sedentary herds/flocks, as found in parts of Pakistan and North India, require standardization of two kinds (assuming they can be disaggregated). First, the separate species (cattle, camels, sheep etc.) and classes of each species have to be standardized in terms of some common animal unit (AU) basis[2] and then, as discussed above, the budgets for each of these (standardized) species-enterprises might have to be compared on the basis of some common input or production factor (such as land or labour or cash required or generated etc.).

In the following example, a farm's herd of five head of mixed cattle and a flock of 16 head of sheep are each standardized (on the basis of approximate feed requirements) by taking one lactating cow as equivalent to one animal unit (AU). Each other type of animal is then expressed as AU relative to a lactating cow, for example:

Cattle	Equivalence Factor	Sheep	Equivalence Factor
Milk Cow	1.0 AU	All types	0.15 AU
OX	0.9 AU		
Calves	0.3 AU		

Population equivalence in AU:
Cows: 2 head × 1.0 AU = 2.0 AU
Oxen: 2 head × 0.9 AU = 1.8 AU
Calves: 1 head × 0.3 AU = 0.3 AU
Total cattle in AU: = 4.1 AU
Sheep: 16 head × 0.15 = 2.4 AU
Total cattle and sheep in AU = 4.1 + 2.4 = 6.5 AU.

It is important to note, however, that from a farm management as opposed to an animal nutrition point of view, it may sometimes be more relevant to standardize livestock on some such basis as labour required by each species/type, or cash inputs required by each, etc. The above nutrition-based equivalence factors are for purposes of illustration only.

Long-term crop and livestock enterprises require a somewhat different approach in budgeting.

- Evaluation budgets of long-term enterprises (or activities) are usually prepared on an annual or seasonal basis and relate to the performance of the enterprise over its most recent operating phase. These single-phase budgets are the same as budgets prepared for short-term enterprises (or activities) and ignore what might have happened to the enterprise in earlier phases and what might happen to it in future phases.
- Planning budgets of long-term enterprises (or activities) are a different matter. Here the inputs/outputs of the enterprise (or activity) must usually be specified for each year of its future life—over 20 to 25 years for coffee, 20 to 40 years for cardamom, 60 to 70 years for coconut, etc.

LEVEL OF BUDGET DETAIL

The necessary degree of detail in a budget is determined by the mode and purpose of analysis. Thus Table 5.1 would probably be adequate for descriptive purposes and for planning purposes, but too detailed for accounting evaluation and too vague for diagnostic purposes. Table 5.1 offers much information relating to labour: jobs to be done, monthly timing of operations, whether family or hired. This might or might not be necessary for planning. On the other hand, the budget says nothing about the type or quality of labour to be employed. Are these workers to be men, women or children?...or do the various tasks specifically require women or men? This would be important on an estate; or if the budget referred to a crop such as coffee requiring school children as harvesters. Regarding yield, 6 825 kg of good ginger is projected to be produced, but how much sub-standard ginger will also be obtained?... and would this be enough to provide a basis for a small kitchen-scale oil extraction activity?

Explicit and Implicit Information

In addition to offering explicit information, a budget should be amenable to implicit extension. Such measures as activity gross margin should permit derivation of further, more detailed measures: gross margin per hectare, per day of family labour, per ₹ 100 of operating capital etc. This is essential in comparative analysis.

UNIT BUDGETS

In order to apply some important planning methods, Table below contains too much information and is too awkward to be used directly. For such purposes, unit-vector budgets are needed. These are simplified, stripped-down versions of a budget such as that of Table from which the following unit-vector budget for ginger has been developed: In the above unit budget, the inputs of Table are consolidated under the headings 'land', 'family labour', 'operating capital' and 'other'. Labour and capital are given a time-dimension (for reasons discussed previously). Also, all information relating to costs versus returns is now consolidated into a single item 'gross margin ₹ 6 634', *i.e.*, no separate cost or return items are shown. Information relating to some items, *e.g.*, hired labour, is now discarded because item-specific costs have been consolidated in the single gross margin item. All other data of Table are now discarded (but of course they would not be discarded if the purpose were detailed post-production evaluation rather than planning). On the other hand, some resources which might only have been implied in Table might now become important. Ginger storage was listed in Table but not the amount or quality of storage needed. If it is possible that these aspects of storage could prove limiting factors to future or expanded production, they would be entered as explicit resources in the unit-vector budget. Use of this type of budget in farm planning is illustrated.

Identification:			
	Date:		Feb. 93
	Crop:		Ginger
	Level:		One acre
	Production period:		11 months, Mar. 93 to Jan. 94
Gross margin:			6 634 ₹
Resource requirements:			
	Land		1 acre
	Family labour		
		Mar.	25 AME
		Apr.	19 AME
		May	10 AME
		Jul.	18 AME
		Dec.-Jan.	30 AME
	Operating capital		
		Mar.-Apr.	4 995 ₹
		Jul.	369 ₹
		Jan.	287 ₹
	Other		
		Storage	1 acre equivalent

EXTENDING BUDGET SCOPE PROCESSING AND MARKETING

In the conventional pre-systems approach to farm management, analysis was largely restricted to field production operations; the post-harvest aspects of an enterprise such as on-farm storage, kitchen processing, family consumption, transport and disposal of commodities beyond the farm gate were regarded as falling within the province of specialists in other fields - marketing experts, processing engineers, family nutritionists etc. Such a compartmentalized approach is possibly appropriate on those farm types where products are simply sold off the farm, *e.g.*, sugarcane to a mill or raw milk to a bottling plant.

However, as emphasized, such a level of structural simplicity is rare on small mixed Asian farms where products and by-products are used and disposed of in many different ways. Here, to define the boundaries of an enterprise as encompassing only field production operations would be quite inadequate. On Type 2 (semi-subsistence) farms it would tell only half the story and on Type 1 (subsistence-oriented) farms only a fraction of it. More specifically, it would overlook the possibilities for household income generation through on-farm or kitchen processing and local marketing, and at village level of establishing cottage industries; moreover, where agricultural resources are already exploited to their potential, local further processing of crop outputs often offers greater scope for rural development than does farm development *per se*.

A Bhutanese farm wife making corn cakes in her kitchen and selling them around the streets of Tashigang is as important a component of the farm's corn enterprise as her husband's corn-growing activity. In this hill country, too, it is not unusual to come across a group of farmers who have each carried out a sack of oranges or potatoes to the nearest road, maybe walking for two or three days, in the hope of selling them. Farm production problems become rather irrelevant. The people know these things; why not the universities?

Clearly, under these 'beyond-the-field' circumstances—and they are often the norm not the exception—if an enterprise is not to lose its 'pith and moment', a systems approach to farming and farm development is called for. But while systems concepts are increasingly accepted, their actual application in farm development projects is not remarkable. It remains at best a field in which the coconuts have only nodding acquaintance with the pineapples and the carp or tilapia, and at worst an arena in which the 'two and forty jarring sects confute'.

Flowcharts

As an aid in understanding the often complicated post-harvest flows of products and byproducts from an enterprise, a useful first step is to sketch them before attempting to incorporate their main elements into a budget.

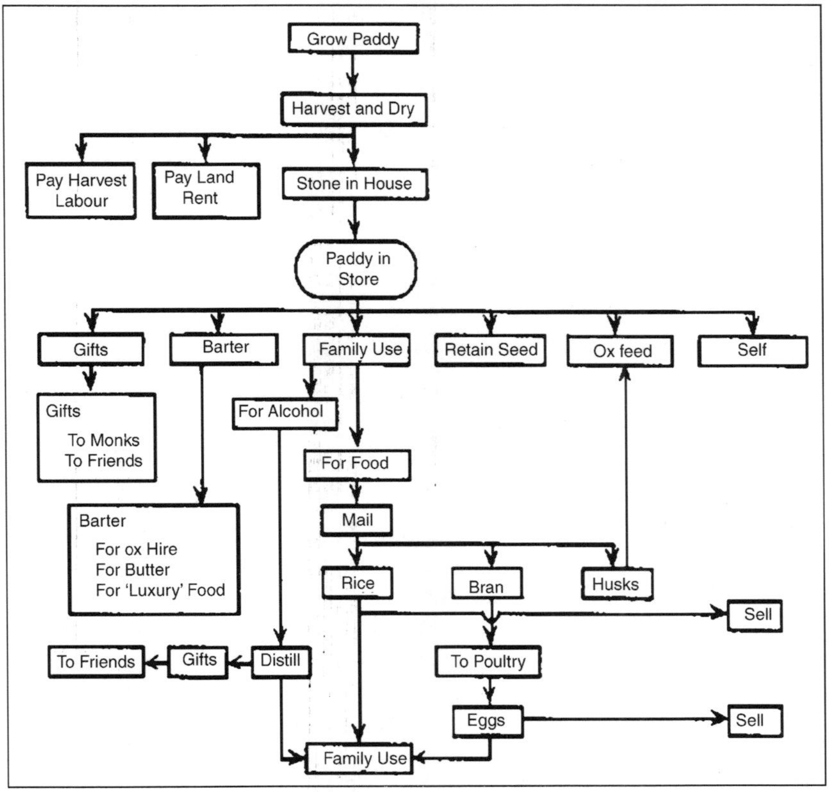

Fig. Example of a Flowchart Post-harvest Handling and Disposal of a Paddy Crop, Bhutan

An example is shown in the flowchart of Figure for post-harvested paddy on a small Type 2 farm in Bhutan. The chart emphasizes those portions of the paddy crop retained for family use; quantities are not indicated.

ECONOMIC AND FINANCIAL BUDGETS

Table 5.1 is an *Economic Budget.* As a planning budget, it lists all the planned inputs and outputs and their values whether or not these will incur actual out-of-pocket costs or will yield actual cash receipts.

For some purposes a *financial budget* will be required. This is an edited version of an economic budget which lists only actual financial outgoings (or costs) and income (or returns). For example, in Table 5.1 if the seed is to be retained from the previous crop and the tools are on hand, these economic 'costs' would now be excluded. Similarly if the cost of the watcher's hut in Table 5.1 is based on providing an annual depreciation amount for this capital item and is not an actual cash outlay, this also would be excluded from the financial budget.

On commercial farms, since all or most inputs are bought and outputs sold, economic and financial budgets are practically equivalent (except that non-cash charges such as depreciation are excluded from the latter). At the other extreme, on Type 1 farms there will be few if any purchased inputs and few sold outputs so that financial budgets are hardly relevant.

REAL AND IMPUTED INPUT COSTS AND OUTPUT VALUES

In a non-commercial environment and where no actual markets exist for inputs or outputs, their values must be imputed. In Table 5.1 straw was valued at 10 cents per bundle. If the farm had not actually bought the straw this might be based on an estimate of what it was worth if used on some other crop (such as mushrooms) or what the farmer could have earned by working for a neighbour instead of staying home bundling straw for his ginger.

Usually the most important economic input is family labour. In Table 5.1 the 256 days of family labour cost nothing in terms of cash outlay and the enterprise gross margin is ₹ 16 586. This conveys an accurate picture only if family labour in fact has no value; but if some realistic value for family labour could be imputed (*e.g.*, by what it could earn off the farm or from the farm's roadside boutique) then Table conveys a false picture of ginger economics: *e.g.*, if family labour had a real value or opportunity cost of ₹ 10 per day, the gross margin would be decreased by ₹ 2 560.

On Type 1 and 2 farms there is often no reference point for the valuation of resources. In consequence, deciding on an appropriate opportunity cost or shadow price for labour, oxen, buildings etc. can be quite subjective. The facts alleged in a budget relating to subsistence-oriented farming, whether for a single farm or for the sector as a whole, will often not stand their ground. This is especially so in Fields C (*i.e.*, sectoral development) and D (*i.e.*, advice for policy making), and not infrequently—sad to say—the 'economies' of an enterprise (or farm or industry based upon it) are nudged up or down to serve a non-objective purpose.

BUDGET-BASED MEASURES OF PERFORMANCE

Depending on the purpose of analysis there are four ways in which an enterprise (or activity) can be evaluated, or four measures of economic performance which can be applied: enterprise net return *(NR)*, gross margin *(GM)*, operational gross margin (*OGM* or 'activity price') and cost of production *(COP)*. *NR, GM* and *OGM* are outlined in this section. *COP* is discussed.

Net Return

Net return *(NR)* is the most appropriate measure if the purpose is an accounting evaluation of past or future projected performance. It is obtained as *NR* = *TGR* - *TC* where *TGR, total gross return* of the enterprise, is the sum of all outputs times their prices, real or imputed, and *TC is* total enterprise cost, again real or imputed. *TGR* needs no further discussion.

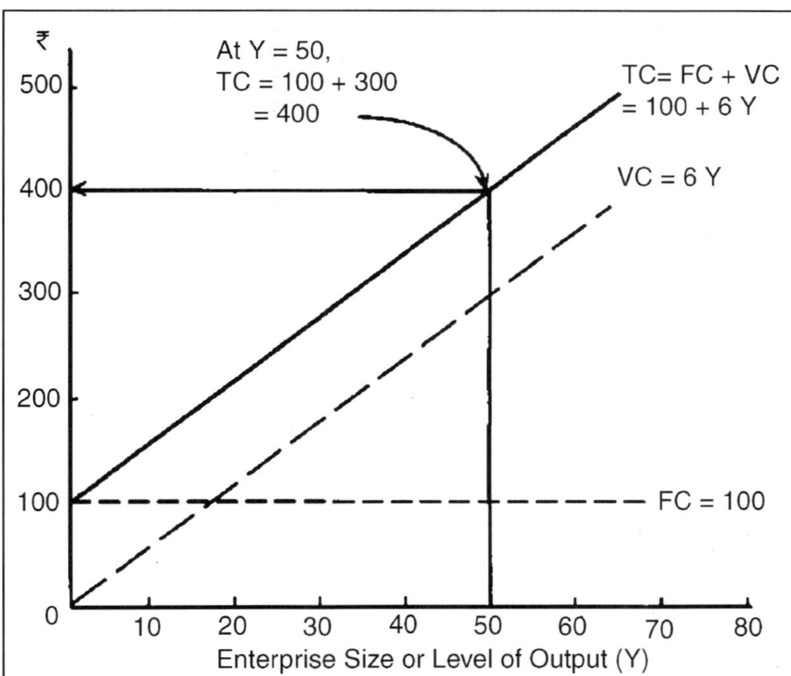

Fig. Example of Relationships between Level of Output and Fixed Costs, Variable Costs and Total Costs

TC consists of two components, total variable cost *(TVC)* and total fixed cost *(TFC)*. *Variable costs (VC)* are those of input items the amounts of which change (usually but not necessarily proportionally) with the size or level of output of the enterprise: the labour, seed, fertilizer, etc. of Table 5.1 are examples. *Fixed costs (FC)* are those of input items, usually services rather than physical things, which remain constant regardless of the size or level of enterprise output: taxes on a barn used to store grain or other produce, the interest costs on an irrigation system, a depreciation amount set aside to eventually replace a cocoa dryer are examples. Fixed costs are further discussed in relation to whole-farm systems.

The relationships between level of output and fixed, variable and total costs are exemplified in Figure. With zero output, variable costs are also zero, but increase as output or size of the enterprise is increased. Fixed costs are constant throughout (but some activities or enterprises will in fact incur no fixed costs). *TC* at any point over the output range is simply the sum of *VC* and *FC*; here, in this particular example, at an output level of 50 units, they are ₹ 300 + 100 = ₹ 400. Note that while *VC* will always increase (*i.e.*, slope upwards) as *Y* increases, the relationship between them need not be linear. This is in contrast to *FC* which will always be linear and parallel to the *Y* or output axis for a given configuration of the production system.

Gross Margin

Gross margin *(GM)* is the most appropriate measure of enterprise performance if the purpose is an operational rather than accounting one, *e.g.*, to make rapid comparisons among three, four, five... enterprises with a view to expanding some or contracting others. *Gross margin* is obtained as total gross returns less variable costs, *GM = TGR - VC*, *i.e.*, fixed costs are ignored since, by their nature, they have to be met whatever is produced (and even if nothing is produced). Justification for this is based on the fact that, by definition, farm fixed capital (ploughs, work oxen, irrigation, etc.) can usually be used by alternative crops; if it is currently used for cotton and cotton prices drop, the farmer will want to evaluate the possibilities of alternative crops—corn, sesame etc. In the short run he or she is stuck with whatever supply of fixed capital is on hand and can budget out the alternatives by considering only those input items which will change if he or she adjusts from cotton to wheat or sesame.

Operational Gross Margin

Operational gross margin *(OGM)* is somewhat equivalent to net return. *OGM = TGR - DC*, where DC is enterprise *direct costs* and consists of variable and fixed components. The difference is only one of emphasis; the *DC* of an enterprise consists of all costs directly associated with that enterprise, usually calculated on a per unit of enterprise basis (per hectare, per head of livestock, etc.). The *DC* of an enterprise thus consists of its variable costs plus some proportion of the farm's fixed costs which should logically be borne by the enterprise. The concept of *DC* is a piece of terminology used with linear programming. An example is discussed in situation (d) of Table below (*See Table 5.2 on page 184*).

Assignment Between Fixed and Variable Costs

The assignment of input items to the fixed or variable categories of enterprise total costs will usually present no problems. However, some items do not fall naturally into one or other category. Whether they should be put in the fixed or variable baskets will depend on circumstances. Four situations are shown in the budgets for a ginger enterprise in (a), (b), (c) and (d) of Table (*See Table on page 184*).

Situation:

(a) Is taken directly from Table. There are no storage costs, variable or fixed, and no other fixed costs, thus net returns of ₹16 586 are the same as gross margin. In situation

(b) The enterprise budget now contains a storage cost of 500. This consists of taxes paid on the storage shed which remain constant regardless of how much ginger is stored or grown. It is thus included as a fixed cost. In situation

(c) At a cost of ₹400, the farmer instead now rents storage on a cost per cubic unit basis; thus ginger storage is here a variable cost because if yield was twice as high or twice as many acres of ginger were to be grown, twice as much storage would be needed and its cost would be twice as much.

Situation (c) is also different in that where previously hired labour was a variable input of 316 days times ₹10 per day, labour is now not casual but permanently attached to the household and must be paid (at ₹10 per day) regardless of how much ginger is grown or its yield. Thus in (c), labour becomes a fixed cost to ginger. (This assumes that ginger is the only crop on the farm: if there were other crops, the fixed labour costs would be shared among them.) This is offered as a caution that some costs do not, simply because of their nature, always belong in either of the fixed or variable categories. An important variation of this occurs on estates where the resident labour force incurs both variable costs (a daily wage) and fixed costs (housing, clinic, worker insurance, retirement fund etc.).

Situation (d) is different again. Here the budget is to be used for planning aimed at selection of the best mix of several enterprises (ginger, corn, cotton etc.) and is on a per unit (acre) basis. Now the storage fixed costs, which were assigned wholly to ginger in situation (b) because this was the only crop on the farm or the only crop to need storage, are shared between ginger and some other storage-using crop, say corn, one fifth or ₹ 40 per acre to ginger and four fifths or ₹ 160 per acre to corn according to their likely relative use of this facility. In (d), the purpose of the budget is to obtain enterprise direct costs and thence the operating gross margin (*OGM* or enterprise net 'price') for use in formulating optimal combinations of several enterprises; the budget is not directed at the evaluation of past performance.

Table Evaluation of a 2.5 Acre Dryland Ginger Enterprise Under Different Cost Conditions

For 2.5 acres of ginger		*(a)*	*(b)*	*(c)*
Variable Cost		(₹)	((₹)	((₹)
	Hired labour	3 160	3 160	(fixed)
	Seed	9 647	9 647	9 647
	Tools	63	63	63
	Watcher's hut	25	25	25
	Fertilizer	544	544	544
	Straw mulch	375	375	375
	Storage	0	0	400
	Transport	63	63	63
	Marketing	250	250	250
Total Variable Costs *(VC)*		14 127	14 127	11 367
Total Fixed Costs *(FC)*		0	500[a]	3 160[b]
Total Costs *(VC + FC)*		14 127	14 627	14 527
Gross Returns *(GR)*		30 713	30 713	30 713
Net Returns *(NR)*		16 586	16 086	16 186
Gross Margin *(GM)*		16 586	16 586	19 346
For 1 acre of ginger			*(d)*	
Gross Returns *(GR)*			12 285	
Total Costs without storage			5 651	
Total Costs with storage of Rs 40			5 691	
Total Direct Costs *(DC)*			5 691	
Operating Gross Margin *(OGM)*			6 594	

[a]For storage

[b]For hired labour

EXTENSION OF ENTERPRISE OR ACTIVITY BUDGETS TO WHOLE-FARM BUDGETS

A *whole-farm budget* is the structural parallel of an enterprise or activity budget, with budgets of the several enterprise and activity subsystems now aggregated. There is only one change: those fixed costs which cannot be logically assigned to any activity are now included as whole-farm fixed or common or *overhead costs (OC)*. This latter term is preferable because it distinguishes more clearly between fixed costs that are specific to an enterprise or activity and those fixed costs which are accrued on a whole-farm basis.

Overhead costs consist of land, water and road taxes, insurance and repair costs of buildings which cannot be assigned to specific activities, and all other input costs relating to the upkeep and maintenance of the whole farm. These overhead costs can be both fixed and operational: *e.g.*, both the annual tax paid on a farm water-supply pump and the fuel costs of operating it. The relevant criterion is that they cannot be logically charged against specific activities or enterprises.

The derivation of a whole-farm budget from the budgets of its constituent enterprises is shown in Table 5.3. In this simple case there are only three enterprises on the farm.

This might convey an impression that enterprises can be clearly separated with well-defined boundaries. On small farms, however, there will usually be a ragtag of miscellaneous activities directed to supplying feed for the oxen, fertility for cash crops etc., so that budgets must be prepared for these also even if they do not generate a final product or positive (imputed or real) gross margin; or they can be aggregated into a smaller number of composite activities; or, when neither of these is possible, they must be included as whole-farm costs.

Table. Whole-farm Evaluation Budget Derived from Enterprise Budgets

Item	Ginger 2.5 acres (₹)	Cotton 1 acre (₹)	Soybeans 0.7 acres (₹)	Whole Farm (₹)
Gross Returns (*GR*)	30 713	20 000	10 000	60 713
Variable Costs (*VC*)	14 127	10 000	5 000	29 127
Fixed Costs (*FC*)	0	3 000	2 000	5 000
Overhead Costs (*OC*)				8 000
Total Costs (*TC*)	14 127	13 000	7000	42 127
Gross Margin (*GR* - *VC*)	16 586	10 000	5 000	31 586
Net Returns (*GR* - *TC*)	16 586	7 000	3 000	18 586
Household Non-farm Income				3 000
Household Total Income				21 586

Whole-farm budgets are used primarily as end-of-year accounting statements or summaries of farm performance over that or some other operating period.

They are generally not operational tools, except when used to project whole-farm performance over several years, *e.g.*, to project the total results of a five, six, seven... year farm-development programme.

EXTENSION OF WHOLE-FARM BUDGETS TO THE HOUSEHOLD

At the whole-farm budget level, one other important element can now be introduced, namely household non-farm income. In Table this is included to obtain household total income. Where the purpose of analysis is not agro-technical farm planning but rather to ascertain the economic wellbeing of the farm household, the next step would be to analyse household outgo or expenditure on non-farm items necessary to keep the whole farm-household system operational—family expenditure on medical services, food, clothing, children's schooling, meeting social obligations etc.

But this step is seldom taken in formal farm management economics (which by-and-large remains preoccupied with agro-technics). This is a pity because it leaves one with an incomplete picture of what is really going on within the most important system component, the household. In particular, it gives no knowledge at all about which beneficiaries are getting what from the system... and, at the end of the day, this of course is what it is all about.

COST OF PRODUCTION

An enterprise or product-producing activity can also be evaluated in terms of its unit Cost of Production *(CoP).* This is obtained as its total costs divided by the quantity of output achieved with those costs, *i.e.*, *TC/Y.* In Table ginger CoP is ₹ 14 127/6 825 kg or ₹ 2.07 per kg.

CoP is usually not a relevant measure of enterprise performance in providing advice to farmers (Field A), especially on small farms where interest is in (net) income rather than what it costs to obtain that income. But in other fields *CoP* can be the most appropriate measure of performance. In Field C the manager of a milk bottling plant will want to know what the milk*CoP* is on farms supplying raw milk to his or her plant (as a basis for setting his or her buying and selling prices and consequent profit margin); he or she will not be interested in farmers' incomes as such.

In Field D, policy makers in Fiji will want to know what the copra *CoP* is on Fijian farms in comparison with Indonesia, Philippines, Malaysia etc. in order to establish sound industry research and development policies—and perhaps even to decide if the Fijian industry has a viable long-term future.

One area where *CoP* is important in Field A is on tea, rubber, cocoa, coconut and other estates where *CoP* rather than net returns or gross margin is the conventional measure of estate performance, both on the same estate over time and in comparison with other estates. But taken by itself *CoP* conveys no information, except perhaps by implication, of the real economics on these estates.

In the 1960s, due largely to political instability, those tea estates of Sri Lanka with the lowest *CoP* per pound of made tea were the worst estates in every other respect, the low *CoP* being due to the fact that the green tea was just being harvested and processed, with little or no expenditure on field or factory or other estate maintenance. In those circumstances *CoP* was, if anything, only a measure of the degree of current system exploitation. (The phase was only a temporary one.)

ACTIVITIES

As noted previously, an enterprise—or any parallel activities of Order Level 4 or 6 making up an enterprise—is a production process directed to the production of one or more final products for sale or consumption (but it might also indirectly generate some amount of resources). All other types of activities in a farm system (*i.e.*, those of Order Level 1, 2 or especially 3) are directed in one way or another to the generation of resources for use on the farm: but they might incidentally also generate some final products.

As with enterprises, these resource-generating activities have to be quantified and evaluated. This requires the construction of activity budgets which are in all essential respects similar to the enterprise budgets discussed above.

TYPES OF RESOURCE-GENERATING ACTIVITIES

The main types of resource-generating activities are now briefly discussed..

Activities and Enterprises as Resource Generators

Those enterprises or activities which also generate some amount of resources fall into three categories:

They Might Generate the Resource

- For their own use or
- For the specific use of some other enterprise or
- For general non-specific use by other enterprises. In the sketch of Figure, situation
  - — Exists in the dairy enterprise: enough of the female calves produced are retained to replace the older cows as these are culled from the herd. In regard to this resource the enterprise is essentially self-perpetuating. Situation
  - — Is represented by the second enterprise, maintaining a beef cattle herd in parallel with the dairy herd in which the latter generates male calves for the specific use of the beef enterprise. Situation
  - — Is represented by the flow of another resource, dairy cow manure, into the general farm resource pool for use by any of the farm's crop enterprises/activities. In all these cases the resource-generation aspects of the dairy cows are incidental to

their main purpose of producing a final product, milk. This type of enterprise (dairy cows) as a resource-generator would be quantified/budgeted/evaluated as was the ginger enterprise of Table 5.1; its total output value would include the value of calves and manure.

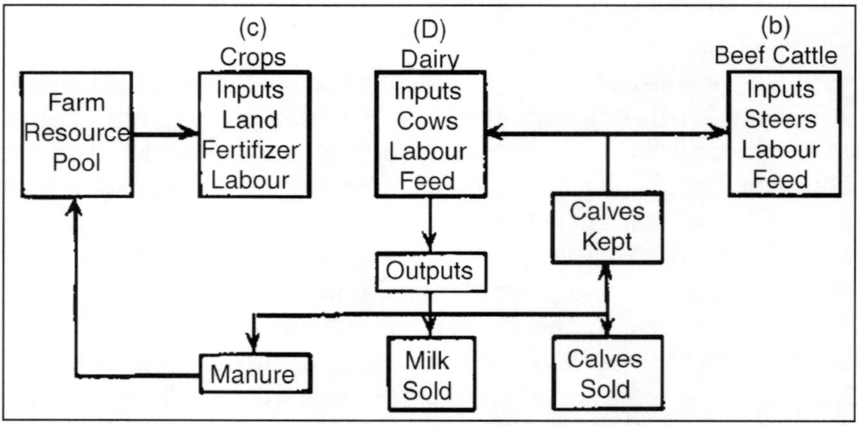

Fig. Example of Enterprises as Resource Generators.

Major Resource-generating Activities

On mixed farms, particularly livestock farms, most resource-generating activities consist of substantial sets of inputs and operations which are similar in all respects to main enterprises except that the main output now is a resource for use on the farm, *i.e.*, an intermediate product rather than a final product. Common examples are a fodder crop grown for dairy cows and a legume crop grown to enhance fertility for some following cash crop.

When financial evaluation of such activities is required, this will proceed as in Table. If no final product is generated, the results of this evaluation will be a negative 'net return' or gross margin equivalent to activity total costs. If some final product is incidentally produced, the value of this will partly offset activity costs; in some activities, costs might be fully offset by the value of final products.

Budget evaluation of resource-generating activities will be necessary in two situations: first, when the activity as a resource generator is to be compared with alternative activities generating the same resource; and second, when cost and return data for all enterprises and activities on a farm, which have been evaluated separately, are to be pooled to enable a whole-farm budget to be constructed.

As with enterprises, it is sometimes not possible to define the boundaries of resource-generating activities, in which case several might have to be aggregated as a composite, or even accounted for on a whole-farm basis.

Resource Generation by Purchase or Barter-exchange Activities

Probably the simplest way for a farmer to acquire a resource is to buy it or exchange some other product or resource for it— payment of money for the use of a parcel of land, exchange of family labour with a neighbour for use of her oxen etc. Such purchase or barter is equally an activity and is quantified and evaluated in terms of a budget, albeit a very simple one. Budgets for two such activities - renting land and exchanging labour for ox draught power.

Table. Example of Budgets for Resource Generation by Purchase or Barter-exchange Activities

Budget Item	Rent land oxpower	Activity Exchange labour for
Input cost	₹600	20 Labour days
Output return	0.25 ha land	4 Ox days
Gross margin	-₹ 600	₹ 0

In the case of renting land, considering the activity only as an activity (and not considering any eventual recovery of the rental cost from the future sale of the crop to be grown on the land), the activity result is an annual cost of ₹600 or a net return or gross margin of -₹ 600 per unit (0.25 ha) of activity. This conceptual approach is appropriate where there are several alternative ways of acquiring land (by rent, lease, outright purchase, clearing jungle etc.) and the costs or returns of each have to be evaluated regardless of what might actually be produced on the land. However, if the renting of land is a normal cost of growing some specific crop, 'renting land' would then be only a normal cost item in the budget for such an enterprise and no separate land-renting activity budget would be necessary.

This also applies to the case of exchanging labour for oxpower. The only difference between the two cases is that the gross margin of exchanging labour is zero because it is assumed that the value of labour exchanged is equal to the value of ox days received (at least in the eye of the farmer). Again, it should be stressed that these resource-generating activities are here quantified and evaluated as activities; if they happen to be integral parts of some specific enterprise then no separate budgets are needed.

ACTIVITY BUDGETS IN LINEAR PROGRAMMING FORMAT

For one important method of analysis used in prescriptive farm planning, *i.e.*, Linear Programming (LP), such budgets as those of Table are reduced yet further. As shown in Table, they are re-written and couched, with slight rearranging, in relation to the farm's resource pool. The *GM* of each activity is the same as before and indicates the money amount by which the value of output of the farm system increases or decreases due to one unit of the respective activity being included as a resource generator in the farm production plan: renting land as an activity in itself would reduce annual farm income by ₹ 600; exchanging labour would have no direct effect. (However, both would have a later indirect effect when actually used in some enterprise.)

Table. Example of Resource-generating Activity Budgets in Linear Programming Format

Budget Item	Rent land oxpower	Activity Exchange labour for
Gross margin ₹	-600	0
Resource pool		
Land (ha)	-0.25	
Labour (days)		20
Oxpower (days)	-4	

In LP format the input and output items of the budgets are stated in terms of their effect on or demand for those corresponding resources shown in the resource pool. Renting land has a negative demand on land in that it contributes to rather than detracts from whatever supply of land is available. Similarly the budget of the labour exchange activity indicates that this barter activity would require or use 20 days of farm labour and that it would generate four days of oxpower. The above activities and their 'budgets' are of an operational nature; their use in whole-farm planning is illustrated.

Resource Generation by Transfer Activities

This again is a very simple kind of activity. It consists of transferring some particular resource now assigned to one activity/enterprise to use by some other activity or enterprise. The ginger enterprise of Table provides an example. About seven tonnes of ginger storage capacity is needed. If this does not presently exist on the farm, a storage shed could be built at some known cost, or alternatively the farmer might be able to convert part of his or her cow barn to storage space for ginger. This type of activity 'generates' resources by transferring them from activities/enterprises where they are not needed or where they have a low use-value to other activities/enterprises where they are needed or have a higher use-value.

Just as for other types of activities, for farm-planning purposes transfer activities need to be quantified in budget form. Thus the above examples of transfer of space from use by cows to ginger is quantified by the following simple budget of this transfer activity:

Budget Item	Transfer of space from cows to ginger
Gross margin of activity (₹)	0
Cow shelter lost (m^2)	1
Ginger storage gained (m^2)	-1

The above example might appear trivial, but resource generation by use-transfer is a powerful tool in more sophisticated analysis of farm systems using linear programming.

External Activities

All the activities noted so far have been internal to the farm. In addition, where the opportunities exist, households often supplement these on-farm activities by off-farm work and petty trading. However, such off-farm activities are usually undertaken more to supplement household income than to obtain resources for the farm component. An exception could be when an above-normal amount of resources is needed temporarily for farm development as distinct from routine farm production.

Application and Use of Resource-generating Activity Budgets

Budgets for the various types of resource-generating activities outlined above are applied in whole-farm planning.

FURTHER EXTENSIONS OF ENTERPRISE OR ACTIVITY BUDGETS

Using a budget such as that of Table 5.1 as a base, several extensions can be made from it for operational purposes, viz.:

- Preparing *partial budgets*;
- Developing *conditional* or *parametric budgets*, equations or graphs;
- Deriving further *performance factors* for use in *comparative analysis* of farm subsystems;
- Preparing *long-term evaluation budgets* for *ex ante* appraisal of investment in an activity or enterprise which extends over many years; and
- Assessing an enterprise or activity under *conditions of uncertainty.*

PARTIAL BUDGETING

As the term indicates, partial budgeting is concerned with the evaluation of only selected parts of a system—only parts of a process, activity, enterprise, farm service matrix or of the whole farm. In farm management in Field A (*i.e.*, advising farmers) partial budgeting is most commonly used to test possible adjustments to farm-level systems which are presently not working well. At higher levels it is widely used as the basis for structuring agricultural development projects (*e.g.*, to assess the impact which a dam or a new road system might have on some parts of existing farm-level systems).

In Table 5.6 partial budgeting is applied to the 2.5 acre ginger enterprise of Table to evaluate the likely impact which irrigation might have on this presently dryland enterprise. Part:

- Of Table is the base budget for this activity, the present 'without irrigation' situation. In making the comparison it is necessary to consider only those few elements or parameters which might change if irrigation were to be used. These changes comprise additional yield whose value is partly offset by additional labour, transport and marketing costs and the lower price for irrigated ginger. As shown in part

- Of Table, the net effect of these changes, *i.e.*, 'after' versus 'before', is an increase in gross margin of ₹4 422.

Table. Evaluation of Adjustments to an Enterprise or Activity by Partial Budgeting

(a) Base budget (unirrigated ginger)		Change from (a) to (b)	(b) Partial budget (irrigated ginger) showing changes in input costs and returns	
Input cost (₹)			Extra labour (₹)	
Hired labour	3 160	+	Water channels	700
Seed	9 647	0	Water application	600
Tools	63	0	Extra harvest	100
Watcher's hut	25	0		
Fertilizer	544	0		
Mulch	375	0		
Storage	0	0		
Transport	63	+	Extra transport (₹)	15
Marketing	250	+	Extra marketing (₹)	80
Total cost (₹)	14 127	+	Total extra costs (₹)	1 495
Output			Output changes	
Ginger (kg)	6 825	+	Extra ginger (kg)	1 500
Price (₹/kg)	4.50	-	Lower price (₹/kg)	4.40
Gross value (₹)	30 713	+	New gross value (₹)	36 630
Gross margin (₹)	16 586	+	New gross margin (₹)	21 008
			Extra gross margin (₹)	4 422

At process level, partial budgeting is a useful tool for adjusting systems of Order Level 1 and 2 which do not warrant the use of more sophisticated methods of response analysis. At whole-farm level, partial budgeting can be used for adjusting the enterprise or activity mix of a system if this does not warrant the use of the more powerful programming methods.

CONDITIONAL OR PARAMETRIC BUDGETING

The type of budget of Table refers to an activity as formulated at some specific point in time. Obviously it will cease to be valid if there are changes to prices, costs, technology or the underlying production conditions. In most situations such changes will in fact occur either through the influence of the market on prices and/or costs, through changes in technology introduced by the farmer causing changes in yield and cost, or through yield changes due to Nature. If the budget is going to be needed for future or continuing use, it is desirable to anticipate likely future changes in the relevant *critical parameters* and build these into the *base budget*. This is done by adding, at the time of budget construction, conditional (or parametric) extensions to it. On the other hand, one might not be concerned with future change but only with considering several alternative cost/price/technical scenarios at the moment of budget construction (*e.g.*, What if costs were to double? What if yields increase/decrease by 20%?...). Conditional extensions to reflect such possible changes in critical parameters are a useful analytical tool.

SINGLE-PARAMETER EXTENSIONS

The steps in conditional extension of an enterprise or activity budget are straightforward, viz.:

- Identify the parameter which is most significant in terms of its impact on budget results and likelihood to change. In the example of Table 5.1 this is, say, ginger sale price.
- Specify the range over which this parameter is likely to change; here, say, from ₹ 3 to ₹ 6 per kg.
- Specify the budget result (*e.g.*, ginger gross margin per acre) as a simple equation in terms of the parameter of interest (*e.g.*, ginger price). Thus, for the particular example being used here, from Table.

Gross margin/acre = Total revenue/acre - Variable cost/acre, *i.e.*, $GM = TR - VC$ = (Yield/acre)(Price/kg) - $VC = (Y)(p_y) - VC = 2\,730p_y - 5651$ where Y denotes ginger yield per acre in kg and p_y denotes ginger price per kg in ₹.

(iv) Graph the single-parameter equation from (iii) as shown in Figure and use this graph as an alternative to solving the equation for all likely prices. Such a parametric-budget approach permits the validity of the base budget to be maintained even though the variable of concern might change over time.

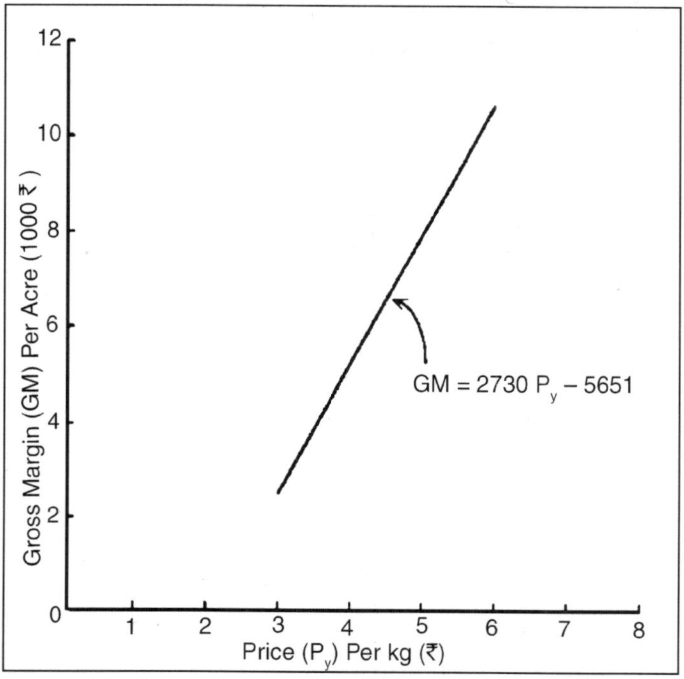

Fig. Example of a Single-variable Parametric Budget Showing Ginger Gross Margin Per Acre for Ginger Prices Ranging from 3 to 6 `/kg

TWO-AND THREE-PARAMETRE EXTENSIONS

Parametric budgeting is readily expanded to accommodate two or three variable parametres—beyond three variables, graphical presentation of results is usually too complicated. As an example, Figure 5.6 shows a three-variable parametric budget relating to the growing and chipping of cassava tubers by an estate for sale as livestock feed. The objective of this budget is to allow rapid determination of total estate net returns.

The unstable parameters of concern to management on this particular estate are: annual field yield of fresh cassava tubers per acre, the percentage of dry processed chips recovered per ton of wet tubers, and the sale price of dry chips.

The graphs of Figure show how the results of a base budget for this enterprise might be parametrized in order for the budget to be 'solved' for any combination of the three unstable parameters: *e.g.*, at a yield of 10 tons per acre, with a chips recovery rate of 35 per cent and a chips sale price of \$13 per picul, total annual net returns for this particular West Malaysian estate would be approximately \$330 000. Analogously to the case of single-variable parametric budgeting (Figure), the graphs of Figure are based on the net returns equation,

$$NR = TR - TC = (Y) \rightarrow (p_y) - TC$$

where Y is tuber yield in tons per acre per year, r is the dry chips recovery coefficient and p_y is chips sale price per picul. Y, r and p_y are variable (*i.e.*, parametrized in the budget over their relevant ranges) and total costs are given.

Picul is a common weight measure in parts of South East Asia. It equals 100 catties of 1.3 pounds each and is thus equivalent to about 60 kg.

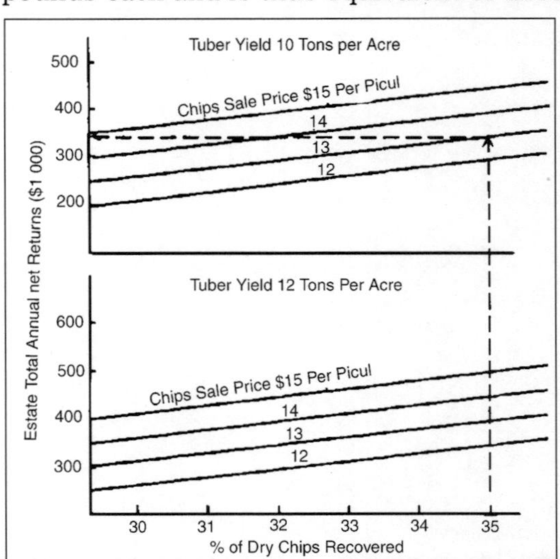

Fig. Example of a Three-variable Parametric Budget showing Annual Net Returns on a Cassava Estate by Tuber Yield, Dry Chips Recovery Rate and Sale Price

DO'S AND DONT'S OF ENTERPRISE AND ACTIVITY BUDGETING

Because budgets are the basis of most of the subsequent farm-household system analysis presented in the following chapters, it is appropriate to conclude this chapter with a list of do's and dont's as a guide to good budget construction.

This applies specifically to enterprise and activity budgets but also generally to other types of budgets such as whole-farm, partial, evaluations-over-time etc.

- The first requirement is for an accurate and unambiguous *heading* or *title* to the budget, *e.g.*, not just Tea' if reference is to some specific type of tea grown at a specific location and elevation.
- Specification should be given of the *level* or *size* of the enterprise or activity to which the budget data refer— *e.g.*, whether to one, two, six, seven or 100 hectares; or whether to one or 100 head of camels. It is not helpful when one encounters budgets headed simply 'Sheep' or 'Economics of Goats' etc. without indication of the number, type, breed and location of the animals under consideration.
- If the budget contains standardized or converted units —*e.g.*, when all the cows, calves, oxen, buffalo etc. on a farm are converted to common animal units—the *basis of standardization* should be specified in the table or a footnote.
- Where appropriate, a listing should be given of the *separate operations* performed within the budgeted enterprise or activity. When input requirements are time-specific, this should be accompanied by a *calendar of operations* showing when each operation is performed.
- A list should be given of *all inputs* and, if appropriate, as in an enterprise budget, their unit costs and the total of these costs.
- A similar *listing of all products generated* (by-products as well as main products), their respective unit prices if they are sold and the total value of the output should be given.
- The *manner of disposal* of the items mentioned in (6) above, together with the quantities disposed of by cash sale and various other means, should be shown. This is particularly important in traditional farming systems.
- *Grade and price classifications* should be given for that part of products sold. Sometimes a farmer will sell his or her produce ungraded, in which case an average price is appropriate. Often, however, he or she will do his or her own grading, resulting in two or more product categories, each with its respective price. This level of detail is often necessary in diagnostic analysis where it will serve as a pointer to specific system weaknesses.
- An aggregation should be given of cash sales to obtain total *cash returns* for the budgeted enterprise or activity.

- An aggregation should be given of all *economic returns* (cash receipts plus the real or imputed values of those parts of production which are used on the farm or bartered or given away). If only produce which is sold is considered, this might grossly underestimate actual total production and thus the real efficiency of an enterprise or activity.
- A statement should be given of enterprise *net returns* or *gross margin*, preferably both.
- A budget prepared for diagnostic purposes must obviously contain *sufficient detail to permit problem diagnosis.* To describe an input as 'fertilizer—100 kg' might be sufficient for some purposes but it would be near useless if a specific fertilizer problem exists on a farm and there is a need to know what kind of fertilizer is being used and perhaps even when it is being applied and how frequently.
- Although budgets prepared for financial accounting or economic evaluation need not contain *physical data*(*e.g.*, ox days used, kg of crop harvested etc.), it is generally desirable that they do so, especially if they might be used at some future date to chart the progress of the farm over time. Because of price changes, inflation and devaluation, the information— drawn from comparison of 'then-and-now' budgets— that a Javanese paddy farmer advanced from having an income of ₹ 80 000 in 1975 to one of ₹ 300 000 in 1995 would be spurious; what would be important is whether his or her paddy yield increased or actually declined, and by how much.
- The *time-dimension* of the enterprise should be noted, preferably in the budget heading. This is often essential information in relation to short-term and annual field crops: a one-hectare bean crop which occupies the land for six weeks will, on an annual basis, require only one quarter of the land resources required by one hectare of a six-months paddy crop; and, other things equal, where land is in short supply a four-month paddy crop will be superior to a five-month crop. Some livestock enterprises also will require a time specification, *e.g.*, 10-, 11- or 12-week batches of broiler chickens. Most livestock enterprises, however, will be operated on a continuing indefinite basis and with these, as well as tree crops, the time basis of most budgets will usually be a one-year period.
- Finally, the *date of construction* and the *sources of data* contained in a budget should be indicated—whether from records of a single farm, from a survey of several farms or simply the analyst's estimates. This can serve two purposes. It will provide the opportunity for independent check of the data should this become necessary, and it will indicate at least implicitly the degree of reliability that can be attached to the respective data items and to the results of any analysis based upon them.

4

Soils of Drought Areas and their Management

SOIL AND WATER CONSERVATION MEASURES

The problem of conserving soil and moisture is also of very great importance in the extensive regions of low and uncertain rainfall, forming parts of Punjab, Madhya Pradesh, Maharashtra, Andhra Pradesh and Karnataka. These tracts are characterized by scanty, ill-distributed and highly erosive rains, undulating topography, high wind velocity and generally shallow soils. The period of heavy downpours from August to October is the period of the heaviest erosion in these regions.

Wind erosion also has been responsible for destroying the valuable top soil in many areas. Halting the march of desert in Rajasthan is one of the vital and outstanding problems facing the country today. An extreme example of sand movement from the coast is to be seen in the Saurashtra region of Gujarat where the once-flourishing ports are now covered with advancing sand-dunes.

In addition to the erosion of the cultivated fields, neglected pastures and wastelands, considerable roadside erosion also takes place owing to the defective highway engineering. Defective drainage and water-logging throw appreciable areas out of cultivation every year and indirectly increase the erosion hazards.

In India, there is very little area free from the hazard of soil erosion. It is estimated that out of 305.9 million hectares of reported area, 145 million hectares is in need of conservation measures. Severe erosion occurs in the sub-humid and per-humid areas due to high rainfall and improper management of land and water. Agricultural land in the major part of the country suffers from erosion. Apart from reducing the yields through the loss of nutrients, erosion destroys the soil resources itself every year.

For example, in Maharashtra over 70 per cent of the cultivated land has been affected by erosion in varying degrees and 32 per cent of the land having been highly eroded is no longer cultivable. In the Sholapur district, nearly 17 per cent of the land of medium depth (more than 45 cm) has deteriorated into shallow soils (less than 45 cm) in 75 years from 1870 to 1945. Similarly, in Akola, Buldana and Yeotmal districts, the number of fields with less than 37.5 cm soil depth increased during the same period by 54, 16 and 8 per cent respectively.

SOIL AND WATER CONSERVATION ON AGRICULTURAL LAND

Broadly speaking, the practical methods of soil and water conservation fall into two important classes, *viz.* Agronomic measures and mechanicla measures.

AGRONOMIC MEASURES FOR SOIL AND WATER CONSERVATION

Agronomic practices for soil and water conservation help to intercept rain drops and reduce the splash effect, help to obtain a better intake of water rate by the soil by improving the content of organic matter and soil structure, help to retard and reduce the overland run-off through the use of contour cultivation, mulches, dense-growing crops, strip-cropping and mixed cropping.

Contour-farming

During intense rain storms, the soil cannot absorb all the rain as it falls. The excess water flows down the slope under the influence of gravity. If farming is done up and down the slope, the flow of water is accelerated, because each furrow serves as a rill. The major part of the rain is drained away without infiltrating into the soil. The top fertile soil, along with plant nutrients and seeds, is washed off. All this results in a scanty and uneven growth of a crop.

A simple practice of farming across the slope, keeping the same level, as far as possible (which is technically called contour-farming) has many beneficial effects. The ridges and the rows of the plants placed across the slope form a continual series of miniature barriers to the water moving over the soil surface. The barriers are small individually, but as they are large in number, their total effect is great in reducing run-off, soil erosion and loss of plant nutrients. It has been experimentally proved that contour-farming reduces run-off and prevents soil erosion as compared with the up-and-down cultivation in the major groups of soils in India, *viz.* Alluvial soils, black soils and deep lateritic soils.

Apart from conserving the water and soil, contour-farming conserves soil fertility and increases crop yields.

Contour-farming on alluvial soil, 2.2 per cent slope at Kanpur has conserved 11.3 kg of N, 11.7 kg of P_2O_5, 44.4 kg of K_2O, 398.1 kg of CaO, 118.1.kg of MgO in one season alone. These nutrients converted into fertilizers amount to 56.5 kg of sulphate of ammonia, 70 kg of single super-phosphate and 74 kg of muriate of potash per hectare in one season.

Contour-farming has also given 490 kg of johar grain and 273 kg of johar stalks more than the up-and-down cultivation at Kanpur. Thus every mm of rain-water conserved by contour-farming gave 22.5 kg of johar grain and 12.5 kg of johar straw more than the up-and-down cultivation. It has been proved that much less power is required to be exerted by man, animals and machines, if the cultivation is done in the contour instead of up-and-down the slope. There is less wear and tear of the implements and the same job is done in less time when contour-farming is practiced.

Table. Effect of Contour Cultivation on Run-off and Soil Erosion

Treatment	Rainfall causing run-off (mm)	Run-off (mm)	Soil loss (tonnes/ha)
Alluvial soils - 8 per cent slope - Dehra Dun			
Maize (up-and-down cultivation)	1,223	670	28.5
Maize + cowpeas (contour cultivation)	1,223	511	19.3
Deep lateritic soil - 25 per cent slope - Ootacamund			
Potato (up-and-down cultivation)	1,295	52	39.3
Potato (contour cultivation)	1,295	29	14.9

How to Practice Contour-farming

On long slopes, bunding is usually done to reduce the length of the slope. These bunds will serve as a good guide for contour-farming. All the cultural operations have to be done parallel to these bunds. On gentle slopes (between 0.5 to 2.0 per cent) bunding may not be essential. Contour (the line passing through the points having the same level) guidelines can be marked with the help of a hand level. On uniform slopes, these lines are to be marked about 50 m apart.

Farming is done parallel to these lines. The establishing of contour-farming on undulating land (having many depressions and ridges) is somewhat tedious. The water from each furrow collects in the depressions and results in breaches. The depressions are required to be filled up by levelling or may be left under grass.

Mulching

Surface mulches are used to prevent soil from blowing and being washed away, to reduce evaporation, to increase infiltration, to keep down weeds, to improve soil structure and eventually to increase crop yields. Inter-culture kills weeds and produces a five or seven cm thick soil mulch which helps to reduce evaporation from the top soil. It also breaks the surface crust which forms after each downpour. Studies on mulching carried out in India under rain-fed agriculture have concentrated on the measurement of crop responses rather than on the manner in which crop responses are influenced.

At Dehra Dun, mulching with maize residues did not significantly influence the yield of the succeeding yield crop. At Kota, mulching, in general, gave a higher yield of wheat grain and stalk than no mulching. At Bellary, mulching with different materials (*e.g.,,* paddy husk, Encap Esso mulch, grass mulch, johar stubble) did not give encouraging results in increasing the yields of cotton and johar crops. Mulching with straw og Encap Esso mulch increased the infiltration rate, improved soil moisture and increased the yields of wheat, barley, gram and linseed, succeeding the maize crop on eroded soils at Ranchi.

Growing of Crops which Provide the Maximum Cover, Reduce Run-off and Soil Loss

Cultivated legumes, in general, furnish a better cover and hence, better protection to cultivated land against erosion than ordinary cultivated crops. The crops and the cropping systems will naturally vary from region to region, depending on the soil and climatic conditions.

At Dehra Dun, cowpeas provided the maximum canopy with or without the application of phosphate fertilizer. This was followed by mung, urad and dhaincha. At Vasad, cowpeas provided the best vegetative cover for the soils. Sunnhemp was the next best; mung and groundnut were effective to some extent. At Kota, velvet bean formed the canopy effective to the maximum extent. Cowpea was the next best. At Kanpur, mung served as the most effective canopy, followed by urad and guar. The application of phosphorus increased the canopy. At Rehmankhera, cowpea formed the best canopy, followed by Styzolobium mung, groundnut, urad, moth, and soybean. Sunnhemp, mung and Styzolobium helped to conserve soil moisture well, leading to a higher yield in the case of the succeeding barley crop. All the legumes were equally effective in reducing the loss of soil and nutrients.

Thus among the legumes, cowpea and mung proved to be important crops for providing a good cover for the land during the rainy season. Bidi tobacco, being a clean-cultivated crop, resulted in the maximum soil loss and water loss. The soil and water losses were very much reduced, especially the water loss, when a cover-cum-manure crop was grown during the early monsoon before tobacco was transplanted. The inclusion of a cover-cum-green-manure crop increased the yield of tobacco from 1,585 to 1,850 kg/ha (*i.e.*,, an increase of 16.7 per cent) and reduced the need for nitrogenous fertilizer dose by 45 per cent. Bajra+mung strip-cropping also reduced the water loss considerably.

Table. Soil and Water Loss Under Various Crops and Cropping Systems

Treatment	Run-off (mm)	Soil loss (tonnes/ha)
Alluvial soil - 2 per cent slope - rainfall (June to March) 791.1 mm rainfall causing run-off 385.9 mm - Vasad (average of 8 years		
Bajra-fallow	167.7	2.3
Bajra-mung strips (3:1 ratio)-fallow	121.0	2.2
Bidi tobacco-fallow	205.3	4.8
Sunhemp (cover-cum-green-manure crop)-*bidi* tobacco-fallow	142.6	4.4
Black soil - 1 per cent slope - annual rainfall 656.8 mm - Kota (average of 4 years)		
Groundnut	73.9	1.9
Black-gram (*mash* or *urad*	102.6	2.1
Johar	103.3	2.4
Red soil - 2 per cent slope - monsoon rainfall 1,002 mm - Deochanda (DVC) (average of 3 years)		
Maize	64	3.33
Maize and *urad* (for seed) intercropped	64	3.0
Maize and *urad* (for green-manuring) intercropped	66	2.9
Maize and *arhar* intercropped	66	2.5
Maize and *arhar* (maize stalks or stubble mulched) - intercropped	86	3.3
Red soil - 5 per cent slope - monsoon rainfall 1,129 mm - Deochanda (DVC) (average of 3 years)		
Maize	326	23.6
Urad	418	47.0
Groundnut	325	13.9
Gora paddy	385	21.1

Groundnut grown under two soil-climate conditions has been shown to reduce both the soil and water loss. Urad grown under two soil-climate conditions has been shown to be a run-off and soil-loss-permitting crop like maize. Intercropping maize with urad or arhar did not reduce the loss of soil and water.

Strip-Cropping

Strip-cropping is essentially another form of rotation. Its importance in controlling the run-off erosion and thereby maintaining the fertility of the soil is now universally recognized. Strip-cropping, in effect, employs several good farming practices, including crop rotation, contour cultivation, proper tillage stubble-mulching, cover-cropping, etc.

Strip-cropping is of the following different forms:

- Contour strip-cropping
- Field strip-cropping
- Wind strip-cropping
- Permanent or temporary buffer strip-cropping.

Contour Strip-cropping

Contour strip-cropping is the growing of soil-exposing and erosion-permitting crop in strips of suitable widths across the slopes on contour, alternating with strip of soil-protecting and erosion-resisting crops. Contour strip-cropping shortens the length of the slope, checks the movement of run-off water, helps to desilt it and increases the absorption of rain-water by the soil.

Further, the dense foliage of the erosion-resitant crops prevents the rain from beating the soil surface directly. It is advisable to rotate the strip-planting by sowing a non-resistant crop, following an erosion-resistant crop and vice versa.

Very little experimental work has been done to determine the best combination of crops and other factors in a strip-cropping programme. The data collected at the Dry Farming Research Station, Sholapur, Maharashtra, have given the following indications:

- Groundnut, Moth bean (Phaseolus acontifolius) and Horse gram (Dolichos biflorus) are the most efficient and suitable crops for checking erosion.
- The normal seed-rates of leguminous crops, other than groundnut, do not give sufficiently dense canopies to prevent rain drops from beating the soil surface in much cases. The seed-rate should be trebled.
- The most effective width of the contour strips for cereals, such as jowar and bajra, is 21.6 m and for the intervening legume 7.2 m.

The results have also shown the following strip widths as suitable for erosion-permitting and erosion-resistant crops on different slopes:

Slope	Width of erosion-permitting crops	Width of erosion-resistant crops
1/2 per cent and below	45 m	9 m
Between 1 and 2 per cent	24 m	6 m
Between 2 and 3 per cent	13.5 m	4.5 m

Field Strip-Cropping

It is the planting of farm crops in more or less parallel strips across fairly uniform slopes, but not on exact contours.

Wind Strip-Cropping

It consists of planting tall-growing crops such as jowar, bajra or, maize, and low-growing crops in alternately arranged straight and long, but relatively narrow, parallel strips laid out right across the direction of the prevailing wind, regardless of the contour.

Permanent or Temporary Buffer Strip-cropping

In the case of permanent or temporary buffer strip-cropping, the strips are established to take care of critical, *i.e.,* steep or highly eroded, slopes in fields under contour strip-cropping. These strips do not form part of the rotation practiced in normal strip-cropping, and they are generally planted with perennial legumes, grasses or shrubs on a permanent or temporary basis.

MIXED CROPPING

The main reason for the lack of interest in strip-cropping in India is the small size of the holdings of the farmers. Instead, the Indian farmers have been interested in mixed farming which is very extensively adopted by him. Some of the important objectives of mixed cropping are a better and continuous cover of the land, good protection against the beating action of the rain, almost a complete protection against soil erosion and the assurance of one or more crops to the farmer.

The roots of various species in a mixed crop feed at different depths in the soil.

Improvements in the practice of mixed cropping tend towards the rationalization of the mixtures with respect to composition and content and towards better arrangements than from the usual medley of crops. The line-sowing of mixed crops gives rise to the practice of intercropping.

Effects of intercropping on the yields of crops - Black soil at Kota.

	Yield kg/ha (average of 5 years)
Wheat (pure crop)	314.9
Gram (pure crop)	314.6
Wheat + gram (in alternate rows)	439.7

Out of five years of trial, the wheat crop failed in one year owing to the extreme drought, and gram failed in one year because of the incidence of gram wilt. In both these years, the other mixed crops was a success, thus ensuring at least one crop to the farmer when mixed cropping was practiced. The wheat+gram mixture gave a consistently higher yield than the pure crops individually. The increase in net profit as a result of mixed cropping was 89 per cent and 183 per cent over the pure crops of wheat and gram, respectively.

Mechanical Measures of Erosion Control

Mechanical measures (also called engineering measures) play a very vital role in controlling erosion on agricultural land. They are adopted to supplement the agronomical practices when the latter alone are not adequately effective. These measures include basin-listing, subsoiling, contour-bunding (also called level terraces, ridge terraces, absorptive-type terraces), graded bunding and bench-terracing on steep slopes.

The main objectives of the mechanical measures for controlling erosion are:

- To increase the time of concentration by intercepting the run-off and thereby providing an oppurtunity for the infiltration of water, and
- To divide a long slope into several short ones so as to reduce the velocity of the run-off and thus prevent erosion.

Basin-Listing

Basin-listing consists in making of small interrupted basins along the counter with a special implement, called a basin-lister. Basin-listing helps to retain rain-water as it falls and is specially effective on retentive soils having mild slopes.

Subsoiling

This method consists in breaking with a subsoiler the hard and impermeable subsoil to conserve more rain-water by improving the physical conditions of a soil. This operation, which does not involve soil inversion and promotes greater moisture penetration into th soil, reduces both run-off and soil erosion. The subsoiler is worked through the soil at a depth of 30-60 cm at a spacing of 90-180 cm.

Contour-Bunding

This practice consists in making a comparatively narrow-based embankment at intervals across the slope of the land on a level that is along the contour. It is an important measure that conserves soil and water in arid and semi-arid areas with high infiltration and permeability, and is commonly adopted on agricultural land up to a slope of about 6 per cent. The cross-sections of bunds adopted in the dry areas of Maharashtra are given below.

Type of soil	Top width (cm)	Bottom width (cm)	Height (cm)	Side slope	Area of section (sq m)
Very shallow soils	45	195	75	1:1	10.00
Shallow soils	45	255	82.5	1.25:1	13.75
Medium soils	52.5	300	82.5	1.50:1	16.00
Medium heavy soils	60	420	90	2:1	24.00

These cross-sections of the bunds can be used as a guide in similar situations. It may be noted here that, as no specifications for bunding in deep black soil are available so far, no large-scale bunding on them can be recommended, pending further research. As regards spacing between bunds it should be not exceed 150 cm vertical drop or 67.5 cm horizontal spacing, whichever is less. The following schedule, which is used in Maharashtra, can be used as a fair guide:

Percentage slope	Vertical drop
0 to 1	1.05 m
1 to 1-1/2	1.20 m
1-1/2 to 2	1.35 m
2 to 3	1.50 m

Where the rainfall is more than 62.5 mm and moisture conservation is important, bunds may be constructed at shorter intervals. In the alluvial soils of Gujarat, a vertical interval of 1.83 m and a cross-section of 1.3 sq m were found to be suitable for land with slopes ranging from 6-12 per cent and for slopes less than 6 per cent contour bunds with cross-sections of 0.9 to 1.3 sq m spaced at 0.9 to 1.2 m vertical interval were found to be effective. Observations and experiments at Sholapur, Bellary and Kota have shown that even in semi-arid climate, contour-bunding in deep black soils, with montmorillonitic type of clay is not suitable. The low rates of permeability and infiltration in these soils cause a prolonged impounding of water on the upstream side, and the crops are consequently damaged.

Graded Bunding or Channel Terraces

Graded bunding has been used in areas receiving rainfall of more than 80 cm per year, irrespective of the soil texture. In clay soils, graded bunding has to be used even for areas having less than 80 cm of annual rainfall. Graded bunds may be narrow-based or broad-based. A broad-based graded terrace consists of a wide-low embankment constructed on the lower edge of the channel from which the soil is excavated. The channel is excavated at suitable intervals on a falling contour with a suitable longitudinal grade.

At Dehra Dun, studies on the channel terraces in the alluvial soils of the valley with 3-4 per cent slope have shown that the two vertical intervals (V.I.)* tried, *viz.* 0.3 (S + 2) and 0.3 (S + 3) did not show much difference in run-off, whereas the soil loss per mm of run-off was more from the V.I. = 0.3 (S + 3). However, the annual soil loss was within the permissable limits and, therefore, V.I. of 0.3 (S + 3) can be adopted safely. *V.I. = Vertical interval in metres. S = Slope per cent Frequency of run-off (cm) and soil loss (tonnes/ha) for two vertical intervals (Dehra Dun)

Vertical interval (m)	Run-off (cm) Frequency (years)				Soil loss (tonnes/ha) Frequency (years)			
	10	5	2	1.25	10	5	2	1.25
0.3 (S+2)	35.0	30.0	17.5	11.0	5.6	4.2	2.5	1.5
0.3 (S+3)	40.0	32.0	19.0	12.5	7.0	5.4	3.2	1.8

The channel grades of 0.4 per cent and 0.6 per cent did not show any signs of scouring. Observations on cross-section revealed that the broad-based and narrow-based cross-sections functioned well without any special maintenance. Broad-based terracing is recommended where farming is practiced with tractors. Studies on broad-based channel terraces constructed on black soils (land slope, 1 per cent) in the semi-arid climate at Bellary showed that a V.I. of 0.6 m was better than that of 0.75 m and that the channel terrace with a variable grade showed less of run-off and soil loss than the channel terrace with a uniform grade. At Kota, graded bunds, 0.7 to 1.0 sq m cross-section and with 0.1 to 0.5 per cent channel grade were found suitable for clay loam to clay black soils.

Bench- Terracing

This consists of a series of platforms having suitable vertical drops along contours or on suitably graded lines across the general slope of the land. The vertical drop may vary from 60 to 180 cm, depending upon the slope andsoil conditions, as also on the economic width required for easy cultural operations. The material excavated from the upper part of the terrace is used in filling the lower part. A small 'shoulder' bund of about 30 cm in height is also constructed along the outer edge of the terrace.

Bench terraces may be 'table top' or sloping outward or inward with or without a slight longitudinal grade, according to the rainfall of the tract - medium, poor or heavy, and the soil and the subsoil are fairly absorptive or poorly permeable.

On steeply sloping and undulating land, intensive farming can be practiced only with bench-terracing. The initial cost of bench -terracing is more than that of bunding. However. Bench-terracing helps to retain the soil, moisture, manure and fertilizer better and facilitates the application of irrigation, if available. In rainfed areas, terracing is usually practiced on slopes ranging from 6 to 33 per cent. It may have to be used on gentle slopes, if irrigation is to be applied to the crop. At Ootacamund, studies have been conducted on the optimum length of bench terraces, longitudinal and inward grades of bench terraces.

Effect of the length of Bench Terraces (on 13-16 per cent slope) on run-off, soil loss and the yields of crops - Ootacamund

Length of bench terrace (m)	91.5	122.0	152.0
Run-off (mm)	32.1	26.2	24.2
Run-off as percentage of the total rainfall	2.4	2.0	1.8
Soil loss (tonnes/ha)	0.59	0.55	0.77
Yield of potato (kg/ha)	10,047	9,418	9,692

The difference in the length of bench-terraces did not influence significantly the run-off, soil loss and the total yield of potato growth on them. However, from the analysis of the fortnightly soil-moisture data, it was observed that on benches longer than 91.5 m, the farther ends of the terraces were significantly drier than those near the cross disposal drains. On this consideration, it was recommended to have bench terraces, of about 100 m in length in the Nilgiris. Five longitudinal grades of bench terraces (*viz.* 0.15, 0.33, 0.50, 0.60 and 0.84 per cent) constructed on land having 25 per cent slope and with 2.5 per cent inward slope were compared to Ootacamund. The run-off and the soil loss increased significantly with the increase in the grade. However, the maximum run-off was only 0.9 per cent of the total rainfall and the soil loss was only 0.3 tonne/ha under the maximum grade of 0.84 per cent, both of which are negligible. The differences among the yields of the potato crop from bench-terraces of various grades were also not significant. Similarly, the effect of the inward grade of the bench terraces (*viz.* 1, 2, 4, 6, 8 and 10 per cent) on the yield of potato was not found to be significant.

GRASSED WATERWAYS

A grassed waterway is associated with channel terraces for the safe disposal of concentrated run-off, thereby protecting the land against rills and gullies. A waterway is constructed according to a proper design and a vegetative cover is established to protect the channel section against erosion because of the concentrated flow. In the alluvial soils of the Doon Valley under the humid subtropical climate, Panicum repens was the best-suited grass, followed by Brachiara mutica, Cynodon plectostachyus, Cynodon dactylon and Paspalum notatum. The suitability of a grass was based on the cover it gave, the ease with which it was established and the forgae yield obtained from it.

EVALUATION OF EFFECTS OF SOIL AND WATER CONSERVATION ON AGRICULTURAL LAND

The beneficial effects of conserving soils moisture by constructing bunds and levelling the land have been extensively demonstrated in the semi-arid alluvial plains of Uttar Pradesh where 35 per cent, 63 per cent and 98 per cent increase in the yields of kharif and rabi crops has been obtained by bunding alone, levelling alone and bunding-cum-lenelling respectively. Bunding has increased the yields of Setaria, cotton and johar by 18 per cent, 11 per cent and 17 per cent in large-scale field trials in Tamil Nadu.

Contour-bunding has not only increased the yield of crops in the dry farming areas in Maharashtra, but has also increased the water level in the wells and the employment oppurtunities as the age of bunding increased.

Estimation of Peak Rate of Run-off

For designing various structures and carrying out mechanical measures to control erosion for the safe disposal of run-off, such as grassed waterways and check dams, the estimation of peak rate of run-off is an important design criterion. Three monographs have been developed to estimate the peak rate of run-off by using three different method\s, *viz.* The Rational Method, the Cooks Method and the Hydrologic Soils-Cover Complex Method.

Gully-Erosion Control and Reclamation

It is estimated that about 2.3 m ha (5.75 m acres) of land in India is affected by severe gully erosion. These gullies are an indication of very bad management of the land resources. Apart from the fact that the gullied land has been completely destroyed, the gullies are a menace to the adjoining tablelands.

Whereas, as a result of gully erosion, the land resource, one of the most important natural resources we have, is completely lost, the people along the river banks suffer from innumerable hardships. The ravine lands pose a socio-economic problem as they harbour dacoits and undesirable social elements. Also, the ravine lands are one of the chief sources of sediment which chokes the reservoirs in the country.

The gently sloping nature of the land, the loamy-sand, the sandy-loam and the silty-loam texture of the soil, intense rains in the monsoon, the improper land use by resorting to overgrazing, the biotic interference with the natural vegetative cover and the faulty agricultural practices are the chief causes of gully erosion all over India.

Classification of Gullies

Any system of gullies has an independent catchment, with a regular stream which has been termed the "drainage system". In each drainage system, it has been observed that gullies with defined side slopes, bed width and depths occur in a regular order. In the upper reaches of the drainage system, the gullies are wide and shallow, with varying side slopes.

The middle part of the drainage system is usually deeper, wider and has uniform side slopes normally up to about 15 per cent. The lower portion of the drainage system which is nearer to the main river is usually very deep, has steep side slopes and is associated with intricate branch gullies. The gullies have been classified as follows:

Symbol	Description	Specifications
G_1	Very small gullies	Up to 3 m deep. Bed width not greater than 18 m. Side slopes vary.
G_2	Small gullies	Up to 3 m deep. Bed width greater than 18 m. Side slopes vary.
G_3	Medium gullies	Depth between 3 and 9 m . Bed width not less than 18 m. Side slopes uniformly sloping betweeen 8 and 15 per cent.
G_4	Deep and narrow gullies	(a)3 m to 9 m deep. Bed width less than 18 m. Side slopes vary. (b)Depth greater than 9 m. Bed width varies. Side slopes vary, mostly steep or even vertical; with intricate and active branch gullies.

While the general pattern of land-capability classification is based on the recommendations of the Soils-Survey Manual, the interpretation in relation to slope classes and the susceptibility to erosion hazard by active gullies has been modified to suit the conditions in ravine lands. In ravine lands, the slope of the land and the nearness of gullies are the most important and dominant factors which vary widely and influence land capability.

The land-capability classification specifications for the ravine lands, as influenced by the slope of the land and the gully erosion hazard, are given below:

Land-form	Slope (%)	Distance from gully rim (m)	Land-capability class
Tablelands	0-1%	Beyond 60	I
Tablelands	1-3%	Beyond 60	II
Tablelands and wide humps in between gullies	0-3%	Between 6 and 60	III
Tablelands	3-5%	Beyond 6	III
Tablelands	5-10%	Beyond 6	III
Tablelands	10-15%	Beyond 6	IV
Marginal land between the gully rim and the tablelands	0-15%	Within 6 m of the gully rim	VI
Tablelands	15-25%	Within 6 m of the gully rim	VI
Very small, small and medium gully sides and beds (G_1, G_2 and G_3	--	--	VI
Tablelands	25%	--	VII
Deep and narrow ies	--	--	VII

Land-capability classes II, III, IV, VI and VII are to be annexed by symbol "e", indicating damage by the past erosion, the present hazard and the future susceptibility to gully erosion.

Control of Gullies and their Reclamation for Various Land uses

The practices described below are arranged in the order in which they should be adopted; the cost of their execution increases progressively.

Closure to Grazing and other Biotic Interference

A study of the natural flora of the eroded areas has shown that only poor types of annual and unpalatable grasses are growing in place of the desirable climax associations which should normally exist in the prevailing soil-climatic environment.

It is reported that at Vasad in Gujarat, as result of closure to grazing and other biotic interference:

- Aristida funiculata and Themada triandra were first replaced by Apluda mutica (a tall annual grass) and then by the perennials, such as

Eremopogon foveolatus, Heteropogon contortus, Dicanthium annulatum and Cenchrus sp.,

- The loss of soil and water progressively decreased from the area as the natural vegetation improved,
- There was not only qualitative but quantitative increase in the yield of grasses.

Similar results have been reported on the clay loam and clay soils of the Chambal ravines where closure to grazing and biotic interference resulted in the qualitative and quantitative increase of useful species, such as Dicanthium annulatum, Cenchrus ciliaris and Apluda mutica. Under the upper Damodar catchment conditions, it has been observed that closure to grazing reduced the soil loss from 3.3 tonnes/ha (under overgrazing condition) to only 0.6 tonnes/ ha.

CHECKING THE GROWTH OF GULLIES

Contour and Peripheral Bunding

After the closure of the ravine lands, the immediate problem to be tackled is to stop the devastating rate of soil erosion and the growth of gullies and the conversion of the cultivated tablelands into wastelands for this purpose, it is essential to retain as much precipitation a possible on the land in the semi-arid and sub-humid areas and safely dispose of the excess run-off in humid areas. In the semi-arid and the sub-humid area of India, contour and peripheral bunds of various cross-sections have been found ideal for this purpose.

In Gujarat, it is now recommended that for alluvial soils the contour and peripheral bunds should be 0.9 sq m to 1.2 sq m in cross section and should be spaced at 90 cm to 120 cm vertical intervals. The contour and peripheral bunds are stabilized by sodding with Dicanthium annulatum, Cenchrus ciliaris and Panicum antidotale. It has been observed at Vasad in Gujarat that land directly under bunds can give a net annual income of ₹ 385 per ha from the sale of these grasses. The excess run-off is safely disposed of through grassed ramps or pipe outlets. In the Chambal ravines, where the soil are relatively fine and the rainfall is heavier, graded bunds in association with grassed waterways and drop structures for the safe disposal of water have been found to be better than the contour lands.

Gully Plugging

The eroding and deepening of gully beds can be prevented with gully plugs. Gully plugs protect the gully beds by reducing the speed of run-off water, redistributing it, increasing its percolation, encouraging silting and improving thesoil-moisture regime for establishing a plant cover. Gully plugs of various materials, *e.g.,*, brushwood live hedges, earth, sand bags, brick masonry and boulders have been tried in India. The size and material of the gully plugs depends on the width, length, and the bed slope of a gully and the anticipated run-off. All types of gully plugs are effective either in retaining or retarding the run-off. Earth is the cheapest and most readily available material and it is, therefore, easire and economical to construct the earthen gully plugs, wherever possible.

Boulder gully plugs are equally effective if the material is available. Brushwood is often available, but there is likely to be a shortage of wooden posts. Moreover, brushwood gully plugs cannot survive the severe attack of white ants, in spite of the fact that the wooden posts are coated in tar, they disintegrate in a couple of years. In the long run, they prove to be costly.

For the same considerations of short life and high costs, the sand-bag gully plugs are not recommended. Gully plugs of brick masonry are constructed at the confluence of all gully branches of a compound gully. For gullies where no run-off is expected from the top, earthen gully plugs of 1.1 sq m cross-section (with a grassed ramp, 22.5 cm below the level) and spaced at 45-60 m horizontal intervals are suitable; for gullies in which run-off from the top is expected, an earthen gully plug of 2.2 m cross-section with a pipe outlet is to be provided. The diameter of the pipe shall be determined by the catchment area (15 cm diameter A.C.C. spun pipe up to a discharge of 2 to 3 cusecs from an effective catchment of 1.6 ha is suitable). A composite check dam of earth and brick masonry (spillway portion) is necessary for larger catchments (more than 1.6 ha). This is located at the confluence of a big compound gully with the main drainage system or in the bed of the main drainage system at 1.2 m vertical intervals or 120 m horizontal intervals.

Reclamation of Gullies for Cultivation

The belief that all the gullied land can be reclaimed for cultivation by making level benches in gully beds is not feasible. This may be possible if no limit is fixed on expenditure. It has been observed that small and medium gullies can be conveniently, safely and economically reclaimed for cultivation, whereas deep and narrow gullies should be retired to a permanent vegetative cover of grasses and trees.

Reclamation of Small Gullies

Small gullies are reclaimed by clearing, minor levelling with bulldozers and constructing diversion-cum-check bunds of 1.5 sq m cross-section spaced at horizontal intervals of 30-45 m. Grassed ramps are provided for the disposal of excess run-off at the ends of bunds near the gully sides. Consecutive grassed ramps are diagonally opposite to one another so that the path of run-off is lengthened and its flow velocity is reduced so as not to cause any scouring. At the end of the small gully, a composite check dam of earth and brick masonry spillway portions constructed.

Reclamation of Medium Gullies

A small gully gets transformed into a medium gully along the length of the main drainage system. A medium gully is reclaimed by clearing and levelling the bed and constructing a series of composite earth and brick masonry check dams at vertical intervals of 1.2 m (which gives a horizontal interval of 120 m on 1 per cent slope of the gully bed) and terracing the side slopes.

Design of Composite Check Dams

The design discharge (maximum run-off) through the drainage channel is computed from the empirical formula:

Q = 0.0028 C.I.A.

Where

Q = Run-off in cubic metres per second (m^3/sec)

I = Rainfall intensity in mm/hr

A = Watershed area in ha

The length of the spillway is determined from the formula:

Q = 1.70 LH3/2

Where

Q = Run-off in cubic metres per second (m^3/sec)

L = Length of the weir notch in metres H = Height in metres of water flow above the spillway level

Terracing of Side Slopes

The uneven side slopes of the medium gullies having 8 to 15 per cent slope are bench-terraced into level terraces at 0.9 to 1.2 m vertical intervals. The terraces are given a back slope of 1 in 50 and a longitudinal grade of 1 in 200 towards the grassed outlet. A ridge bund of 0.3 sq m cross-section is provided at the edge of each terrace. Terrace faces are given a slope of 1.5: 1. Bench terraces are constructed when the gully sides are having a uniform slope for a length of at least 120 m to justify the cost of terracing. The terrace faces, grassed outlets and earthen checked dams are stabilized by sodding or growing them with suitable grasses. Dicanthium annulatum and Cenchrus ciliaris have been found suitable for this purpose, specially in Gujarat and in the ravine son the banks of the Jamuna river. Bench terraces and the check dams require careful maintenance for the first two years in view of the unsettled conditions of the soil.

Reclamation of Deep and Narrow Gullies

As mentioned earlier, the best land use of ravine lands is to retire them to permanent vegetation comprising grasses and trees. This type of land use is a must for the deep and narrow gullies. The natural tree species of the ravine lands of Gujarat comprise Acacia nilotica, A. senegal, A. leucophloea, Azadirachta indica, Albizia lebbeck, Feronia elephantum, Prosopis spicigera, etc. With closure to grazing and other biotic interferences, these species make very good growth which is further helped by silvicultural operations, such as climber-cutting and thinning. Afforestation with a number of species has been tried. Acacia nilotica, Ailanthus excelsa, Albizia lebbeck, Azadirachta indica, Dalbergia sissoo, Dendrocalamus strictus, Eucalyptus camaldulensis, E. citridora, E. hybrid, Pongamia glabra, Phyllanthus embilica, Salmalia malabarica and Tectona grandis are quite promising species for ravines in Gujarat. For the afforestation of ravines along the banks of the Yamuna river at Agra, Dalbergia sissoo, Acacia nilotica, Azadirachta indica, Albizia lebbeck, Pongamia pinnata, Holoptelia integrifolia, Dendrocalamus strictus and Eucalyptus hybrid have been found to be the most suitable species.

In Kota, Rajasthan, Dendrocalamus strictus, Salix tetrasperma in gully beds and Acacia nilotica on the top and marginal lands have been found to be very suitable.

Landslide Control

Landslides pose an immense threat to highways, villages, agricultural lands, lines of communication, etc. The problem of landslides is more serious in the Himalayan region than anywhere else in India. One landslide about 4 ha in area in Nalotakhala watershed at Dehra Dun has been controlled.

The Nalota Nala landslide was controlled by protecting the landslide against the scouring action of the torrent (by training the lower reaches of the torrent, stabilizing the debris cone, stabilizing the middle reaches of the torrent), by stabilizing the landslips and landslides (by wattling to provide temporary support to bare erodible slopes with grass and brush, by planting deep-rooted shrubs and grasses, such as Pennisetum purpureum, Ipomoea carnea, Vitex negundo and Pueraria hirsute). Based on the observations on the landslide control, it is recommended that the control methods may be adopted, depending on the kinds of materials available in the area, the cause of the problem, the type and the rate of the movement of the slide. These factors vary so greatly from slide to slide that details of remedial measures are required to be tailored to deal with each slide.

Torrent-training and Stream-bank Erosion

The torrent problem is of immense magnitude, extending all along the foothills and the plains abutting the Himalayas and the Siwaliks in Northern India. A study was, therefore, undertaken at the Soil Conservation Research Centre, Dehra Dun, in the lower reaches of a torrent (Bainkhala Torrent) to develop a co-ordinated technique based on suitable vegetative and engineering measures for torrent-training and stream-bank protection. The Bainkhala Torrent-treatment measures were observed for 10 years.

Their performance and utility were evaluated as under:

- Out of the various species tried, for planting live hedges and rainforcing spurs, Vitex negundo was found to be most suitable followed by Arundo donax and Ipomoea carnea. Ipomoea carnea in the case of its planting along spurs was found to be damaged by the abrasive action of debris and boulders moving with flood waters.
- The species found suitable for planting on sloped banks were Aristida cynantha, Chrysopogon fulvus, Arundo donax, Pennisetum purpureum (Napier) and Cynodon plectostachyus (giant star grass).
- Boulder rip-raps on sloped banks invariably gave way owing to scouring at the toe, in spite of the 1 m deep foundation. Even the planting of a live hedge at its base was not much help, unless the main current was deflected from the bank by erecting spurs, etc.
- Jetted posts and jacks provided good protection against bank erosion by inducing siltation, but these structures were usually damaged by the villagers and graziers who often took away the wooden posts for use as fuel. Jacks were found particularly suitable for a straight reaches of the banks.
- The repelling type of spurs were found to be most suitable for quick reclamation of concave banks, since, these spurs induced heavy siltation both on the upstream and downstream sides. However, they needed special protection of their nose which was subjected to excessive scouring.
- The wooden posts in the log spurs and cross barriers started rotting after 2 to 3 years.
- Out of the various species tried for wooden posts, Salmalia malabarica, Cordia myxa and Broussonetia papyrifera gave better performances. It was seen that shoot development took place in most of the species tried, but it was not followed by root development. The shoot died within a few months. On the whole, posts from younger branches were better in sprouting and surviving than those from the older branches.
- Out of the various types of spurs tried, the boulder spurs reinforced with vegetation and gabion spurs (both with 'nose' protection) gave better performance.
- The best months for erecting vegetable structures and making planting was found to be in January and February, when some winter showers are received and the vegetation can get sufficient time to get established before the floods during the monsoon.
- Pennisetum purpureum (Napier) was found to be the best species for stabilizing fresh deposits of silt near the spur and other structures. For a site having coarse deposits (shingle and boulders), Aristida

cynantha and Saccharum spontaneum proved to be useful. The data on the forage yield of Napier from the torrent bed have shown that an average yield of about 4,000 kg/ha can be obtained.

- For the utilization and stabilization of the reclaimed areas behind the banks, fuel-cum-fodder plantations of Dalbergia sissoo (sisham) and Chrysopogon fulvus (gorda grass) were found to be quite suitable.

LAND-CAPABILITY CLASSIFICATION

Any soil and water-conservation project includes two distinct sets of operations, viz.

1. The mapping of land for classification according to its capability,
2. Planning and executing measures to check erosion, improve land productivity and reclaim wasteland.

The farm plans for effective soil and water conservation are based largely on the capability of the land. The land-capability classification map is normally prepared by interpreting a standard soil-survey map. Land-capability classification is a systematic arrangement of different kinds of lands according to those properties that determine the ability of the land to produce crops on a virtually permanent basis.

The Factors Determining Land-capability

These are the major soil characteristics of the land, *e.g.,,* the texture of the top soil, its effective depth, permeability of the top soil and subsoil, and associated land features, *e.g.,,* the slope of the the land, the extent of erosion, the degree of wetness and susceptibility to overflowing and flooding. The grouping of soils into capability classes is done primarily on the basis of their capability to produce common cultivated crops and pasture plants without deterioration over a long period.

Land-capability Classes

The land-capability classes are based on the intensity of hazards and the limitations of use. The land-capability classes range from the best and most easily farmed land to that which has no value for cultivation, grazing or forestry, but which may be suited to wild-life, recreation or for watershed protection. They all fall into 2 broad groups: one suitable for cultivation and other land uses, and the other not suitable for cultivation, but suitable for other land uses.

Land Suitable for Cultivation and Other Uses

Class I (Green Colour)

Soils in class I have very few or no limitations that restrict their use.

This type of land is nearly level and the erosion hazard is low. The soils are deep, well-drained, easily worked, hold water well and are either fairly well supplied with plant nutrients or highly responsive to the application of fertilizers. The soils are not subject to damage because of overflow. The local climate must be favourable for growing many of the common field crops. In irrigated areas, the soils may be in class I, if the limitation of the arid climate has been removed by relatively permanent irrigation works.

These soils need ordinary management practices to maintain productivity. Such practices may include the use of one or more of the following: fertilizers, lime, cover and green-manure crops, conservation of crop residues and crop rotations.

Soils in this class are suited to a wide range of plants, may be used for cultivated crops, pastures, forests, and wildlife, food and cover.

Class II (Yellow Colour)

Soils in class II have some limitations which reduce the choice of plants or require simple conservation practices.

The limitations of soils in class II may result from the effects of one or more of the following factors:

- A gentle slope,
- A slight susceptibility to erosion,
- Less than ideal soil depth,
- Occasional damaging overflow,
- Wetness which can be corrected by drainage, but existing permanently as a moderate limitation,
- Slight to moderate salinity or sodium, easily corrected but likely to recur,
- A slight climatic limitation on soil use and management.

These soils require careful management. The limitations are only a few and the practices are easy to apply. They may need one or more of the following practices: terracing, strip cropping, contour cultivation, water disposal area, covered with vegetation crop rotation, cover and green-manure crops, stubble mulching, the use of fertilizers, manure and lime. These soils may be used for growing cultivated crops, raising pastures, forests, and for wild-life, food and cover.

Class III (Red Colour)

Soils in class III have moderate limitations which reduce the choice of plants or require special conservation practices. Soils in class III have more restrictions than those in class II and, when used for cultivated crops, the conservation practices are usually more difficult to apply and to maintain.

Limitations of soils in class III may result from the effects of one or more of the following factors:

- A moderately sloping land,
- Moderately susceptibility to water or wind erosion,

- Frequent overflow accompanied with some crop damage,
- Very slow permeability of the sub-soil,
- Wetness or continuing water-logging after drainage,
- Shallow soil depth up to the bed-rock, hard-pan or clay-pan which limits the rooting-zone and water storage,
- Low moisture-holding capacity,
- Moderate salinity or sodium,
- Moderate climatic limitations.

Class IV (Blue Colour)

Soils in class IV have severe limitations that restrict the choice of plants and require careful management. The restrictions in the use of these soils are greater than those in class III and the choice of plants is more limited. When these soils are cultivated, very careful management is required and the conservation practices are more difficult to apply and to maintain.

The use of these soils for cultivated crops is limited as a result of the effect of one or more of the permanent features, such as:

- Steep slopes,
- Severe susceptibility to water or wind erosion,
- Severe effect of past erosion,
- Shallow soil,
- Low moisture-holding capacity,
- Frequent overflow accompanied with severe crop damage,
- Excessive wetness or continuing hazard of water-logging after drainage,
- Severe salinity or sodium,
- Moderately adverse climate.

These soils can be used for crops, pastures, forests, and wild-life food and cover.

Land Not Suitable for Cultivation but Suitable for Other Land Uses

Class V (Dark Green or Uncoloured)

Soils in class V have little or no erosion hazard, but have other limitations, the removal of which is not practicable. They are used largely for pastures, forests, and wild-life food and cover. Such land is nearly level and is not subject to more than slight wind or water erosion. Cultivation is not feasible because of one or more limitations, such as overflow, stoniness, wetness or severe climate.

Examples of class V land are:

- Soils of lowlands subject to frequent overflows which prevent the normal production of cultivated crops,

- Nearly level soils with growing season that prevents the normal production of cultivated crops,
- The level or nearly level stony or rocky soils,
- Ponded areas where drainage for cultivated crops is not feasible but where soils are suitable for grasses or trees.

Soils in class V are not suitable for raising cultivated crops, but are suitable for perennial vegetation (grazing and forestry, with few or no limitation). Pastures can be improved, and benefits from proper management can be expected. Physical conditions of soils are such that it is practicable to apply pasture improvements, if needed, such as seeding, liming, fertilizing, and water control with contour furrows, drainage ditches, diversions of water spreaders.

Class VI (Orange Colour)

Soils in class VI have severe limitations that make them unsuitable for cultivation and limit their use largely for pastures, or forests, or wild-life food and cover. Soils in class VI have continuing limitations which cannot be corrected, such as:

- Steep slope,
- Very severe erosion hazard,
- Very severe effect of past erosion
- Stoniness,
- Shallow rooting-zone,
- Excessive wetness or overflow,
- Low moisture capacity,
- Salinity or sodium,
- Severe climate.

Soils in this class are subject to moderate limitations under grazing or forestry use.

Class VII (Brown Colour)

Soils in class VII have very severe limitations that make them unsuitable for cultivation and restrict their use largely to grazing, or forestation, or wild-life food and cover. The soils in this class are subject to severe limitations or hazards under either grazing or forestry use. The physical condition of soils is such that it is not practicable to adopt pasture improvements and water-control practices. Soil restrictions are sever e than those in the case of class VI soils.

Class VIII (Purple Colour)

Soils and land forms in class VIII have limitations that preclude their use for commercial plant production and restrict their use to recreation, wild-life food and cover or to water-supply, water shed protection or for aesthetic purposes. Significant return on site benefits from soils and land forms in class

VIII cannot be expected from management of crops, grasses or trees, although indirect benefits from wild-life, watershed protection or recreation may be possible.

Limitations which cannot be corrected may result from the effects of one or more of the following factors:

- Erosion or erosion hazard,
- Severe climate,
- Wet soil,
- Stones,
- Low moisture capacity,
- Salinity or sodium.

Bad lands, rock outcrops, sandy beaches, marshes, deserts, river wash, mine tailings and other nearly barren lands are included in class VIII in order to protect other more valuable soils to control water or for wild-life or for aesthetic reasons. The land-capability class is indicated on the maps by roman numerals I to VIII or by standard colours or by both.

Land-capability Subclass

A land-capability class is determined by the degree of limitations in land use together with the hazards involved. For example, in class III land, we have land suitable for cultivation but subject to moderate hazard of water erosion because of a steep slope or a moderate hazard of wind erosion on smooth land or moderate hazard of water-logging or overflow and a shallow depth to the bed-rock. Each of these kinds of limitations are recognized at the subclass. Four kinds of limitations are recognized at the subclass level.

Subclass (e) Erosion

It is made up of soils where the susceptibility to erosion is the dominant hazard in their use. Susceptibility to erosion and damage due to past erosion are major factors that govern the placing of soils in this class.

Subclass (w) Excess Water

It is made up of soils where excess water is the dominant hazard in their use. Poor soil drainage, wetness, high water-table and overflow are the criteria for determining which soils belong in this subclass.

Subclass (s) Soil Limitations within the Rooting Zone

It includes soils which have such limitations as the shallowness of the rooting-zone, stones, low moisture-holding capacity, low fertility difficult to correct and salinity or alkalinity.

Subclass (c) Climatic Limitations

It includes soils where the climate (temperature or lack of moisture) is the only major hazard of limitations in their use. The land-capability subclass is designated by the small letters which follow the land-capability classes. Roman numerals, *e.g.,*, IIe, IIIs, IVw capability class I has no subclass. Where two kinds of limitation can be modified or corrected and are essentially equal, the subclasses have the following priority e, w, s, c. where soils have two kinds of limitations, the dominant one is shown first.

Table. Effect of Climate

Characteristics of Climate	**Influence on the Capability Group**
Humid climate with well-distributed rainfall	Can start with class I
Humid climate with occasional dry-spell	Can start with class II
Sub-humid, crop yield frequently reduced by droughts	Can start with class II or III
Semi-arid	Can start with class III or IV
Arid	Can start with class IV

SOILS AND SOIL WATER RELATIONS

Most vascular plants are rooted in the soil from which they obtain both water and mineral salts. The entrance of water from the environment into any of the organs of a plant is called the absorption, intake, or uptake of water. In most vascular species the quantity of water absorbed through organs other than the roots is of negligible importance. Any thorough consideration of the entrance of water into roots requires a consideration of the properties of soils, particularly as they affect the movement of water from the soil into the root.

CONSTITUTION OF THE SOIL

The soil matrix which is the habitat of most roots is an extremely complex system. In general five different components of this system are distinguished:1. The Mineral Matter of the Soil.The parent substance of practically all soils is rock, of which there are numerous varieties. By various weathering processes rock strata are reduced to fragments of diverse sizes and these compose the bulk of most soils. The rock particles in soils may vary in size from stones and gravel down to sub-microscopic particles of colloidal clay.

The mineral portion of the soil is customarily classified into several fractions depending upon the size of the particles. Such classifications usually disregard the very large particles of the soil (rock fragments, pebbles, etc.).

The proportions of the different fractions present are very different in different kinds of soils.The clay fraction of the mineral portion of soils requires special consideration.

Unlike the coarser fractions which are composed of small fragments of unmodified rock minerals such as quartz, feldspar, and mica, the clay portion of soils is made up almost entirely of the products of chemical weathering of the rock minerals and hence differs not only in its physical state, but in its chemical composition from the particles in the coarser fractions.

Most of the particles in the clay fraction are of colloidal dimensions and exhibit the characteristic properties of colloidal systems. The particles of the clay complex, like those of many other colloidal systems, retain water by imbibition, *i.e.* within the structure of the particle. On the contrary the sand and silt particles of the soil retain water only on their surfaces. The presence of a considerable proportion of clay in a soil therefore endows it with a high water retaining capacity. Changes in the water content of colloidal clay result in marked changes in its volume. One result of such changes in volume is the commonly observed cracking of a soil rich in clay upon drying. The plasticity and cohesiveness of soils are also due very largely to the colloidal clay present.

Like other colloidal systems colloidal clay is markedly sensitive to the influence of electrolytes. The micelles of colloidal clay usually bear a negative charge when in contact with water. In the presence of calcium ions the individual clay particles are more or less completely flocculated into compound particles. Much of the colloidal clay in most soils exists as enveloping films around the larger soil particles and is also closely associated with organic material in the soil. Flocculation of the clay particles therefore usually results in the formation of compound granules including sand and silt particles and organic matter in addition to the clay.

These are called soil crumbs. For agricultural purposes a well developed granular structure of the soil is highly desirable since such a structure favours both a high moisture-retaining capacity and a good aeration of the soil. Calcium soils, that is, those with a high calcium content, are in general the most suitable and most valuable for agricultural purposes partly because calcium favours the development of a crumb structure. In the presence of an excess of univalent cations (Na^+, etc.), on the other hand, a greater proportion of the clay fraction of the soil disperses into its ultimate particles, and the soil has a single grain structure.

In this condition the soil is in the least desirable structural condition for agricultural purposes. Many soils contain hydrogen ions in excess. Such soils often develop a good crumb structure, but the crumbs are less stable than those developed in a calcium soil. The addition of lime improves the physical structure of such soils. The crumb structure of a soil, especially in its surface layers, can also be destroyed by purely mechanical effects, such as trampling,or beating by heavy rains. The Organic Matter of the Soil.

Most soils contain organic matter which has been derived principally from the partial decomposition of plant residues. Small quantities may also originate from animal residues and excretions. The proportion of organic matter present may vary from almost none as in some sand deposits to 95 per cent or better in some peat soils. In ordinary agricultural soils the amount present seldom exceeds 15 per cent. In forests organic matter comes from falling leaves, dead branches and trunks of woody plants, roots which die and decay underground, and from dead herbaceous vegetation. In grasslands the underground roots and rhizomes as well as the aerial parts of the plants all contribute their quota to the organic matter of the soil. In well managed agricultural soils attempts are made to maintain the organic matter content by supplying them with organic fertilizers.

The organic matter is the seat of most of the microbiol-ogical processes occurring in the soil. One of the most important of these is the oxidation of the organic matter, a process due largely to the metabolic activities of bacteria and fungi, although a limited amount of purely chemical decomposition probably also occurs. Under conditions which are exceptionally favourable for the activities of microorganisms the organic matter of the soil is oxidised completely and disappears.

For this reason the organic matter of soils in tropical regions, particularly when under cultivation, is very low. Even in more temperate regions cultivation of the soils generally results in a rapid reduction inorganic matter content, due principally to the better aeration induced by till age. As a result of the decay process there is present in most soils organic matter in various stages of decomposition. A large proportion of the organicmaterial which is added to some soils survives in the form of a dark-colouredamorphous substance called humus. Humus is composed principally of the degradation products of the cellulose and lignin derived from plant remains.

The accumulation of humus in soils is furthered by conditions unfavourable to the oxidative decomposition of organic matter. The decomposition of organic matter in bogs, ponds, swamps, and water-logged soils under conditions which are largely if not entirely anaerobic results in the production of relatively large quantities of humus, frequently of the type which is called peat. Where the organic matter supplied is distinctly acid, as under coniferous forests, or heath plants, humus usually accumulates as a definite layer at the surface. Decomposition of the organic remains under these conditions is largely effected by fungi. In prairie and steppe regions, where a grassland vegetation is predominant, humus usually accumulates in considerable quantities as a result of the decay of both underground and aerial organs of plants. The amount of humus which accumulates in any soil depends upon the relative rates of the addition of organic residues and of its disappearance as a result of oxidation. Soils with a low humus content may result from a sparse contribution of organic matter, as in desert or semi-desert regions, or from a rapid oxidation of organic material which prevents accumulation of humus even when the supply of organic residues to the soil is large.

This latter condition obtains in many tropical and sub-tropical soils. Humus is essentially colloidal in its properties and possesses an even greater imbibitional capacity than the colloidal clay particles of the soil. The plasticity and cohesiveness of the colloidal organic matter, while considerably less than that of the colloidal clay, is much greater than that of the non-colloidal fractions of the soil. Humus is rather inert chemically, its influence on the soil being largely a physical one. Its presence in soils favours a looser structure and hence better aeration, a higher water holding capacity and a reduction in cohesiveness as compared with heavy clay soils.

Since the clay fraction and the humus are the two essentially colloidal fractions of the soil, and are associated in an intimate physical relationship many soil scientists refer to these two soil fractions, considered jointly, as the colloidal complex of the soil. A large part of this colloidal complex occurs in many soils, as films enveloping the larger soil particles. The relation of these films to the maintenance of the crumb structure of the soil has already been mentioned. Many other important soil properties are either due to or greatly influenced by the colloidal complex.

SOIL WATER AND THE SOIL SOLUTION

Water is universally a component of soils, although the amount present may vary from the merest trace to a quantity sufficient to saturate the soil, *i.e.* completely fill all of the spaces between the soil particles. Dissolved in the soil water are varying quantities of numerous chemical compounds. These originate principally from the dissolution or chemical weathering of the rock particles, from the decomposition of organic matter, from the activities of microorganisms, and from reactions between the roots of plants and the soil constituents. It is thus more accurate to speak of the soil solution than of the soil water, although in discussions of the water relations of soils it is often a common practice to disregard the presence of solutes in the soil water.

The concentration of the soil solution in any given soil varies with the proportion of water present. While in most soils the soil solution is very dilute, in saline and alkaline soils it maybe so concentrated that only a few species of plants can survive with their roots in contact with it. The principal cations found in the soil solution are Ca_{11}, Mg_{11}, K1, Na1, Al^{+1+}, and Fe^{111} (or Fe^{++}); the principal anions are HCO_3Th $P0_4$, Cl, $N0_3$, $S0_4$, and 5i03. Other solutes too numerous to mention may also occur in the soil solution but are usually present only in very low concentrations.

THE SOIL ATMOSPHERE

The irregularity of the soil particles in size shape, and arrangement insures the existence of a certain amount of space between them, even in the most tightly packed soils. This is termed the pore space of a soil. The pore space of soils varies from approximately 30 per cent of the volume of the soil in sandy soils to about so per cent of the volume in clay soils, or even higher in soils which are very rich in organic matter. The pore space of any given soil depends upon the physical and chemical conditions to which the soil is subjected. Conditions favouring a crumb structure of a soil, for example, usually result in an increase in its pore space.

The interstitial spaces of a soil may be occupied entirely by air, as indesiccated soils, entirely by water, as in saturated soils, or, as is most usually true, partly by water and partly by air. The relative proportions of water and air present in any given soil vary depending upon the water content of the soil.

The air present in the soil is generally referred to as the soil atmosphere.The soil air usually contains a higher concentration of carbon dioxide and a lower concentration of oxygen than the above ground atmosphere. Concentrations of carbon dioxide as high as 5 per cent have been recorded for the soil atmosphere; such values are far in excess of the average value of 0.03 per cent for the air. The accumulation of carbon dioxide in soils is due more to the metabolic activities of micro-organisms than to respiration of soil animals and the underground portions of vascular plants. Except in very dry soils the soil atmosphere is usually saturated or nearly so with water-vapour.5. Soil Organisms.

The soil flora includes bacteria, fungi, and algae. The bacteria are generally the most abundant of all the living organisms present in any soil. Among them are the nitrifying, sulfofying, nitrogen fixing, ammonifying, and cellulose decomposing bacteria. The bacteria accomplishing the oxidative decomposition of cellulose and similar compounds are the most important agents in the production of humus. The numbers of bacteria present vary greatly from soil to soil, and in any one soil vary with seasonal and other fluctuations in soil conditions. Most soils contain between two million and two hundred million individual bacteria per gram of soil.

The number of bacteria decreases rapidly with increasing depth, sub soils being sterile or practically so. In general an abundant representation of most species of bacteria is favoured in soils by warm temperatures (3 - 400 C.), good aeration, and a good but not superabundant water supply. A high calcium content of the soil is also favourable to the development of most species of bacteria, apparently because it favours a granular structure of the soil, thus improving aeration. Some species of bacteria, on the other hand, are anaerobic,and thrive when aeration of the soil is deficient. The denitrifying bacteria and certain of the nitrogen-fixing bacteria (Clostridiurn spp.) are examples of anaerobes. Fungi are, in general, most abundant in soils of acid reaction. In such soils they largely replace bacteria as agents of decomposition of organic matter.

The soil fauna includes protozoa, nematodes, earthworms, insects, insect larvae, and burrowing species of the higher animals. The earthworms are generally credited with having the most important effects on soil structure, at least in many soils. Their activities result principally in a general loosening of the soil, which facilitates both aeration and distribution of water. Many of the other soil animals have similar effects on the structural organisation of the soil.

SOIL WATER RELATIONS UNDER FIELD CONDITIONS

In a region of moist climate, if a hole be dug or bored into the ground at almost any place where the soil is deep enough a level at which the soil is completely saturated with water will be encountered at some depth or other. Water will stand in this hole up to this level of complete saturation which is called the water table. In river valleys or in close proximity to large bodies of water the water table will usually be reached at a depth of only a few feet under the soil surface. Even in regions of arid climate there are some local situations in which a water table is present. The depth of the water table in any locality usually fluctuates, sometimes very markedly, with seasonal and periodic changes in the relative rates of rainfall, evapouration, transpiration and other factors.

Relatively impermeable soil layers sometimes impede downward percolation of water sufficiently to cause the development of temporary water tables which may be far above the level of the true water table. Such temporary water tables have essentially the same effects on soil water relations as true water tables, except that their influence is often only a transient one.

For many years an important role was ascribed to the capillary rise of the water from the water table into the soil above in maintaining the moisture conditions within that soil. Recent investigations have shown, however, that the importance of this source of water in soils has been overemphasised. Experiments upon the rise of water through columns of soil indicate that water seldom rises through the soil by capillarity from the water table at an appreciable rate for heights of more than a few feet. In a typical loam soil the absolute maximum capillary rise of water is about 8 feet. Such capillary rise as does occur takes place most slowly, but to the greatest height in clay soils, and most rapidly but to lesser heights in sandy soils, loam soils occupying an intermediate position.In many soils the water table lies so far below the soil surface that it has little or no effect on the soil moisture conditions in the soil layers which are penetrated by the roots of most plants.

Generally speaking even in loam or clay loam soils, a capillary rise of water from a zone of complete saturation is probably ineffective in providing the roots of most species of plants with any considerable part of the water which they absorb unless the water table is within about 15 feet of the surface. Some of the more deeply rooted species may obtain some water from a water table located at depths as great as about 30 feet, but the presence of a water table at greater depths than this is an egligible factor in supplying the roots of any species of plants with water. A capillary rise of water from a water table is usually an important source of water for plants in such locations as river bottom lands or in fields or forests in close proximity to ponds or lakes. In many and perhaps most agricultural soils in moist climate regions plants obtain some water from the water table at least during the earlier part of the growing season.

However the widespread practice of drainage of agricultural regions has often resulted in such a marked lowering of the water table as to greatly reduce the possibility that capillary rise of water from below will supply crop plants with any significant part of the water which they absorb. The other important source of soil water is that part of the precipitation usually rain, although often melting snow or ice, which percolates downward into the soil. In dry regions this is the only source of water available to plants.

Even in more humid regions this is the principal or only source of available soil water in most soils during the dry season of the year. Not all of the rain which falls on the surface of a soil penetrates into it. Some maybe lost by surface run-off and a portion usually evapourates before it can sink into the soil. The proportion of the precipitation which is lost in the run-off is in general much less with open, porous soils such as those found in most forests than with those of a lower porosity.

A smaller proportion of the water is lost in the run-off when it falls as a gentle rain than when it comes as sudden downpour. The proportion of the precipitation which is lost by evapouration from the surface layers of the soil depends in part on the colour, texture porosity, and other properties of the soil, and in part on the temperature and vapour pressure of the atmosphere, as well as upon the impinging solar radiation.

Let us now consider how percolating rainwater becomes distributed in as oil. We will assume that the soil under consideration is approximately air dry, that it is essentially homogeneous to a depth of several feet, and that Let us now assume that another two inches of rain falls on this same soil before any appreciable amount is lost from its upper layers by evapouration or transpiration. After a new equilibrium has been attained the upper foot of soil will not have increased in water content, but a layer of the soil approximately two feet in depth will now be moistened up to its field capacity. In other words addition of a second increment of water equal in volume to the first does not increase the water content of the already moist layer of the soil above its field capacity, but results, due to further capillary movement, in raising to its field capacity a second layer of soil, lying directly under the zone which had been moistened by the addition of the first increment of rain, and approximately equal to it in thickness.

Although the exact mechanics of the distribution of water under these conditions is probably more complicated, the effect produced is as if the second increment of water simply flows through the moist blanket of soil, after which it is distributed to the dry soil layer underneath by capillarity. Successive rainfalls would thus continue to deepen the layer of soil which has been moistened up to its field capacity. If the water table is not too deep, and if sufficient rainfall penetrates the soil, not too much of which is utilized by plants growing thereon, eventually the entire soil from its surface down to the water table will be moistened up to its field capacity. A zone several feet in height just above the water table may be enriched somewhat above field capacity by upward capillary movement from the water table. If additional water is applied to the soil, after the entire soil mass down to the water table has attained its field capacity, this water percolates down through the soil under the influence of gravity and becomes apart of the ground water. Such conditions obtain in many of the soils of more humid regions at least during the wetter seasons of the year, provided that the water table is not located at too great a depth. This downward percolation of water to the water table is an important factor in influencing its depth below the soil surface, which usually fluctuates considerably from season to season.

In the preceding discussion we have assumed, in the interests of simplicity a homogeneous soil. However, most soils consist of a vertical succession of several distinct horizons, each with more or less distinctive physical and chemical properties. Even after long continued disturbance of a soil by plowing or other cultural activities at least some semblance of the original soil stratification usually persists. In the horizons below those reached by the plow the original structural organisation of the soil is usually maintained practically intact. Although the individual horizons of a soil are often fairly homogeneous within themselves, each such horizon in a given soil may have a distinct field capacity of its own.

The water contents of the different horizons, even after an equilibrium in the capillary distribution of water has been attained, may therefore be very different. A somewhat erratic distribution of rainfall to an underlying soil often results from cracks or channels which are opened into the soil by one agency or another. Many soils crack upon drying, sometimes to depths of several feet. Such cracks often facilitate a mass flow of rainwater to a considerable depth in the soil.

Similarly in forest soils the decomposition of roots may leave channels through which water flows down into the deeper layers of the soil. The burrows of animals may also facilitate the entry of water into a soil.The presence of rock strata, or of relatively impervious layers of soil close to the surface, will also modify very markedly the simple picture which has been presented of soil water conditions.

THE EFFECTIVES OF INDIGENOUS SOIL AND WATER CONSERVATION TECHNIQUES

From 1997 to 2001, the second phase of the Indigenous Soil and Water Conservation (ISWC 2) programme had been operating in seven countries in both Anglophone (Ethiopia, Tanzania and Zimbabwe) and Francophone Africa (Tunisia, Burkina Faso and Cameroon). The programmes had taken an approach to agricultural research and development through building on local innovation and encouraging farmer experimentation and Participatory Technology Development. This paper describes the main components of this farmer innovation approach.

This presentation of ten components of a farmer innovation approach to agricultural research and development does not mean that these were or should be neatly implemented one after the other. In practice, several components run parallel to each other or are repeated several times within the approach. Nor does it mean that each country involved in ISWC 2 and PFI has given the same attention to each component. The vastly differing socio-economic and agro-ecological conditions in each of the countries involved have led to different accents being placed. The three country programmes under PFI followed the steps fairly closely, whereas each of the seven countries under ISWC 2 designed its programme in the light of its own perceptions, experience and history, as well as the capacity and orientation of the partner organisations.

Members of the ISWC 2 European Consortium (see Box 1.1) gave some advisory support or 'backstopping', but it was up to the National Coordinator and Steering Committee in each country to determine how they would combine the components of the farmer innovation approach to suit their own circumstances. During the annual review meeting and via the joint ISWC/PFI newsletter on farmer innovation in land husbandry, the partners in the country programmes could compare and analyse their different experiences and learn from each other. Also the backstopping missions following Consortium meetings and the sharing of reports between country programmes contributed to this exchange.

Within each country, the ISWC 2 and PFI programmes have concentrated their initial work in selected regions, for example, the Southern Highlands in Tanzania, parts of the Central Plateau of Burkina Faso, the Tigray Region in northern Ethiopia, the Kabale District in southwest Uganda. An exception has been the Zimbabwe programme, which already had considerable experience in participatory research and extension in Masvingo Province before the programme began and used the ISWC 2 phase for scaling up. Most of the components described below refer only to activities in the action areas, but the lobbying for policy change and institutionalizing the farmer innovation approach (Components 9 and 10) have reached out beyond the action areas, with a view to further expansion of the activities.

Training in PRA and PTD

Although there are outstanding exceptions, many scientists and extension agents have difficulties to communicate eye-to-eye with farmers. Their conventional training and vision of development through transfer of modern 'improved' technologies have imbued them with a sense of superiority. They tend to regard themselves as the teachers of farmers, as the agents of change to draw farmers out of the stagnancy of tradition. Most of them cannot imagine that they can also learn from (illiterate) farmers.

With a view to changing these attitudes, the ISWC 2 programme organized training-of-trainer workshops in PRA and PTD. Two courses were held on a regional level for the anglophone and francophone countries in Zimbabwe and Burkina Faso, respectively. The trainees from each country programme came from research, extension and development organisations, both governmental and non-governmental. They then collaborated in planning and facilitating PRA/PTD training and awareness-raising workshops at national and/or provincial (regional) level. Some countries have invested more time in PRA/PTD training than others. For example, ISWC-Ethiopia built up a local training capacity through a series of workshops and by including new people as co-facilitators of training workshops. It was thus able to train numerous government extension agents (called Development Agents or DAs) in all four regions of Tigray. The philosophy behind this was to create a broad basis for identifying local innovations and for supporting farmer-led experimentation and farmer-to-farmer exchange, rather than starting a few isolated PTD experiments involving only a small number of farmers and DAs and then trying to scale up to include a larger number.

Likewise, in Tanzania, a major output of the training activities has been the firm establishment of local PRA/PTD training capacities: already ten professionals from research, extension and training organisations are well practised in facilitating participatory training events. ISWC-Tanzania developed a sequence of training events focused mainly on scientists, extension staff and farmers directly involved in the programme. An introductory PRA/PTD training was followed by a refresher training to review experiences and increase insights. This, in turn, was followed by training in farmer experimentation and by review and planning workshops based on the experiences in farmer experimentation. Thus, training and learning have been closely integrated with exchange, joint review and planning, with the latter gradually assuming more importance than training *per se*.

Because one external training course is not enough to impart all the necessary skills, most of the ISWC National Coordinators asked the external backstoppers to support them in implementing follow-up sessions at national level. These usually focused on specific aspects of PTD, such as how to design experiments together with farmers. In Cameroon, the backstopper was directly involved in facilitating a workshop to raise awareness about PTD at national level. However, in most countries, the PRA/PTD training events at national level were carried out by the participants in the initial training-of-trainer workshops and other local facilitators, with the backstoppers giving advisory support often only from a distance through electronic means of communication.

In the case of ISWC-Tunisia, the scientists had little experience with participatory research and were hesitant to facilitate the training on their own. For the first national PRA/PTD training workshop held in southern Tunisia in October 1997, trainers were flown in from Senegal and Burkina Faso – an innovation in itself, in the sense that experts from South of the Sahara were training scientists in North Africa. The workshop was an eye-opener for most of the participants, who were astounded at the level of local knowledge they discovered during the fieldwork. After this workshop, however, only a small number of participants continued to use PRA techniques in their regular work. The reasons have not yet been analysed, but it is likely that isolated trainees could not easily apply their new knowledge and skills in an unchanged institutional setting. The few trainees who did continue to use their new skills managed to identify interesting innovations and innovators, and this had a decisive positive impact on the future of the ISWC programme in Tunisia.

Not only in Tunisia but across all seven countries in the ISWC programme, the success of the training events in changing the participants' attitudes depended on the personalities of the individuals and the extent to which the institutional contexts in which they operate gave them space to use participatory approaches. The National Coordinators and external backstoppers observed in many cases that, when scientists and extension agents were interacting directly with farmers in the field in post-workshop activities, they treated the farmers with greater respect than previously. In some cases, they gave the innovators nicknames, such as 'professor', to express admiration for the farmers' wealth of knowledge, experience and creativity, as well as for their capacity to express what they know and do. Indeed, it became evident during field days and travelling seminars that some farmer innovators have oratory and presentational skills far superior to those of many scientists, college lecturers and professors.

Identifying and Verifying Farmer Innovators

The process of identifying farmer innovators is not an easy and straightforward one, because farmers are not necessarily aware that they are innovating. In each country, all partners first had to agree on the concept of innovation and innovators. For example, as a working definition for an innovator, ISWC-Ethiopia used 'someone who develops or tries out new ideas without the support of formal extension services.' 'New' was defined as 'something that has been started within the lifetime of the farmers – not something that s/he has inherited from parents or grandparents'. This definition helped to focus the search on the dynamics of indigenous knowledge, not just looking at what is traditional but seeking endogenous change. In contrast, ISWC-Tunisia decided to include also technologies inherited from parents in the inventory of local innovations in land husbandry.

Many types of actors were involved in the identification of farmer innovators: they included extension agents, NGO field staff, students doing fieldwork, teaching staff and scientists. In the search, the detailed local knowledge of field agents in NGOs and government services was an important asset.

They could sometimes name innovators whom they already knew from their day-to-day work. However, this was not always the case. Some field agents initially had eyes only for the technologies that they themselves were promoting and for the 'progressive' farmers who adopted these technologies. For example, NGO staff members in Cameroon were surprised to hear about the existence of farmer innovators; one of them said: 'We are always in the field and we have never seen them.' However, once they became familiar with the concept of farmer innovation and had actually met some local innovators and seen their accomplishments, the same staff members began to recognize innovators (both men and women) regularly. Some of them even commented that they were now noticing small differences in farming practice almost every time they went to the field.

Not only a wide range of actors was involved in the identification process; also a wide range of means was used: direct observation, interviews with farmer groups and with key informants, contests, peer identification, invitations for self-identification through rural and regional radio programmes. In Tunisia, for example, men and women farmers responded to the weekly radio programme on Agriculture and Innovation by writing to the broadcasting station that they, too, had innovated and wanted to tell others about this.

Some methods worked well in some countries but not in others, for readily understandable reasons. For example, farmers in Ethiopia could readily identify innovators in their midst but when innovative farmers in Burkina Faso were asked to identify other innovators, they tended to name relatives. This was a logical thing to do, because ISWC-Burkina provided credit to innovators. In Ethiopia, an annual contest was set up: village elders, local leaders and DAs identified top innovators in each district. The winners were distinguished in public ceremonies, as an expression of recognition by their fellows and to encourage them to continue innovating and interacting with their communities (Mitiku 2000). ISWC-Ethiopia deliberately avoided offering credit to individuals, in view of the DAs' negative experiences in having to convince farmers under the Sasakawa Global 2000 scheme to take up credit for purchasing external inputs. This illustrates how each country designed its programme in the light of its own experience.

One issue that was much discussed by the partners in the ISWC 2 programme was whether the focus should be on individuals or on groups of farmers in identifying and giving public recognition to innovators. Most countries initially focused on identifying outstanding individuals. There was sometimes a tendency for scientists and extension agents to select those farmers with whom they were already in contact. Other countries tried to spread the search as widely as possible, relying mainly on extension agents and village leaders but rarely involving 'ordinary' farmers in the identification process. In its work in Tigray, the ISWC-Ethiopia team encouraged partners to identify innovations by both individuals and groups of farmers (eg, in modifying traditional irrigation systems), as well as innovations by husband-wife teams. However, in most countries, it was often only later, after starting to work with male innovator in participatory research, that the important role of wives in local innovation and experimentation was realized.

In both ISWC 2 and PFI, an innovation was generally defined as something new to the particular locality, but not necessarily new to the world. For example, an Ethiopian farmer who saw a *shadouf* (an ancient Egyptian device for lifting water) while he was a refugee in the Sudan and who developed a *shadouf*-based irrigation system when he returned to Tigray, was regarded as an innovator in his home area. In the PFI programme, farmers who simply copied what another farmer in the same village had developed or introduced were not regarded as 'first generation' innovators, even though what they did was new for their particular farms. A first round of identifying farmer innovators by the PFI programme therefore had to be followed by a process of verifying that they were indeed 'first generation' innovators in the eyes of their fellow villagers.

In most countries in the ISWC 2 programme, the distinction between 'first-generation' and 'second-generation' innovators (adopters, adapters) was not made. The focus was on identifying new ideas that had been developed or tried by a few farmers but could be of interest to many: in other words, the programmes were more concerned with verifying the usefulness of the innovation rather than whether a particular individual was a genuine innovator. In order to assess whether an innovation was likely to be more widely accepted, some countries, such as Ethiopia, Cameroon and Tanzania, studied the social setting and resource endowments of the innovators.

A total of over 800 farmer innovators have been identified in the seven countries involved in ISWC 2 and the innovations of most of them have been documented in reports, database entries and photographs. In some cases, documentation had taken the form of video films. Not only scientists but also field agents have been preparing this documentation. These few hundred innovators represent only 'the tip of the iceberg', because the programme covers relatively small parts of each country. Most innovators and their innovations continue to be hidden, overlooked or ignored. The main aim of the programme is not, however, to identify only outstanding innovators. It is to stimulate the innovative capacities of *all* farmers, by encouraging as many scientists and extension agents as possible to recognize local innovation and to work with farmers in ways that promote innovation, as outlined in the following components. In this context, it is important that farmer innovations are 'verified' by other farmers as part of a process of stimulating more widespread innovation in a village (see Component 6).

Analysis of Innovators and Innovations

Because relatively little is known or documented about farmer innovation in Africa, the ISWC 2 and PFI programmes tried to gain a better picture of the characteristics of outstanding innovators and their motivations for innovating. As pointed out by Yohannes, every farmer has to be an innovator to some degree, but some farmers are well known in the community as being particularly innovative. What triggers these farmers to develop new ideas or try out something new, while others operating under similar conditions do not? Is it because they are particularly rich or particularly poor in productive resources? Are most of the outstanding innovators old or young, educated or illiterate, men or women? Do innovations by women differ from those by men? Do the more innovative farmers have certain characteristics that can be cultivated, eg, through education and training? In which domains do farmers innovate? What is the potential of local innovations to be adopted or adapted by other farmers?

The viewpoint of the ISWC 2 and PFI programmes from the viewpoint of doctoral research on the subject. Generally, the men and women who were found to be outstanding innovators are people with strong personalities, who have sometimes had to withstand initial resistance by other villagers. This was particularly the case among the women innovators in Tigray who dared to challenge cultural taboos by taking on the male task of ploughing or using donkeys for traction. Some also had to deal with the resistance of family members. For example, a man in Tigray who spent several years developing an intricate system of lifting, storing and distributing water to irrigated plots was threatened with divorce by his wife, because her family thought he was wasting his time on the farm instead of going to town to earn money in construction work. Only after he started to sell fruit, vegetables and fodder from the irrigated land did his wife return to live with him. She now collaborates closely with him in maintaining the irrigated plots and selling the produce.

In Tanzania, a systematic study was made into the socio-economic background of the farmer innovators identified through the programme activities. Students from Wageningen Agricultural University found that the innovators included both rich and poor farmers. The former appeared to be innovating because they are curious and enterprising and had the resources to experiment; the latter appeared to be innovating because they were highly motivated to improve their situation and, having no resources to apply solutions offered from 'outside' (the extension service), used their creativity to find their own solutions.

Discussions among partner organisations in the two programmes often revolved around the question whether there was a tendency to work primarily with richer farmers who had developed more spectacular innovations, or whether outstanding innovators were richer because they were so innovative. There was a concern that the smaller improvements in their farming systems made by farmers with fewer resources were being overlooked. When country programmes such as Tunisia and Ethiopia began to seek out especially women's innovations, they found that these tended to be low-cost, making use primarily of local resources. Such innovations are particularly promising for resource-poor farmers, not only women, and have a good potential for spreading, but these innovators usually do not have the same confidence and means to make their ideas more widely known as do richer, male farmers. Extension agents can play a particularly important role in encouraging farmer-to-farmer communication about the low-external-inputs options developed by the less wealthy local innovators.

Setting up Monitoring and Evaluation Systems

When all is said and done, it must be possible to show all stakeholders in agricultural development whether or not the programme has enhanced the capacity of farmers to experiment and to innovate, and whether this increased capacity and the emerging innovations indeed contribute to improving natural resource management and the well-being of the farm families. It is important to produce numbers, especially for donor agencies and political decision-makers, but it is just as important to analyse the processes, as a source of learning and guidance for future work.

It is therefore necessary to document *who* has done *what, where, how* and *why*. If monitoring and evaluation (M&E) of the programme activities is to be done well and be useful, then all partners must be involved. They must feel both capable and willing to do the work. Therefore, the observations made and recorded have to be limited to the smallest possible number of key indicators of interest to those involved, and the questions need to be readily understandable. Only in this way can the learning aims be achieved.

Members of the ISWC 2 Consortium proposed questions and forms to facilitate monitoring of the process and outcome of the various programme activities, as well as to assess their impact. The proposals included more conventional aspects of M&E – collecting information defined by outsiders for analysis by outsiders – and some participatory aspects of M&E, so that the farmers and national partners could record and assess according to their own criteria and using methods they chose or developed themselves. It was up to each country programme to adapt the questions and forms to the local conditions as well as to the local capacities to handle and analyse the information generated.

An initial assumption of the ISWC 2 Consortium was that farmers would perceive the recording of data as a burden. However, the experience in, for instance, Burkina Faso, Cameroon and Uganda has been that, when the farmers were involved in determining what data to collect, they were keen to keep the records. The farmers regarded this as a new and useful skill that helps them manage their farms better, because recording allows them to keep track of and analyse levels of inputs, outputs and crop performance. All the farmer innovators involved in joint experimentation in the Yatenga region of Burkina Faso insisted on keeping the records themselves. After one season, one innovator remarked: '*On ne mange même plus au hasard*' (even our meals are no longer unplanned). Some farmers in Uganda seemed to be more interested in improving their capacities to keep their own records than in improving their yields through the particular technologies they were testing. Many farmer innovators also keep visitors books, so that they can record who visited them over the years.

Exchange Visits and Study Tours for Farmer Innovators

Both the ISWC 2 and the PFI programmes gave innovators an opportunity to visit each other's farms and to exchange information and experience about their innovations. After their return, many innovators started to try out for themselves what they had observed.

Farmer exchange and study visits have been highly effective in disseminating local innovations or the principle ideas behind them. The major question is how to widen the impact of this farmer-to-farmer communication. Three phases can be distinguished in the process: preparation, implementation and follow-up. In exchange visits in general, and this is also true for some of the exchange visits under ISWC 2, most attention is given to implementation and little to adequate preparation of both the visitors and the hosts. What do both sides hope and expect to gain from these visits? Also an adequate follow-up is important. What did the visitors and hosts find useful about the exchange? How and to whom did they report their impressions? Did the visitors adapt the techniques to their specific conditions back home? Some tentative observations in Zimbabwe are that women seem to be more likely than men to share their impressions with others, although not necessarily in a formal way, and that women tend to share with women while men tend to share with men.

It is also important to know whether some additional technical training or other forms of support may be required as a follow-up to a visit or study tour. In Tunisia, some farmer innovators have trained other farmers, eg, in grafting fruit trees, immediately during the visits, but often such training will be possible only after the actual farmer-to-farmer visit.

In the PFI programme, innovators are encouraged to organize themselves into clusters of usually eight farmers, and they exchange experience within and between these clusters. One advantage of such small groups in one locality is that the members can meet easily and at little expense, at least in the case of groups in more densely populated areas. The ISWC programme in Uganda follows the PFI approach and includes 32 farmer innovators in four networks of eight innovators each.

In the other ISWC 2 countries, it was left up to the innovators to decide if and how they wanted to organize themselves. In Ethiopia, participants in the first travelling seminar decided to form an association and to meet annually to discuss progress in their innovation activities. In contrast, the farmer innovators involved in joint experimentation with scientists in Cameroon were selected by their peers within an existing farmers union and, in Zimbabwe, they were selected by self-selected groups of farmers with common interests. In Tanzania, three cases were recorded in which farmer innovators, after returning home from exchange visits, started up a local group of one or more innovators and a large number of neighbouring farmers. They not only wanted to share what they had learn about techniques; they also found that participation in the visits had encouraged them to undertake joint development activities.

Farmers' Evaluation of Local Innovations

This component can be a preparatory step to the selection of promising ideas for farmer-led experimentation as well as to farmer-to-farmer exchange on innovations. In most cases, innovations were initially assessed by outsiders. Then the farmers themselves – both the outstanding innovators and their neighbours – were given an opportunity to assess the innovations jointly. This was not limited to comparing yields and other technical parameters. For example, Yohannes found the values and experience of the communities strongly influenced their acceptance of local innovations.

Village workshops have proved to be a useful tool for farmers' assessment of innovations. In Tigray, for example, the Bureau of Agriculture and Natural Resources (BoANR) organizes Farmers' Fora during which farmer innovators and their neighbours come together to examine both local and external innovations and to discuss what is useful for which categories of farmers in the community. Such workshops for farmers at village or district level can also help to counteract the isolation from their fellow villagers that many outstanding innovators feel because they are doing something different from the norm.

In Zimbabwe, for example, local innovators were often regarded – at least by government officials – as 'off-types', because the policy environment discouraged the application of indigenous knowledge. The emphasis of ISWC-

Zimbabwe on group formation and joint experimentation served to enhance the social standing and confidence of innovators and strengthen their position vis-à-vis the government services. A group approach also reduces the risk that farmer innovation programmes focus on only a few privileged farmers.

Innovation assessment workshops at village level can be starting points for designing experiments implemented by farmers who have been selected by the community. This embeds the experimentation by individuals within a wider social process. In Cameroon, for instance, the priorities for experimentation were set during a workshop involving scientists, extension agents, farmer innovators, other male and female villagers, representatives of the traditional authorities and, for some time, the *Fon* (the king) himself. This was deliberately done to avoid isolation of the innovators and their experiments from the rest of the community.

Stimulating and Supporting Processes of Joint Experimentation

The original assumption in the ISWC 2 programme document was that joint experimentation by scientists, extension agents and farmer innovators. This was far too optimistic. The entire process of gaining a common understanding of concepts, training in PRA/PTD, identifying and understanding farmers' innovations and informal experiments, organizing exchange visits and building up partnerships between farmers, extension agents and scientists requires much more time.

If the joint experimentation had started earlier, there would have been a greater risk that the scientists defined the experiments and imposed them on the farmers. Ideally, the innovators and other interested farmers should set the research agenda and it should be based on their priorities.

Scientists have a role in:

- Proposing elements for testing, which the farmers might like to include;
- Advising farmers how to design simple experiments, so that both farmers and scientists have a firmer basis for evaluating the results; and
- Explaining reasons for the farmers' findings and thus helping farmers better understand some of the principles and less visible factors influencing the outcome of their experiments.

In addition, the scientists can assist in generating 'hard' data to validate the findings in conventional scientific terms, in order to convince other scientists, policy-makers and donor agencies. A further role of scientists, especially in the initial stages of collaboration with farmers and extension workers, is to observe and analyse the process in order to develop the farmer innovation methodology and to describe it clearly to others wanting to engage in it.

The actual process of setting the joint research agenda differed from country to country. In Cameroon, for instance, village workshops were held to elicit the priorities of farmer innovators. One innovator, Samuel Toh, clearly formulated their priorities and told the scientists: 'We are aware that the researchers have their priorities ... Let's first address our priorities and then we will also work with the researchers on what they want to study.' The scientists agreed and a process of PTD was commenced. The situation was quite different in Tunisia. Here, the National Coordinator is a scientist who has developed both simple and complex, but effective, technologies that reduce maintenance requirements of a traditional water-harvesting system and allow more efficient use of the limited water resources available in the region. He strongly influenced the research agenda, but this was based on farmers' practice. One farmer innovator in Tunisia observed the scientist's experiments and started his own, in a kind of competition, claiming: 'What you can do, I can do better and cheaper'. It was not initially a strategy of ISWC-Tunisia to set up competition between formal and informal research, but this served to spur on both the scientists and the farmer innovators.

In Tanzania, a series of workshops was organized for the 'experts' (scientists and extension agents) to bring them to acknowledge and appreciate the potentials and important roles of farmers in agricultural research and development. At the same time, workshops and exchange visits were organized for farmers to build up their confidence and assertiveness, so that they would be better able to articulate their position and argue for their interests. Once these two parallel processes had matured, the experts and farmers were brought together in a workshop to set priorities for joint experimentation.

At the start of the ISWC 2 programme, the country with the most experience in stimulating and supporting processes of joint experimentation was Zimbabwe. Here, the PTD activities were inextricably linked with the development of local institutions and were carried out with groups of farmers defined by the communities. PTD thus became a tool not only for developing techniques but also for developing communities (Murwira et al 2000).

In some cases, the joint experimentation focused primarily on scientific validation on the local innovation. Here, the procedures were more conventional and it was important to collect data that could be subjected to statistical analysis. In other cases, the process of experimentation was designed to allow primarily farmers to assess the local innovations and/or to investigate farmers' and scientists' ideas to improve them still further. This had the additional purpose of strengthening local capacities to test and assess new ideas. Here, it was more important that the procedures and measurements could be managed completely by farmers, also eventually on their own, and it also meant that farmers were given the chance to learn about experimentation by analysing their own experiences and mistakes. The workshops for farmer experimenters organized by ISWC-Tanzania reflect this latter approach: with the support of scientists and extension agents, the farmers examined each other's experiments and themselves recognized where improvements should be made (eg, Malley and Mruma 2000). In Tanzania, after a small number of joint experiments by farmers and technical specialists in 1997/98, more than 30 joint experiments on a wide variety of topics were carried out in the following two growing seasons. In addition, some individual farmers did their own experiments on the same topics, without direct support from the specialists.

The studies on the maize-pit system are showing astounding results, which are now being acknowledged by the scientific community. Results achieved in farmers' trials with irrigation to induce flowing in coffee are also very promising, and have led to new research questions needing attention, particularly with respect to soil fertility. At the same time, partners in the ISWC-Tanzania programme see a need to stimulate continued experimentation and innovation by farmers, in addition to this more systematic joint experimentation. For example, while the joint experiments with the maize pit system was confined to an agreed set of dimensions for the pits, several farmers have independently tried out other dimensions and ways of making the pits. Discussion between farmers and scientists about the reasons for these changes and the results obtained could enrich the learning process.

Farmer-to-farmer Dissemination of Innovations

A key aim of both ISWC 2 and PFI is to disseminate useful innovations. Various forms of farmer-to-farmer communication are facilitated, primarily through visits and workshops. The PFI programme organizes three types of exchange visits: farmer innovators visit other innovators to learn from each other (FIs to FIs), 'ordinary' farmers visit farmer innovators to learn from their experience (Fs to FIs), and farmer innovators visit other farmers to inform them and to train them in the use of improved technologies (FIs to Fs). The first type, involving only farmer innovators, comes under Component 5, while the second and third types are examples of wider farmer-to-farmer extension.

In the ISWC 2 programme, each country has developed its own variations. In Ethiopia, Components 5 and 8 were combined in the travelling seminars, during which innovators visited other innovators and, at each site of innovation, met with a wider group of people in that community. In Zimbabwe, mixed groups of farmer innovators and other villagers visited other sites of innovation, and the villagers rather than the programme chose the farmers to be involved. In Uganda, study tours were also organized to take farmers to other parts of the country: exchange visits were made between the farmer innovators working with the PFI programme in the north and those working with the ISWC programme in the south. A large number of farmers have been involved: in

Kenya alone, over 2500 farmers (1600 men and 900 women) have visited farmer innovators in the framework of PFI.

The original idea was to disseminate farmers' innovations that had been scientifically validated, but it soon became obvious that farmers do not wait until a technology has been tested and given a stamp of approval by scientists. A farmer who thinks that a technology is interesting and possible to apply will try it out, and may adapt it, or may choose some elements to adopt. In Tanzania, seeds and planting materials were exchanged informally during farmer-to-farmer visits and subsequently planted. Some of the local innovations viewed by other farmers have already been widely adopted. Follow-up enquiries after an exchange visit revealed that 79 farmers in Njombe District alone had started trying out the sowing of many maize plants in a pit, an innovation developed by a farmer in Njombe, and also farmers in other districts and regions had started using this technique, although scientists had not yet validated it.

In Tanzania, this component is closely linked with Component 6. The village workshops for evaluating local innovations automatically led to sharing of ideas between farmers. However, most of this sharing probably took place outside of the activities supported directly by the programme. In additional to informal communication between farmers, this included the increased opportunities for farmer-to-farmer exchange within the regular research and extension activities of the partner organisations. For instance, during the regular farmer field days, farmer innovators are asked to explain what they are doing. Information about local innovations and innovators has also been spread via the existing journal of the farmer network Mviwata.

Reactions of different categories of farmers to local innovations still need more investigation. The impact study in Uganda found that women were more responsive than men to adopting new ideas and those who tried out local innovations tended to be poorer in resources than the original innovators. The reasons behind this are not yet clear. It may be that the wealthier farmers are in a better position to take the risks involved in innovating, while the poorer ones are prepared to adjust their practices when they see good alternatives that suit their needs. However, this will apply only where the richer farmers' innovations can also be realized with the limited resources available to the poorer ones. For example, it is unlikely that complex innovations that require high investments, such as those developed by some male farmers in Tunisia, will spread easily through farmer-to-farmer extension without external financial support. Men in Tunisia can take advantage of government subsidies and credit schemes that are not available to most farmers, male or female, in the other countries in the ISWC 2 and PFI programmes.

It is quite a different case in West Cameroon, where – after prices for the men's customary cash crops (coffee and cocoa) fell – some men started innovating with cost-effective ways of growing women's crops. Barthélemy

Djambou is one innovator who is exploring better ways to grow vegetables as market crops, and his innovations are of interest mainly to resource-poor women, who customarily grow food crops and vegetables. Here, too, it has yet to be investigated whether women were also innovating with these garden crops and, if not, what was constraining them from doing so.

A fundamental issue that will determine the success of farmer-to-farmer dissemination of local innovations is whether innovators are willing to share their knowledge and experience with others. A woman innovator in Tunisia had not been willing to tell other farmers about how she uses decomposing manure to hatch eggs, until she was offered an opportunity to present her innovation on the radio. Some individuals are not at all willing to inform others about their innovations, and some will do so only for payment (farmers can hire their services as consultants). Nielsen found that the most innovative farmers were the least keen to share their knowledge.

In most cases, however, the ISWC 2 and PFI programmes found that farmer innovators were eager to promote their own innovations. In some cases, they did so because this gave them public recognition and social esteem; in others, because they felt it was their duty to their community. Some farmers deliberately share their knowledge with others in their village in order to avoid jealousy and possible ensuing difficulties (witchcraft).

Women whose innovations go against social norms are initially reluctant to share their ideas openly. The poorer farmers, especially the female household heads, often find it difficult to spare the time to teach other farmers. In one case in Ethiopia, the community decided to send someone to work on a woman innovator's farm when she was asked to teach other farmers, eg, to train other women how to plough in their own fields (Mamusha Lemma, pers. comm., February 2000). In areas like Tunisia, where the communication radius of women is confined, radio may be the best means for them to share beyond their immediate family and female neighbours.

Farmers share their knowledge informally in various ways, but the most common forms appear to be:

- Farmers discuss new ideas during market visits or at small social meetings, eg, Ethiopian women who meet for the traditional coffee ceremony;
- Farmers visit other farmers who are doing something that appears to be interesting; and
- Farmers speak to a larger group about what they have seen or are doing, eg, during a village meeting, possibly held for another main purpose.

In Burkina Faso, outstanding personalities have innovated in developing extension approaches to share experiences with improved traditional planting pits (*zaï*). One innovator initiated an annual *zaï* market day, which is attended by all farmers interested in exchanging information about this technique and its numerous variations. Another has created a kind of 'field school': farmers jointly treat a piece of degraded land with *zaï* and learn by working together. A third innovator coaches a number of other farmers, one of whom has started to experiment with the layout and configurations of *zaï*. These models retain many of the characteristics of informal learning between farmers: social gathering, learning by seeing and doing, and personal mentoring. The value of dialogue between recognized equals and personally experiencing new ways of working, rather than being told how something should be done, is expressed in the farmer's statement: 'Learning from exchange visits is better than being visited by a village extension worker'. While both ISWC 2 and PFI have placed great emphasis on facilitating farmer-to-farmer exchange, designed to reinforce the above-mentioned informal processes, PFI has taken a more structured approach to this.

Raising Awareness and Lobbying for Policy Change

The eight countries participating in the two programmes have pursued various paths to raising awareness about farmer innovation and trying to influence policy in its favour. Much attention has been given to documentation and publication in the form of working papers, project reports, workshop proceedings, papers for conferences and articles in newsletters and journals. The programmes in Cameroon and Ethiopia even started up their own local newsletters. All the ISWC 2 teams have gained access to radio, television and the press. As soon as ISWC-Ethiopia had identified some outstanding farmer innovators, it arranged radio interviews that were broadcast in the local language (Tigrigna). ISWC-Tunisia launched a two-hour programme on Agriculture and Innovation, which is broadcast by a regional radio station to most of central and southern Tunisia. The Tunisia experience stimulated ISWC-Cameroon to appoint a media advisor to maximize access to mass media and stimulated ISWC-Burkina to start, in late 2000, a radio programme in the Yatenga region using the station *La Voix du Paysan* (Voice of the Farmer). Such radio programmes are likely to be noticed also by decision-makers at regional and national level; however, the impact in this respect has yet to be investigated.

Several ISWC 2 teams have produced one or more video films about farmer innovation in their country and, in some cases, at least excerpts have been shown on national television. PFI has produced a broadcast-quality video on farmer innovation in East Africa, which has been aired on television in all three countries involved in that programme. It has also published a book outlining the theory and practice of its approach (Critchley et al 1999) and more than half of the 10,000 copies had been distributed by the end of 2000.

Various other activities also contribute to enhancing policy dialogue. The National Coordinators have organized meetings with and field visits by policy-makers. The President and Vice-President of Uganda visited farmer innovators under the PFI programme. In most other countries, meetings have been held with Ministers of Agriculture or with senior staff responsible for national programmes of research and extension. Upon the invitation of the country programmes, these policy-makers opened national or international workshops on farmer innovation.

The Head of the BoANR in Tigray plays a very active role in the Steering Committee of ISWC-Ethiopia. The national ministers of both Agriculture and Education have visited farmer innovators in the field. The Integrated Food Security Desk (IFSD) in Tigray recently decided to introduce the approach of promoting farmer innovation and farmer-to-farmer extension in the 16 most drought-prone districts. According to Mengesha Haile, the Head of the IFSD, the performance of the DAs will no longer be evaluated according to how many farmers they draw into the Global 2000 scheme, which may not be appropriate for drought-prone areas.

In trying to initiate an approach to PTD through identifying farmer innovation, ISWC 2 deliberately commenced work below the national level (ie, in only certain provinces or regions of a country) in order to develop successful cases of proven local innovation capacity, as this is essential for effective lobbying work. Within three years, the country programmes collected substantial evidence that the farmer innovation approach produces results of interest to smallholders and supporting organizations, and that it can be an alternative to the conventional ToT model of agricultural research and extension. They are providing the accumulated evidence in various forms to decision-makers in their countries, and are exposing them to examples of farmer-led experimentation and innovation.

Important events for raising awareness about the farmer innovation approach on national and regional levels were the two conferences on farmer innovation held in November 1999 in Cameroon for francophone (primarily West) Africa and in February 2000 in Ethiopia for anglophone (primarily Eastern and Southern) Africa. These meetings gave an opportunity for exchange of experience between the countries in the two programmes, but also broadened the participation to include other projects and, above all, policy-makers who could have a positive influence on institutionalizing the farmer innovation approach. Also for this purpose, one day of the annual review meeting in the third and fourth years of the ISWC 2 programme was opened up to policy-makers from the host country.

Institutionalising the Farmer Innovation Approach

Ultimately, the ISWC 2 and PFI programmes are working towards incorporating the farmer innovation approach into the regular activities of agricultural research, extension and education in the countries where they are operating. Only in this way will it be possible to ensure the long-term sustainability of the approach. This requires a shift away from the conventional ToT towards the promotion of farmer-led experimentation based on both indigenous and exogenous ideas. Both programmes seek to strengthen the capacity of scientists and extension agents to recognize the problems being addressed by local innovators in their informal experimentation and to participate in and support farmer-led research, as outlined in Component 7. In this collaboration, one role of extension agents will still be to make information, from whatever sources, more easily available to farmers. However, this will be with the aim of enriching farmers' experimentation, ie, feeding farmers' hunger for useful new ideas to try out, rather than prescribing introduced 'improvements' which may not prove to be such. Virtually all persons who have been directly involved in the two programmes have become excited about the approach. Especially the scientists and extension agents involved at field level became enthusiastic when they started to recognize the knowledge and skills of local innovators. Both programmes have contributed to building up national capacities to give training in PRA and PTD. This can form a basis for further expansion of activities within countries currently in these programmes and to new countries in Africa and elsewhere.

However, real progress and substantial scaling up can be achieved only when the methods of promoting farmer innovation are included in the curricula of research, education and training institutions. Mekelle University in Tigray, the lead agency of ISWC-Ethiopia, has started to incorporate PRA/PTD training into its curricula; so has the Cooperative College Moshi, the lead agency in Tanzania. Some students of Mekelle University have already done their practical attachments on indigenous knowledge, farmer innovation and informal experimentation; and scientists have become involved in studies related to farmer innovation. ISWC-Cameroon has recently trained staff of the National Agricultural Extension and Research Programme (PNVRA) funded by the World Bank and IFAD and, in the next phase, the farmer innovation programme will become a semi-autonomous project under the PNVRA. The involvement of Masters students from Wageningen Agricultural University in the Netherlands has led to an increased understanding of and interest in the farmer innovation approach among staff of the Department for Communication and Innovation Studies. These are encouraging steps forward, but there is still a long road to travel to institutionalize the farmer innovation approach in these and other countries in Africa and Europe and to make the approach less dependent on external funding and technical support.

MEANING AND SCOPE OF WATER CONSERVATION

Water conservation is a broad term involving all the measures which aim at arresting maximum amount of run-off water, storing or collecting it in safe, artificially raised structures and recycling the stored water again to the field in times of need. The ultimate aim of water conservation is to produce maximum from the limited availability of water, by using it most efficiently. An efficient system of collecting, storing and reusing run-off water is sometimes also referred to as water harvesting.

From the point of dry land agriculture, water harvesting indicates not only storing rain water in irrigation tanks/ponds but also employing mechanical and cultural manipulations of soil to improve its rainfall absorption and moisture retention capacity. However, the measures adopted are location specific. To decide on the suitable measures to be taken a preliminary inventory of soil water and other resources, a study of the land use pattern, a dialogue with the target group and a study of socio-political, economic and cultural setting are a must. This implies a scientific approach to water conservation. The need for educating, and organizing people to make them accept necessary reforms for effective implementation of integrated water conservation programmes need not be over-emphasized.

The chief agent of soil erosion is water. It is estimated that about 5333 million tonnes of soil (amounting to about 16 tonnes/ha) is eroded from Indian territory. Nearly 29 per cent of this is carried into the sea and nearly 10 per cent is deposited in surface reservoirs resulting in loss of storage capacity of reservoirs and occurrence of floods. Conservation of water virtually reduces the soil erosion. Thus the scope of conservation is very wide, encompassing all the measures of soil conservation, moisture retention and nutrient preservation in the soil.

NEED OF WATER CONSERVATION

Water is absolutely essential for utilization of all other natural resources including land. Agriculture depends on the availability and supply of water either from rainfall or from surface or underground fresh water resources. Most of the water is received through monsoon rains and is obtained from July to September. Only in some rivers of North India, water is received through the melting of snow in summer.

Because of high intensity of monsoon rains coupled with poor infiltration rates of soils, there is a heavy run-off of water. Run-off occurs when amount of precipitation is more than infiltration of water into the soil. Run-off is very heavy particularly in first rains. As a consequence of heavy run-off, the discharge in rivers increases during rainy period. The experience of last 2-3 decades, shows that every passing year the amount of run-off water discharged into the rivers is in creasing. It indicates that the amount of water which was conserved earlier in the site of rainfall (catchment area) has been reduced.

Our country receives more annual rainfall than the global average of annual rainfall. Therefore, water conservation has to be adopted as a national objective, not only for the sake of water availability but also for protecting the soil which is a precious resource.

WATER EROSION PROBLEM IN INDIA

Out of the total 328 m ha of geographical area of the country, about 143 m ha is cultivated and about 65 m ha is barren uncultivable waste and cultural wastelands. By and large these lands are more or less devoid of protective vegetation and physical barriers and hence are subjected to very serious water erosion. Nature takes 500 to 1000 years to develop 2.5 cm top soil but gets eroded in a course of a year or two. As a result it becomes the most harmful single factor in the deterioration of productive land. Along with the loss of run-off water a colossal amount of soil is also lost.

Overgrazing, deforestation, faulty cultivation, shifting cultivation and carelessly built roads in catchment areas have led to devastating down streams. These include gullying and floods leading to destruction of farm lands and villages, drop in flow during the dry season and consequent loss of crops, and siltation of reservoirs and canals. The problem has been further aggravated due to high rate of population growth: both human and livestock, resulting in indiscriminate exploitation of natural sources, for meeting the ever-increasing demand for fodder, fuel, fibre and fertilizers. Thus continuous degradation of production base and imbalance in land - water -plant-man-animal system is leading to ecological imbalance and economic insecurity through severe soil erosion both by water and wind and threat to the quality of our life and cultivation.

Even though no systematic survey for accelerating the extent of water and soil loss in different areas of the country, has been carried out, it. is estimated that about 5334 mt of soil is detached annually from its original place. The country's rivers carry 2052 mt of this, nearly 1572 mt is carried away by the rivers into the sea every year and 480 mt is being deposited in various reservoirs.

Soil erosion by water is mainly of four types:

1. *Sheet erosion:* About 4-10 tonnes/ha/year in red soil, 17-43 tonne/ha/year in black soil and 4-14 tonne/ha/year in alluvial soil.
2. *Gully erosion:* About 33 tonnes/ha/year in ravine regions
3. *Hill side erosion:* More than 80 tonnes/ha/year in landslide, mine spoil areas etc.
4. *Stream bank erosion:* Along with soil, about 2.5 mt of nitrogen, 1.5 mt of phosphorus, 2.2 mt of potash, large amount of organic matter and micronutrients are also lost. The loss of nutrients is valued at about Rs.15000 million per annum. Mohanjodaro and Harappa are the examples of this fact. Glaring evidence of neglect of rainwater can be seen in the denuded hill tops all around and the extensive network

of raville in the states of Gujarat, Madhya Pradesh, Uttar Pradesh and Rajasthan. Once a thick forest, Rajasthan is now a desert, Conservation of water is prerequisite to conserve soil which is a natural reservoir of plant nutrients. Taking into consideration the magnitude of problems, there is a great scope to streamline the entire water conservation programme more scientifically on micro watershed basis in cluster instead of sporadic efforts. Watershed management programme to conserve water and soil is a new approach and it is getting popularity very rapidly. The programme involves an appropriate combination of agronomic, mechanical, agrostological and afforestation measures, fitting to soil-climatic and topographical conditions of area and socio-economic conditions of the target group.

TYPES OF WATER LOSSES

Water losses with special reference to soil erosion aloe de- scribed below:

Raindrop or Splash Loss

Raindrops fall on the ground and form a splash along with suspended soil patlicles. Water and soil move away from their original place.

Sheet Erosion

When the intensity of rainfall is bit higher, a fairly uniform layer of soil is lost from the soil along with the run-off water. This type of soil and water loss is serious on slightly sloppy lands. The existence of this kind of soil and water erosion is seldom known to farmers as it does not leave behind any visible change on soil topography. Though the field appears the same as before but the cream of the soil *i.e.* highly fertile upper most layer, is skimmed off along with moving water. The estimates reveal that sheet loss of water erode away many tonnes of soil and has damaged millions of hectares of land in our country.

Rill Erosion

The speed of run-off water is sometimes high enough to create rills on the soil surface. Rills are very shallow finger sized channels which can be smoothened out by ploughing. Rill erosion is the intensified form of sheet erosion and more distinctly noticeable. The width of rills keeps on widening with every passing rainy season.

Gully Erosion

Gully erosion of water and soil is the aggravated form of rill loss. When rills are not smoothened out, water keeps on drawing through them and these shallow rills go deeper and deeper with every passing rainy season. The depth and size of rills go so high that they cannot be smoothened out with ploughing, they are called gullies. The size of gullies may be many metres wide and deep. They provide a big route to run-off water and a huge amount of water is lost through them.

FACTORS AFFECTING WATER LOSSES

Water in motion removes the soil and causes erosion of soil. Water erosion is due to dispersive action and transporting power of water. So it descends in the form of rain and leaves the land in the form of run-off. The intensity and speed of run-off are directly correlated to the amount of soil' and water loss. Some of the factors discussed below greatly influence the extent of soil and water loss.

Climate

The major climatic factors affecting run-off and erosion at'e rainfall, temperature and wind. Of these, rainfall is the most important and the knowledge of rainfall characteristics is important in erosion studies. Raindrop impact on a soil surface has a pronounced effect on erosion. Raindrops cause soil splash, detach soil particles and make them available for transport. The amount of soil detached by the rain depends on the intensity of rain, its duration and the protective value of any cover present.

Erosive capacity of rain drops results from three factors, namely:

1. Amount and intensity of rainfall,
2. The diameter of raindrops, and
3. The velocity of drops as they strike the soil.

The amount of soil transported by raindrops is governed by the transporting capacity of the raindrop energy; the case with which detached patlicles are called; and the resistance afforded by the vegetation and other obstructions.

The amount, intensity, frequency and duration of rainfall have very definite effects on the amount and rate of resultant run-off. As large total. rainfall may not cause excessive erosion if the intensity is low. Likewise, an intensive rain of short duration may not produce sufficient run-off to cause erosion. When both amount and intensity factors are high in a given storm, run-off erosion will be serious.

Topography

Sloppy soils frequently permit run-off, resulting in the loss of water and soil, while on flat lands erosion is comparatively negligible. The degree of slope and length of slope are the main features of topography affecting erosion. Velocity of run-off water is influenced mainly by the degree of slope. If the land slope is increased four times, the velocity of water flowing over it is approximately doubled. When the velocity is doubled the erosion capacity as represented by the kinetic energy of flowing water is increased about four times, tile amount of material of a given size that can be carried is increased by about 32 times, and the size of particles that can be transported by pushing or rolling is increased by about 64 times. There is a definite limit to the amount of suspended material that can be carried by given stream of water. When this limit is reached, more material cannot be picked up without increasing either the velocity or the depth. Any reduction in velocity on the other hand, will result in deposition of the suspended soil.

Vegetation

Vegetation is one of tile most efficient means to conserve water. A thick growth of grass or a dense forest may negate the effect of all those factors which accelerate water erosion.

Vegetation reduces water erosion through the ways mentioned below:

- *Interception of rainfall:* The foliage of vegetation intercepts tile raindrops, retains a portion of water and evaporates it back into the atmosphere. However, the plant absorbs some of this water through foliage and utilizes it for metabolic purposes. The amount directly evaporated does not contribute to the run-off water.
- *Decreasing run-off velocity:* Vegetative cover serves as a hindrance to run-off water. A weIl distributed, close-growing vegetation not only slows down the rate at which water travels down the slope, but also tends to prevent " the concentration of water in a particular area. These two effects greatly reduce the erosive capacity of the run-off water.
- *Root effect:* Roots of grasses and other vegetation make the soil porous and permeable to water. The roots die and decay in the soil leaving behind numerous small cavities which increase the pore space and consequently the absorption of water.
- *Biological effect:* Remnants of vegetation serve as the food material for numerous organisms inhabiting the soil. These organisms range from large sized earthworms to microscopic bacteria, fungi, algae and actionmycetes. Macroorganisms work the soil and make it porous and permeable. Microorganisms decompose organic matter of the soil, and humus is formed as a decomposition product. Humus is very efficient in retaining water. It can retain water as much as 100 times of its own weight.

Soil

The amount of water left on the soil surface for run-off very much depends on soil properties. If the infiltration capacity of the soil is high, a large amount of water is soaked in by the soil and there is little run-off.

In case soil is very compact or hardpan lies in the subsoil, a large amount of water is lost by run-off. The infiltration capacity or permeability of soil depends on number of factors such as soil structure, texture, organic matter content, moisture content and slope percentage.

AVENUES OF WATER LOSS FROM SOIL

Factors which influence behaviour of water in soil in the context of soil erosion have been discussed above. Here, it is useful to briefly highlight the avenues through which water disappears from the soil.

Infiltration

The downward entry or movement of water into the soil is called infiltration. When the water is introduced to the soil either by irrigation or rain, it penetrates the surface of the soil. The speed of movement or the depth covered in a unit time is termed as infiltration rate. It is usually measured in centimeters per hour. The infiltration rate is greatly influenced by the moisture content of the soil. The soil takes in or absorbs water rapidly, when water is just applied on the field surface.

If water supply continues, surface becomes saturated and infiltration rate decreases until it becomes merely constant. The soil layer with the lowest transmission rate, either at the surface or below it, usually determines the infiltration rate. Surface sealing which is the formation of a thin compact layer on the ground surface rapidly reduces the rate of infiltration. The surface seal results from a breakdown in soil structure due to the beating action of raindrops and the action of the water flowing over the surface whereby, the fine particles are filtered around the larger particles to form a relatively impervious seal. Very sandy soils may have infiltration rates of over 25 cm per hour, whereas clay soils may have rates approaching zero. Poor soil structure, salinity and alkalinity reduce infiltration rate.

Run-off

Run-off may be defined as the portion of rain or irrigation water which leaves the field either as surface flow or subsurface flow. As long as the rate of rainfall (or irrigation water) reaching the soil surface is less than the infiltration capacity, all the water is absorbed into the soil. When the rate of rain- fall exceeds the rate of infiltration, shallow depressions are filled to overflow level, water begins to flow over the land towards streams. The water required to fill depressions prior to the beginning of surface run-off is called initial detention or 'depression storage'. Overland run-off usually reaches a tiny rivulet or channel which connects to the big rivers and ultimately to ocean. The time of travel from raindrop to stream channels depends on distance, slope, surface condition and depth of flow.

Surface run-off is the run-off which travels over the ground surface to the channel of a watershed. The channels may range from rills to major streams. Subsurface flow is that portion of infiltrated water which penetrates to a shallow depth, travels laterally and is intercepted by channels or emerges to the surface. Appreciable amount of subsurface flow, relative to total run-off, is likely to occur where permeable surface soils lie over slowly permeable or impervious horizons at shallow depths.

Evaporation from the Soil

Evaporation is the process of vaporization by which liquid water is transferred into the atmosphere. The rate of evaporation of water depends on atmospheric temperature, soil humidity, organic matter content and wind velocity. Dry air has a greater capacity for absorbing moisture than moist air, hence evaporation increases under conditions of low humidity. High evaporation occurs at places of high temperature, low atmospheric humidity and high winds.

Transpiration by Plants

Transpiration is the discharge of water as vapour into the atmosphere by the leaves and stems of living plants. The amount and frequency with which irrigation water must be applied will be governed in part by the rate at which crops transpire. This rate of transpiration varies from practically nothing at young seedling stage during cold cloudy weather to a maximum during hot windy weather at a time when crops are growing most luxuriantly. Rapidly growing crops of a leafy nature may use about 5 cm of water per week during the peak growing season. The volume of water transpired by the plants depends mainly on the water at their disposal and also on temperature and humidity of the air, wind, intensity and duration of sunlight, stage of development of the plant, species of the plant and nature of the leaves.

Deep percolations

When the amount of water entering the soil becomes greater than its water holding capacity, deep percolation occurs. This is an intensified form of infiltration in which a great loss of water takes place. Water goes beyond the exploration capacity of plant roots. This water moves due to the force of gravity.

WATER CONSERVATION METHODS AND PRACTICES

It is estimated that about 46 per cent of the water received through rainfall is lost through surface run-off. Now it is visualized that if the rainfall water is obstructed and stored in soil at the place where it is received (in situ) it can help to reduce not only soil erosion but siltation of river beds and to tanks and ultimately control floods in plain. In addition to ! this, the water stored in soil can support good crops and increase the production markedly.

The term conservation means preservation of something against loss or deterioration. Water can be well-preserved by utilizing the lands appropriately and erecting some structures. The concept of using the lands according to their capacity in order to conserve soil and water is termed as 'land capability classification.

Table. Land Capability Classification.

Sl. NO	Class of land	Slope %	Adopted land use and soil conservation meausres
A. Land Suitable for Cultivation			
1	Class I	0-1	Any crop can be grown with proper crop rotation and green manuring to maintain soil fertility
2	Class II	1-3	Contour farming, contour strip cropping and cover cropping contour-bunding.
3	Class III	3-5	Intensive agronomical measures such as contour cropping, contour strip cropping, terracing or contour bunding
4	Class IV	5-8	Contour bunds or terraces and intense agronomic measures. Mostly soil building and soil maintenance crops are to be sown.
B. Land not suitable for cultivation			
5	Class V	8-12	Permanent pasture with controlled grazing
6	Class VI	12-18	Pasture, grasses and forestry. Grazing should be restricted
7	Class VII	18-25	Forest with restricted felling. Contour trenching as conservation measure.
8	Class VIII	>25	Forest with complete closure to grazing and felling of trees.

Using lands according to their capability, ensures use of land without its damage and sustains crop production on a pennanent basis.

Some of the very useful water and soil conservation techniques which can be adopted at the individual watershed level, according to their suitability to the local agro-climatic conditions are put under (A) agronomic measures, (B) agrostological measures, (C) mechanical or engineering measures, and (D) afforestation measures.

Agronomic Measures

Following agronomic measures can be adopted for con- serving water and soil.

Contour Farming

Contour farming is practiced in sloppy or hilly regions. In such areas, the rain water is absorbed in very little amount because of its quick downward movement on the slopes. If these areas are ploughed up and down the slope, tile heavy rainfall may cause gully development. Taking into consideration this effect, the sloppy areas are ploughed and seeded across the slope *i.e.* in circular furrows around the slope. This process is termed as contour farming. The contours (circular or spherical furrows) catch the downward moving water until it is absorbed in the soil. The ridges reduce the flow of water. The circular rows of the crop plants across the slope, reduce the speed of moving water. Greater amount of water is soaked by the soil. Reduction in amount and speed of run-off results in considerable reduction in soil and water loss. Contour is an imaginary line which connects the points located on the land surface at the same heights. Before raising a furrow or ridge, contour line should be marked with the help of wooden sticks or small brick pieces/pebbles. Furrows should be opened parallel to this marked contour soil. These furrows or ridges should be made sloppy towards the main waterways. Tillage should then be done parallel to the contour line on both sides. On small fields of uniform slope, one guideline may be sufficient, on large and more regular fields, several lines may be required. On a hillside, first contour should ordinarily be laid about 1 to 1.5 m vertically below the top of the hill. Additional contour lines are located with the same spacing as the first. In ploughing, the best plan is to start back furrows on the guidelines and work around them.

Tillage Operation

Tillage operation includes ploughing, discing, harrowing and cultivating. The effect of tillage on water conservation may be both useful and harmful. Tillage is useful when it increases infiltration rate of water into the soil. It is harmful when it destroys soil structure, seals soil surface consequently decreasing infiltration and increasing run-off.

The concept of minimum tillage can be advantageously applied for soil and water conservation. In this process the land surface is left least disturbed.

As a measure of tillage operation, surface mulches are also used to prevent water and soil against draining away. These mulches reduce evaporation, increase infiltration capacity of soil, keep down weeds, improve soil structure and virtually increase crop yields. Crop residues like the stubbles, leaves, twigs etc. are used for mulching.

Crop Rotation

Crop rotation involves incorporation of legumes with cereals in a sequence in order to take advantage of different feeding zones of soil, both for, nutrients and water and to off-set disadvantages of mono-cropping in controlling insect pests and diseases. In an experiment at Dehloadun it was found that maize - pea rotation gives a net return of ₹ 1622/ha as compared to maize - fallow ₹ 988/1111 or maize - wheat ₹ I079/ ha. At another place, two year rotation of green manured bidi tobacco - kodo millet (I year) and pigeon pea mixture of Sundia sorghum (II year) under rainfed conditions has been found suitable for rainfed condition. Another rotation *i.e.* pearl millet mixed with green gram rotated with green manured bidi tobacco, is also found suitable for dryland regions.

Crop rotation helps in water conservation by improving soil structure. It improves soil aggregation which results in increased soil permeability and increased water retention.

Besides crop rotation, mixed cropping is also useful from the point of view of conserving moisture and soil. Advantages of this type of croppings are good crop cover, feeding of crops from different soil layers and under fainted condition ensures the farmers against a total crop failure. In medium black soils of Kota, cultivation of sorghum mixed with pigeon pea has been found useful in reducing run-off.

Strip Cropping

This system of cropping involves growing of a few erosion resisting and erosion permitting crops in alternate strips on contour or across the slope with the objective of breaking long slopes on farm and preventing water and soil loss.

Crops that can be grown with minimum stirring of soil are, in varying degrees, erosion resisting or soil conserving crops. These crops are often close-growing, and nutrient enriching. Most of the legume crops and grasses are erosion resisting, whereas the tall growing, widely spaced crops like maize, cotton, jowar, bajra etc. are erosion permitting crops.

Strip cropping is quite often used in conjunction with other water conservation measures like crop rotation, contour farming, cover cropping, terracing, bunding etc. The following are the four general types of strip cropping.

1. *Contour strip cropping:* In contour strip cropping, the crops are arranged in strips or bands laid on the contour line, just across the natural slope of land. In one strip, erosion resisting crop is grown and in next strip erosion permitting crop is grown. Usually the strips are cropped in a definite sequence.
2. *Field strip cropping:* Field strip cropping consists of strips of uniform width running generally perpendicular to the direction of the erosive force. For the control of erosion by water, the strips run across the general slope, but do not necessarily curve to follow any contour line. This practice is recommended only in areas where the topography is too irregular or undulating to make strip cropping practical.
3. *Wind strip cropping:* It is a farming system in which the strips of crop are raised across the direction of wind.
4. *Buffer strip cropping:* In buffer strip cropping, some grasses or legume crops are laid-out between contour strips of crops in the regular rotations. They may also be used as correction strips where the slope is irregular. The buffer strips may be wide or narrow. They may be even or may have variable depths. They may be placed only on the steep, badly eroded parts of a slope or they may be at more or less regular interval on the slope. The buffer strips are used to give more protection against water erosion than is afforded by a solid planting of grain or inter- tilled crop.

Addition 'If Organic Matter

Organic matter can be added to the soil in the 101m of farmyard manure, compost and green manure. Organic manures not only supply plant food elements but also help in improving the soil physical condition. They improve the rate of water infiltration by bringing about desirable change in soil structure and its permeability.

Organic matter helps in retaining moisture in the soil and greater amount of run-off water infiltrates into the soil. This infiltrating water contributes to the underground reserves of water. These reserves can be tapped in times of need.

Agrostological Methods

The following are the important agrostological practices that check water erosion.

- *Lay farming:* This method consists of growing grasses in rotation with agricultural crops. This practice improves water holding capacity and fertility of soil, helps in binding the soil particles and reducing loss of water and soil.
- *Retiring the land:* This practice helps in generating grass cover on the soil. Under favourable climatic conditions grazing should also be restricted. Numerous researchers have shown that grasses have good soil binding capacity and they greatly help the soil to absorb a large amount of rainwater. In different places, doobgrass (*Cynodon dacrylon*), *Dacrylis glome rata*, *Eragrostis amabitis* and *Eragrostis cerbula* have proved their worth in conserving soil and water.
- *Afforestation and reforestation:* Tree plantations help a great deal in conserving rain water. The stems of the growing plants create a hindrance for moving water thereby allowing greater infiltration. Percolating water helps further vegetation to come up in the soil. Roots of vegetation hold the soil and water. After their death and decay, empty cavities are left which accelerate water retention in the soil. A large amount of organic matter is contributed by the trees too, which helps in moisture conservation.

  Extensive plantation strengthens ecology and the hydrogen cycle of the region. The chances of rainfall and consequent acceleration of further vegetative growth are greatly in- creased.
- *Restricted grazing:* Excessive grazing not only removes vegetation from the soil but also scratch and loosens the soil surface. In such a situation, rainwater finds easy way to run-off along with valuable upper soil. Since grazing cannot be completely avoided a system of restricted or rotational grazing must be adopted. In this system an area open to grazing for sometimes should be closed for the following years to

facilitate regeneration of trees and grasses and restore a thick ground vegetation.

Mechanical Methods

Following are the mechanical or engineering methods adopted to conserve water and soil.

Contour Bunding

This practice of soil water conservation is widely practiced in Maharashtra, Gujarat, Tamil Nadu, Karnataka and Andhra Pradesh, Contour bunding consists of consllllcting an earthen embankment across the slope of the land following the contours as closely as possible. A series of such bunds divide the area into strips and act as barriers to the flow of water, thus reducing the amount and velocity of the run-off.

Cultivation is not done on the contour bunds, therefore, about 5 per cent of the land is lost under the bunds for cultivation, about 25 to 162 tonnes of soil and a large quantity of water can be saved annually by constructing contour bunds. In addition to controlling erosion and maintaining soil fertility, the construction of bunds helps in better infiltration of water into the soil, ultimately replenishing the underground water table. Experiences have shown that contour bunds constructed in shallow, medium (depth 45 cm) and medium deep soils have stood well and have been beneficial to farmers. Bunds in deep black soil have been a failure because of the nature of the soil which cracks during hot weather and cakes during the monsoon. This results in the bunds having series of cracks especially during first few years of their construction. Bunds can be constructed by manual labour or by animal or mechanically operated machines. Bulldozers and motorgrades are employed in large scale contour bunding works, When animal power is employed the buck scrapper is the most efficient implement. In case of manual handling, burrow pits are dug towards upper slope of the bund and the soil is laid on the contour lines. When two men operated mould-board plough is used, furrow slice is thrown towards the bund from both sides. The spacing between contour bunds depends on slope per cent and the specification on the depth of soil.

Table. Spacing of Contour Bunds.

SI.NO	Slope of land (%)	Vertical Interval (VI) between Two Bunds (in metres)	Horrizontal Interval (HI) between Two Bunds (in Metres)
1	0 to1	1.05	105
2	1 to 1.5	1.20	98
3	1.5 to 2	1.35	75
4	2 to 3	1.50	60
5	3 to 4	1.66	52

Table. Specification for Bund Cross Section

Sl. NO	Depth of Soil (Metre)	Base Width (Metre)	Top with Ratio	Side Slope	Height (Metre)	Area o Cross Section
1	Shallow soils (7.5 to 22.5 cm)	2.67	0.38	1:5:1	0.77	1.14
2	Medium soils (22.5 to 45 cm)	3.12	0.60	1:5:1	0.85	1.56
3	Medium deep (45-90)	4.25	0.60	2:1	0.90	2.18

Graded Bonding

Graded bunds are extensively used in India with a view to making safe disposal of excess run-off in high rainfall areas. The base width of these bunds ranges from one to two metres. They are useful in the areas where soil is compact and less permeable. No cultivation is done on bunds. The designs of the graded bunds involves the fixing of the dimensions and the slope of the disposal channel so that the velocity of run-off flow can be kept under control. On steep slopes, a parabolic channel and an eatlhen embankment are erected. On less steeper slopes, providing the bunds along a suitable grade and allowing the water to flow behind the bund ensures adequately safe disposal of excess run-off water.

Terracing

Ten-ace is an embankment or ridge of earth constructed across a slope to control run off and minimize water and soil loss. A terrace reduces the length of the hill side slope thereby reducing sheet and the erosion of soil and water.

Studies on soil loss. with water have shown that doubling the length at slope increases erosion by 1.4 times and shortening the length of slope through terracing greatly reduces soil and water loss.

Terracing is a costly measure and thus cannot be justified on crop lands that can be protected by less expensive measures. Agronomic measures such as contour tillage, crop rotation and strip cropping are enough in many sloppy areas. These measures alone may furnish enough protection where rainfall intensities are low. But where erodable soil, long slopes and high rainfall intensities prevail, agronomic measures may give only partial control. Terraces should always be supplemented with the best possible cropping practices, since they fail to capture water when used alone.

Following types of terraces are constructed to conserve water:

- *Bench terraces:* This method involves constructing wide step like platforms along the contour line on sloppy land. Bench terraces make possible the growing of cultivated crops in mountainous regions. Based on shape, bench ten-aces are of three types namely
  - Level and table top,
  - Slopping outwards, and
  - Slopping inwards. The first one is suitable for the evenly distributed medium rainfall areas and deep and highly permeable

soils. Slopping outwards type of ten-aces are effective and economical in areas with a permeable soil of medium depth; and slopping inwards types are useful in high rainfall areas.

- *Broad based ridge terrace:* In this practice, ridges or bunds of 25-50 cm height and 5-9 m width with gently slopping sides are constructed. On these bunds cultivation can be done. Under some conditions base width is kept narrow and the distance between the bunds is also less. Such kind of terraces are called narrow based terraces. These are similar to graded bunds.
- *Channel type and ridge type terraces:* The channel type terraces are mostly used on soils where controlled removal of water is of prime importance. The important feature of these terraces is to dig a channel towards the inner end of the platform. Ridge type terraces are usually used where the water holding capacity is the prime function. Since spreading of water over maximum area is the main concern, the ridge is an important item and the channel is only incidental to produce the ridge. The ridge type of terraces are usually built from both sides. The base width of a narrow based terrace is usually 1.2 to 2.5 m and is more for the broad based ones. However, the ridges of narrow based terraces cannot be cultivated unlike broad based terraces.

Gully Plugs and Check Dams

While planning gully controls, the economic factor should be assessed well in advance. Some times gully control measures may cost more than the value of area where the gullies occur. However, in such cases gully control may be justified on the basis of protection to adjacent or downstream land, reservoirs, buildings or other structures.

The various methods employed for controlling run-off have some underlying steps:

- Retention of run-off on the drainage area or catchment area by employing methods like contour farming, contour bunding, strip cropping, terracing etc. -Diversion of run-off from above the gullies.
- Conveying run-off safely through gullies.

Following gully structures which are known as check dams, gully plugs etc. can be erected to reduce amount and velocity of run-off through gullies:

- *Temporary checkdams:* They are constructed across the bed of gully and have two uses:
  - To collect enough soil and water to ensure growth of pro- tective vegetation; and
  - To check channel erosion until sufficient vegetation is established.

The life of a temporary check dam ranges from 3-8 years and during this period enough vegetation is expected to come up. The check dam should be placed in such a way that the top of one elevates the base of another located upslope side.

This criterion is considered in deciding distance between two check dams. The height should be more than 75 cm. In heavy soils, a slope of 0.1 to 0.5 per cent is given. An overall protection is provided by placing wooden planks, loose rocks or constructing platform of sufficient length and width which catches water falling from over the top of the check dam. These are placed towards down stream side of the check dams. Thus three types of temporary check dams can be constructed.

These are described below:

- *Woven wire dams:* Woven wire dams may be used as temporary aids in the establishment of vegetation for the permanent control of erosion.

  To construct the woven wire dam a row of posts 60 – 90 cm deep is set along the curve of the proposed dam at about 1.2 m interval. Heavy gauge woven wire laced over the posts at 25-30 cm apart stmling from 25-30 cm above the bed level. The stakes are then driven down on the bed 30-60 cm deep. Paddy straw, sugarcane tops etc. along with stone pieces and soil are then packed along the row of post. The centre of the dam should be low enough to provide the necessary spill capacity.
- *Ioose rock dams:* In the places where rocks and stones of appreciable size and suitable quality are available, the dams could be constructed using these. The stones are usually encased in woven wire. To construct a dam, a trench is first made in the gully bed across the width to a depth of about 30 cm. This forms the base of the dam on which the stones are laid in rows and are brought to the require height. The centre of the dam is kept lower to provide space for spillway.
- *Plank or slab dams:* In building these dams, the posts are set in a row across the gully to a depth of one meter and about 1.2 m apart. The posts should be so arranged that one of the interval between them will fall in the approximate centre of the gully to form a spillway. After the post is set, a narrow trench is dug along the upstream side. The trench is made about 30 cm deep and just wide enough to permit placing of the headwall. The required spillway notch is cut out after the dam is constructed or a suitable opelling can be left at the headwall during construction. An earthfill is next made against the upstream face of the headwall and brought up to the height of the spillway crest. The fill should have slope not steeper than 2: 1 and should extend well on the gully banks.

Construction of Permanent Structures

Permanent structures to conserve water and soil are built of masonry, reinforced concrete or earth. They serve as efficient supplemental measures in soil and water conservation. These structures are necessary at places where other less costly vegetative measures do not work. Permanent Structures are necessary where a high degree of safety or permanence is required. the main functions of permanent structure are to halt the advance of the vertical over falls at gully heads, to stabilize grades so that a gully can be changed to a regular waterway and in case of drop inlet structures, to control downstream flow.

Three permanent structures are erected to reduce loss of water and soil:

1. Drop spillways
2. Chute spillways
3. Drop inlet spillways

Constructing permanent structures requires skill and thorough understanding of engineering principles and techniques. They art: costly and require substantial investment in the beginning. A well-planned system of water conservation requires supportive permanent structure like the ones cited above. However, their construction should be avoided if other vegetative and simple field structures are adequate to provide enough protection to soil and water.

LAND LEVELING AND GRADING

Land leveling or grading is the process of preparing or modifying the land surface to a planned grade to provide a suitable surface. Leveling requires cutting of elevated surface of land and filling the soil in depressed spots in order to remove surface irregularities and unevenness to make a plain surface. It makes suitable field surface to control the flow of water to check erosion and provide better drainage.

Land leveling is governed by certain factors such as soil characteristics, topography, cropping pattern, method of irrigation, rainfall statistics of the region etc.

The time for leveling should be such that manual, animal or mechanical labour is free from other farm operations. It should be carried out at proper moisture level so as to reduce the energy consumption in leveling. When soil is very dry, the unit draft required is about 3 kg/sq. cm as compared to 1 - 1.5 kg/sq. cm at optimum moisture. Before transferring soil, it should be loosened with disc plough or disc harrow. Bull- dozers are found to be very economical for leveling extensive areas in comparison to other equipments.

Stabilization of Bunds and Outlets with Grass -plantation

Bunds, terraces and other structures are created by manipulating the soil so as to reduce the flow of water. Outlets are the structures through which excess water ponding against a bund or terraces, is safely disposed off. As these structures are earthen, they are vulnerable to erosive action of rapidly moving water. Growing grasses over these structures make them highly stable and resistant to damage. Extensive network of the grass roots keep the bund soil tightly bound together.

Construction of Tanks

Storing water on the surface and artificially recharging ground water reservoir is highly imperative in rain fed, arid and semi arid areas. Constructions of irrigation tanks or percolation tanks provide for the cheapest, considerably effective, hence popular means of harnessing the rain water in minor irrigation and village water supplying schemes.

Selection of Site

Intensive care should be taken while selecting the site of tank construction. It depends upon certain climatic hydrogeological and geomorphological features. Tank construction must be supported by soil survey, measurement of permeability in the zones, water table, infiltration rates in the top soil, rainfall atmospheric humidity, temperature, topography, drainage pattern, etc. Percolation tanks are meant for recharging the unconfined and semi-confined aquifers in areas where the annual rainfall is less than 75 cm and where ground water is over exploited.

Percolation tanks are suitable for the areas where:

- The surface soil is sufficiently permeable;
- There are no layers in the zone above the water table of such low hydraulic conductivity causing perched ground water mounds that rise into the tank and restrict infiltration
- The regional water table is sufficiently deep to keep the rise in water sufficiently below the bottom of the tank and below the root-zone in the command area but not so deep that large quantities of water are needed to wet the rootzone before any recoverable water reaches the watertable;
- The acquifer is unconfined and sufficiently transmissive to allow lateral movement of the recharged water without building up water table right into the root-zone; and
- Permeable formations exist in the down stream side of the tank without any barrier formations like dikes in between.

Field Approach

Following points should be taken into consideration while planning for tank construction:

- If aerial photographs are available one can prepare soil maps, geological maps, bring out' buried channels, know vegetation conditions, bring out structural features and drainage characteristics of larger areas within a short till reducing the quantum of field work.

- Total catchment area and the run-off available should be assessed by using Survey of India top<) sheets and by analysing rainfall data,
- Physiographic features by using toposheets and aerial maps should he traced if available.
- Soil map, soil analysis, determination of soil permeability if possible and geological map of the area including the catchment area with structural details that control occurrence and movement of ground water are determined.
- Detailed inventory is taken of existing wells to know the type of formation to prepare water table maps for at least one complete cycle and conduct pumping tests to determine specific yield etc. and estimate present withdrawals.
- Geo-electrical resistivity and seismic surveys to determine the depth of bedrock, thickness of soil zone etc."

  This information is useful in determining to what depth tank is to be dug, to what depth the foundation of the dam across the stream sources should be laid and to what depth the cut-off trench beneath the bund should be dug for building the core wall.
- The surface and sub-surface soil profiles, geological features and bedrock depths in the tank area, command area and along the stream course have to be determined. In shallow bedrock zones check dams should be provided along the stream course to tap seepage along stream.

Irrigation tank differs from percolation tank in that the main purpose of irrigation tank is to preserve the water surface in order to make its immediate use. Therefore, measures are adopted to reduce percolation or seepage of water from the irrigation tanks. The field approach in locating the site for irrigation tanks is the same as that of the percolation tanks. Irrigation tanks are located in zones where the soils are less permeable and the bedrock is very shallow. The foundation of the dam across the stream course and the cutoff wall should reach more than 98 per cent of the depth to the bedrock to: prevent seepage losses.

Seepage or percolation can be reduced by following means:

- Reducing the wetted surface area in relation to the quantity of water stored (*e.g.* circular design);
- Application of sodium salt to calcium rich clay soils;
- Soil compaction;
- Tank silt or clay soil with bhusa;
- Mud plaster;
- Bentonite application; and
- Soil cement mixture.

WATER HARVESTING PONDS

For collection of run-off water two types of ponds are used namely (a) embankment types of ponds are feasible in hilly, and undulating topography where, by constructing a small length of dam across a water. course maximum storage of water can be affected. Depending on site conditions, storage/ earth work ratios of 5 to 20 can be achieved. In flat areas, embankment type of ponds are not feasible, In such areas, excavated ponds are constructed advantageously. 1n case of these ponds the storage to earth work ratios are relatively much smaller generally around one.

Selection of suitable site is an important phase in the planning and construction of a farm pond, The site selected should ensure that the catchment is neither too smaIl nor too:c, big, Too small a catchment may not contribute sufficient water to the pond while too big a catchment may result in rapid siltation of the pond. Catchments well-protected with conservation measures (*i.e.* bunds and trenches) will contribute less silt to the ponds. Other aspects like willingness of the farmer, both for construction of the pond in his area and for sharing the water with other beneficiaries, availability of sufficient command area with minimum undulation and free from soil problems like salinity, alkaliluty and stoniness are to be considered in selection of pond site. Deciding a suitable size for the pond requires information. on the catchment size, its run-off producing characteristics including type of soils, land use, topography, conservation measures adopted and their effective storage losses (seepage and evaporation) from the pond and control measures adopted, period of storage required, area commanded by the pond and type of crops covered with protective irrigation. If other uses like providing drinking water for livestock and domestic uses are also involved, then these are also to be considered for deciding the total amount of water required to be stored. Usually provision is to be made for meeting all the combined demands for 18 months so as to cover the deficit in case of drought. The size (capacity) of the farm pond is also decided upon the volume of run-off reaching the pond. The pond size is fixed to hold about 50 per cent of the run-off so that the pond gets filled even during lower rainfall years. Except for selected locations, the information on total volume of water expected at different places in India, is not yet available.

Embankment Ponds

In the embankment type of ponds, the total height of the embankment includes the design height of impoundment, a free board of 20 per cent of design height for protecting against overtopping and the occurrence of storms of higher frequency than the designed one and another 5-10 per cent extra height for settlement due to consolidation of the earth work. A sufficient top width is provided to serve as a road connecting both the banks bf the water course. Upstream and down stream side slopes of embankment are usually in the ratio of 3:1 and 2: 1 respectively. In case of embankment with porous soils, a core wall of impervious soil is provided to cut down the excessive seepage loss and also to keep the phreatic line in check. A key trench is provided to secure the embankment with the foundation to overcome sliding action.

Excavated Ponds

These ponds are usually constructed as square or rectangular ponds for easiness of construction. A convenient depth is chosen for the pond. This usually varies between 3 and 5 meters. Greater depths result in excavation costs disproportionate to the additional capacity provided. Greater depths; therefore, reduce the area occupied by the pond and hence the loss owing to evaporation, seepage rates become excessive due to the increased hydrostatic pressure. Excavated ponds are provided with controlled inlets of the chute spillway type so that gully is not formed at the inlet portion. Emergency spillways should be provided in the ponds to dispose off excess water. Measures should also be taken to reduce seepage from the ponds.

USE OF WATER PRESERVANTS

Water preservants are organic polymer compounds endowed with a great capacity to retain water. Their production and consumption is very limited in our country. However, they are very useful for small fields and dryland areas.

A recently discovered and the most efficient water preservant is known as *Jalshakti'*. *Jalshakti* is an off-white free- flowing powder which on absorbing water forms a smooth gel which acts like a water reservoir. It is a polymer, hygroscopic in nature and retains its free flowing character even on absorbing up to 50 per cent by weight of moisture. This granular organic compound is especially designed to improve plant soil relationship. *Jalshakti* is safe to use. It is non-toxic, bio- degradable and has no adverse effects either on the crop or on the soil.

Moisture pre servants are mostly used as soil additives. They are also sometimes used for seed treatment. On finding sufficient moisture in the soil they absorb many times more water than its own weight. They keep the water largely safe against percolation, seepage loss and evaporation when the water level in soil goes down in post monsoon season, moisture preservants act as water reservoirs and meet the moisture requirement of crops.

5

Socio-economic Analysis of Agriculture

COMMERCIAL AGRICULTURE

Although elements of the above ideal type of a competitive food system could be found in parts of the United States at various times, it never did exist in many areas of the country. For an individual farmer, the question was not how many firms were involved in the different stages of the food chain across the country, but rather how much of this commodity chain was accessible to his (sometimes her) farm. AS farmers moved west, one of their major problems was how to transport their products to markets in the eastern cities. The government, wishing to promote increased industrialization, also perceived the problem and subsidized the construction of transportation systems, especially railroads.

This often made the farmer dependent on a monopoly which could exploit him/her because of the unequal balance of economic power. If a farmer had access to only one railroad, the power relationship certainly favored the railroad. That farmer faced a monopoly regardless of how many other railroads existed in the country. Thus, many farmers faced the issue of monopoly control of capital from the time they became commercial farmers and began to be dependent on a single transportation system to move their products to the market.

Railroads in some parts of the country needed the business of farmers, but they had access to hundreds, if not thousands, of farmers. They were not dependent on any single farmer. Their only concern was that farmers might be successful in organizing a united stand against the railroads. Frank Norris' agrarian populist novel, The Octopus:

A History of California (1901), was about a handful of farmers who attempted such a united stand, rising up in direct rebellion, only to be dispatched by the railroads. The whole history of the farmers' movement is largely about the unequal power balance between farmers and the railroads, and, more generally, between the farmers and all the "middlemen" they depended on for transportation, markets, and a host of inputs such as credit and farm equipment.

In southwestern Minnesota, for example, the selling of water fowl to cities to the East and later the selling of agriculture products, especially grain, all depended on the railroad for transportation. In the case of grain, the farmers also depended on the elevators (large silos) to store and to transfer it from farmers' wagons to the train. Many of the transnational corporations (TNCs) of today, like Cargill, exercised economic power in many of the local markets in which they began operating. Most farmers' movements were not successful in establishing alternative economic systems or firms which benefited the farmers, but with the help of legislation to encourage farmer cooperatives, there were some successes.

DIVERSIFICATION AND CROP INCOME STABILITY

The effectiveness of diversification as a self-insurance strategy. Stability is measured in a relative context and is identified with a low coefficient of variation for household crop income. Crop income is measured in two ways, gross returns and net returns to family owned resources which include land, capital, family labour and management. All non-marketed outputs and inputs are valued at their respective opportunity costs in measuring gross and net returns.

Of the 180 cultivator households in the VLS sample, 134 have data on crop income for each of the five years from 1975-76 to 1979-80. The majority of the other 46 households leased out their land for one or more cropping years; a minority left the sample and were replaced.

Therefore, there are 134 cultivators for whom coefficients of variation of household gross and net crop returns are estimated from 1975-76 to 1979-80. CVs are calculated for each household across the five cropping years. It was also expected that crop income stability is a function of some of the resource base determinants. Moreover, differences in crop income stability among farmers can also be attributed to fluctuations in the resource base across cropping years. To assess the impact of diversification on crop income stability, it is important to control for shifts in cultivated area, irrigated area, and land quality over time. This is particularly true for regions such as Sholapur where tenancy is prevalent (Jodha, 1981).

Descriptive information on the CVs' of the dependent and independent variables. The size of the CVs' at about 40 to 50 per cent is another indication of the riskiness of dryland agriculture in the semi-arid tropics of peninsular India. Fluctuations in gross returns are somewhat less than in net returns. Somewhat surprisingly, both average gross and net returns are less stable in the more heavily irrigated Mahbubnagar region compared to the dryland Sholapur and Akola regions.

It is believed that crop income stability can be traced not only to the level of the resource base but also to its intertemporal variation. Because crop and plot diversification are themselves functions of the same resource base viewed in the context of association rather than causation.

It is perhaps heroic to try to explain inter-farm variation in crop income stability within a narrow ecological region based on only five year data. Nonetheless, some of the hypothesized determinants behave as expected and have statistically significant estimated coefficients. Crop diversification is negatively and strongly associated with crop income instability in the more dryland Sholapur and Akola regions. A 10 percent proportional increase in the crop diversification index is associated with 4.8 and 13.0 decrease in the CV of net crop returns in Sholapur and Akola respectively. At the margin, crop diversification is about three times more effective in stabilizing net returns in rainfall assured Akola than in drought-prone Sholapur.

In Mahbubnagar, plot diversification contributes positively to crop income stability. In contrast, in the Akola and Sholapur villages, the results mildly suggest that plot diversification is associated with greater crop income instability. Production conditions for a crop in these more dryland villages must be quite narrowly defined as diversification across space with the same commodity does not dampen fluctuations in income. This is particularly true in Sholapur where field diversification is positively correlated with gross and net return instability. These results support Walker and Singh who found land sharecropped in Sholapur was of inferior quality and was more likely to be the site of crop failure than owner-operated land. Plot diversification appears to be a resource management strategy rather than an action that offers scope for crop income protection.

As expected, the CVs' of the resource base determinants are for the most part-the exception being land value in Mahbubnagar-positively associated with crop income instability. Larger farms having more gross cropped area are characterized by greater crop income stability in the three regions. However, the impact of farm size on crop income stability is not large.

Evaluated at their arithmetic means, a 10 percent increase in gross cropped area leads on are average to about a 2 percent reduction to the CV of net returns. The evidence with respect to irrigation is not as clear, but it weakly suggests that greater access to irrigation is accompanied by greater instability in net returns particularly in the Akola villages where irrigated land accounts for only 3 percent of the gross cropped area. Besides following inter-regional differences were also observed:

1. The impact of irrigation on crop diversification and income stability hinges upon cropping conditions and the existing level of irrigation. When an expansion in irrigation takes place for rainy season paddy production in a region where many farmers have some access to irrigation, irrigation leads to more specialization in paddy production. In contrast, when an investment in well irrigation occurs in a

multicrop predominantly dryland region, it enhances opportunities for further crop diversification particularly in the postrainy season. More profitable production opportunities in turn translate into greater relative variance in net crop returns income and increased crop income instability. The net effect of irrigation on crop diversification and income stability depends on the source of irrigation, ecological location, and level of growth of irrigation facilities.

2. Crop and plot diversification fluctuate more in more drought prone regions like Sholapur. Crop diversification appears to be more sensitive to agro-climatic determinants than plot diversification.
3. Different regional ecological conditions offer differential opportunities for risk averse farmers to diversify. Therefore, it is not surprising to find that risk attitudinal differences vary regionally in their effect on diversification. Where they are significant, differences in risk attitudes do not exert a sizeable influence on decisions on diversification; their proportional impact is about the same as differences in draft power availability.
4. Crop diversification effectively imparts stability to net crop returns in the dryland farming Sholapur and Akola villages. In the more highly irrigated Mahbubnagar villages, income instability and crop diversification are not significantly associated.

The implications of these conclusions are threefold. First, at present levels of technology it appears that increasing land fragmentation associated with plot diversification does not represent a significant cost in terms of income foregone or a material benefit in the form of enhanced crop income stability. Thus a prospective land consolidation programme would not compromise the risk-bearing capacity of farmers, nor would it significantly increase average crop income of farm households at existing levels of technology. These issues require closer scrutiny within a more rigorous household economics framework.

Secondly, the emergence of crop diversification as a strong force in protecting net crop returns in the more rainfall-assured Akola region decreases the demand for government risk-reducing policies, such as crop insurance, because farmers can rely on self-insurance through diversification to enhance crop income stability.

These results further underscore the emerging consensus that the potential benefits of crop insurance programmes will be greater in more risk-prone, dryland regions like Sholapur for three reasons. First, yield variability is the predominant source of risk in these regions (Barah and Binswanger, 1982), yields are more likely to be positively covariate across farmers which augments the efficiency of a homogeneous area approach to dampen fluctuations in crop income and third, there is less scope for crop diversification to be an effective self-insurance measure.

Lastly, an investment in irrigation may have a negative effect on relative crop income stability when instability is measured with respect to the coefficient of variation. The farm-level effects of irrigation may be markedly different from what obtains at the district, state or national levels.

ECONOMIC GROWTH AND AGRICULTURE

Economic growth is an increase in per capita income. Agricultural growth is necessary for economic growth. Nearly every high-income country has a highly productive agricultural sector, and agricultural growth is critical in the process of economic growth. Among other things, economic growth involves the production of more goods and services, and a much wider range of goods and services, than before. Economic growth agriculture's share of the economy declines with economic growth. As per capita income increases, percentage of labour force in agricultural production declines. Agriculture's share of Gross Domestic Product (GDP) also declines. GDP is a widely used measure of national income. Across states at a given point in time, or at a single country over time, the relationship between per capita income and agriculture's percentage of the labour force and GDP looks. Agriculture tends to decline more quickly as a percentage of GDP than as a percentage of the labour force.

POLICIES TO MARKET ACCESS

Poor infrastructure, limited resource base, lack of information, lack of or inadequate support institutions and poor policies affect the livelihoods of small-holder farmers. Other barriers include market standards, limited information, requirements for large initial capital investments, limited product differentiation, and handicapping policies. While almost any of the farm produce sells at the village level market, consumers discriminate against produce that is comparatively inferior, hence farmers have, over time, adapted to selling only that which will sell.

POLICIES RELATED TO GLOBALIZATION

The effect of globalization on any country depends on that country's level of economic development, structures in place during the implementation stage, flexibility of its economy. Globalization has three dimensions: multiplication and intensification of economic, political, social and cultural linkages among people, organizations and states at the world level; the tendency towards the universal application of economic, institutional, legal, political and cultural practices; and the emergence of significant spill-over from the behaviour of individuals and societies to the rest of the world. Due to the interrelation of the various dimensions, policies made in one country are bound to have effects on another. With globalization, comes liberalization of markets. The food security threat caused by liberalization is due to dumping of heavily subsidized produce in developing states and pre-mature exposure of upcoming industries to genuine competition from producers in developing and developed states. In addition, most profits are repatriated by transnational companies reducing the potential for poverty reduction to direct employment alone. In most cases, the pay is low because the national policies do not protect the small-holder.

HANDICAPPING POLICIES

Poor policies have greatly affected the food security in India. This is mainly due to uneven development within states based on political grounds. Certain regions are developed preferentially for political reasons at the expense of others. The problem arises when the focus on policies, structures and institutions is put above that of the people themselves. When policies are not inclusive in their design they tend to handicap the exempted lot by providing barriers.

One such way in which this may take place is uneven development within states where certain regions are preferentially developed for political reasons at the expense of others. Polices that promote monopolistic competition for the large-scale industries hurt the cottage and small industry. When we fail to provide safety nets for vulnerable groups, we doom them to destruction.

CHANGE PROCESS AFFECTING AGRICULTURAL PRODUCTION AND LIVELIHOODS

The lack of transparent, timely and reliable crop and livestock marketing information is seen by many as one of the greatest challenges to the development of the agriculture industry in East India. Without access to information about agricultural products prices at different regional markets, farmers are unable to identify which points-of-sale offer the best prices for their agri-products.

For example, in Mbirikani, Kajiado County, Kenya, Maasai pastoralists once relied on middlemen to gain market information. However, a marketing information system has been developed by the Livestock Information Network and Knowledge System (LINKS) to support livestock producers and traders. Now the farmers use mobile phones to ask for livestock prices in Emali, Mombasa and Nairobi, and this knowledge significantly improves their bargaining power with livestock traders.

INCREASING MARKETING OPPORTUNITIES

Given the high dependency of pastoralists' livelihoods on the sale of livestock and livestock products, LINKS designed and implemented an Information Communication Technology (ICT) infrastructure to collate data on livestock sales and prices from a network of different markets for dissemination using SMS messages. This has been a success and has been used to develop a National Livestock Marketing Information System (NLMIS) in

Kenya. NLMIS relies on a network of County livestock marketing officers and data monitors to transmit data between markets and the database.

The field officers are also trained to download, analyse, and summarize the information to transmit to pastoralists and traders, including information about prices and volumes of cattle, camels, sheep and goats at livestock markets. The market information is also made available online, and may be downloaded for printing and sharing with livestock communities with no internet access. The information is also shared by e-mail, posted on billboards at market places and can be requested through SMS.

Vibrant Markets

This change in communication has also transformed undeveloped markets in other value chains in agriculture. The availability of marketing information through SMS and information boards, competition among agri-products traders has increased, and this has improved and stabilized prices paid to farmers. Women have also benefited by providing animal health services, fodder and small loans to the traders. Empowering producers to negotiate for better prices has equipped market agencies and communities with appropriate tools and information to plan for and respond to changing incomes, and consequently has improved livelihoods.

Policy

The success of the marketing system has equipped planners and policymakers with the tools to track price trends, which are helping them, improve decision-making and devise appropriate interventions to mitigate the effects of deteriorating terms.

IT FOR AGRICULTURAL PRODUCTION AND MARKETING

IT is playing an important and vital role in agricultural production and marketing. IT allows farmers to save time on order and delivery and getting feedback. In the existing competition, there is a need to rapidly attract new customers as well as retain existing customers.

In order to take the real status of agricultural production and marketing, there is an urgent need to develop the following items:

- *Farmers' Crop Database must be Managed*: The database includes the kinds of crops, the size of cultivated area, time of harvest and yield. Farmers or the extension personnel transmit those data via the Internet to database server. Further, information provides the farmer with an important instrument for decision making and taking action.
- *Crops Information Service System should be Created:* This system analyses the crop data to create some statistical tables. Farmers can access these statistical data by browsing the homepage and make their production plan. Changes within the structure of agriculture will

probably have an impact on the selection and types of acquisition of software and other integrated systems made by the farmers.

- *Production Techniques and Information Enquiry System should be Created*: This system integrates the production techniques and information, which are developed by experimental agricultural institutes and agricultural improvement stations. Farmers can find out relevant production information through this enquiry service system.
- *Production Equipment's Enquiry Service System should be Created*: This system gathers information from the companies of seeds and crop production equipment to build the production equipment's enquiry service system. At the same time, allow relevant companies to access this system and enter their own data. Therefore, farmers can order the needed items through this system.

Information is critical to the social and economic activities that comprise the development process. Development economy has witnessed for revolutions in agricultural, bio-technological, industrial and information technology. Good communication system and information system reinforce commitments to sustainable productivity. The Government of India is giving more thrust on agriculture, food and information technology sectors towards achievement of economic reforms to achieve high growth rate in production in the years to come.

The National Agriculture Policy announced addresses the challenges arising out of economic liberalization and globalization. It seeks to actualize the vast untapped growth potential of Indian agriculture, strengthen rural infrastructure to support faster agricultural development, promote value addition and secure a fair standard of living for farmers and farm workers. The National Agriculture Policy lays emphasis on the use of Information Technology for achieving a more rapid development of agriculture in India.

In pursuance thereof, the Department of Agriculture and Cooperation (DAC) has formulated information technology (IT) Vision 2020. This vision *inter alia* envisages that:

- Information relating to agriculture sector would be available to the ultimate users—the farmers—for optimizing their productivity and income;
- Extension and advisory services making use of information technology would be available to the farmers on round the clock basis;
- The tools for information technology will provide networking of agriculture sector not only in the country but also globally and the Union and State Government Departments will have reservoirs of data base; and
- The long term vision on "Information Technology in Agriculture Sector" is to bring farmers, researchers, scientists and administrators

together by establishing "Agriculture on-line" through exchange of ideas/information.

In future, information technology will reduce the cost and time of information system. IT will bring new information services for agricultural development that will enable the farmers to have much greater control over the information channels.

AGRICULTURAL IMPLICATIONS OF IT

Information technology provides answers to a number of questions to the farmers. For example, what are the benefits of more irrigation? Is it cost-effective to apply additional chemicals? When is the best time to sell crops or buy inputs? With improved record-keeping, more detailed cost analysis and more sophisticated marketing strategies, farmers are making better decisions and earning higher profits.

The Internet is increasing communication and business opportunities within the agricultural community, which previously operated in the relative isolation of rural areas. Farmers, agricultural researchers, cooperatives, suppliers and buyers use the Internet to exchange ideas and information, as well as to conduct business with each other. Machinery, seed chemicals and other types of agricultural products can be purchased and sold online. People can search for jobs and employees. It is to be noted that, the farmer is in no position to use IT directly.

The literacy levels, language barrier as most of the application software are predominantly in English, cost of computers, poor communication infrastructure make it impossible for individual farmers, particularly small farmers to directly adopt IT. This calls for institutional effort to harness to create the necessary IT based services to farmers. But in India, one prominent problem is that most of the farmers own small holdings, this seems to be difficult. In this situation, it may be made possible by adopting the corporate farming system, which is the need of the hour with advent of new agricultural policy.

By taking up corporate farming, a group of farmers can install a computer and any educated young man from that group can undergo training of how to browse the Internet.

He can provide the farmers current commodity, analysis reports on world markets and trade for different commodities. Food market overviews provide valuable information about some of the most important export market. IT can help to provide the information on the likely price distribution of key commodities over the coming years. Such information helps farmers and traders make decisions on when and in what ways to market their grain. Whether, to sell at harvest or store on-farm in anticipation of higher later in the season. When combined with enterprise budget data, the information can also be used in deciding which crops to produce in the coming season.

In order to encourage farmers to obtain best possible price, information on various agricultural output markets is also being provided. The objective of this activity is to provide status of price at different markets to facilitate farmer to move his produce to the market where he can expect better price. The entire exercise will not be useful unless necessary arrangements are made to ensure that the farmers utilize this facility. The contribution of information technology in bringing down costs, increasing efficiency and improving productivity and thereby contributing to the bottom line needs no special emphasis.

In the fertilizer marketing context, IT can play a major role in efficient sales operations, checking the marketing costs, safeguarding market share and providing efficient customer services. A well conceived IT set up can endow decision makers at all levels with better reflexes to effectively respond to market conditions. IT helps producers monitor and respond to weather variability on a day-to-day basis.

Solar-powered weather stations in the field can be hooked up to a farmer's computer to relay information about current air and soil temperature, precipitation, relative humidity, leaf wetness, soil moisture, day length, wind speed and solar radiation. Producers use the Internet to monitor prices quickly and as often as they like. Farmers from around the world can exchange ideas, post questions and get answers about specific topics. Thus, it is said that the importance of information technology in the field of agriculture is emerging.

THE COMMERCIAL GRAIN-FARMING AREA

This area covers the outer region in the south and the east of European Russia, the steppe gubernias of Novorossia and the Transvolga. Agriculture is distinguished here for its extensive character and the enormous scale of the production of grain for sale. If we take the eight gubernias of Kherson, Bessarabia, Taurida, Don, Ekaterinoslav, Saratov, Samara and Orenburg, we shall find that in 1883-1887 the net crop of cereals (not including oats) for a population of 13,877,000 amounted to 41.3 million chetverts, *i.e.*, more than one-fourth of the total net yield of the 50 gubernias of European Russia. The crop most commonly sown here is wheat—the principal export grain. Agriculture develops here fastest of all (by comparison with the other areas of Russia), and these gubernias relegate the central black-earth gubernias, formerly in the lead, to the background: Thus there is a *shifting* of the principal centre of grain production: in the 1860s and 1870s the central black-earth gubernias were ahead of all the rest, but in the 1880s they yielded priority to the steppe and Lower Volga gubernias: their production of grain began to *diminish*.

This interesting fact of the enormous growth of agricultural production in the area described is to be explained by the circumstance that in the post-Reform period the outer steppe regions have been *colonies* of the central, long-settled part of European Russia. The abundance of free land has attracted an enormous stream of settlers, who have quickly increased the area under crops. The extensive development of *commercial* crops was possible only because of the close economic ties of these colonies with central Russia, on the one hand, and the European grain importing countries, on the other. The development of industry in central Russia and the development of commercial farming in the outer regions are inseparably connected and create a market for each other. The industrial gubernias received grain from the South, selling there the products of their factories and supplying the colonies with labour, artisans, and means of production (timber, building materials, tools, etc.). Only because of this social division of labour could the settlers in the steppe localities engage exclusively in agriculture and sell huge quantities of grain in the home and particularly in the foreign market.

Only because of their close connection with the home and foreign markets could the economic development of these localities proceed so rapidly; and it was precisely capitalist development, for along with the growth of commercial farming there was an equally rapid process of the diversion of the population into industry, the process of the growth of towns and of the formation of new centres of large-scale industry.

As to the question of whether the growth of commercial farming in this area is bound up with technical progress in agriculture and with the creation of capitalist relations, that has been dealt with above. We saw how large the areas cultivated by peasants in these localities are and how sharply capitalist relations manifest themselves there even within the village community. We saw that in this area there has been a particularly rapid development in the use of machinery, that the capitalist farms in the outer regions attract hundreds of thousands and millions of wage-workers, with huge farms created on a scale unprecedented in agriculture, on which there is extensive co-operation of wage-workers, etc. We have little left now to add in completion of this picture.

In the outer steppe regions the privately-owned estates are not only distinguished occasionally for their enormous size, but are also the scene of farming on a very big scale. Above we made reference to crop areas of 8, 10 and 15 thousand dessiatines in Samara Gubernia. In Taurida Gubernia, Falz-Fein owns 200,000 dess., Mordvinov 80,000 dess.; two individuals own 60,000 dess. each, "and many proprietors have from 10,000 to 25,000 dessiatines". An idea of the scale of farming can be obtained, for example, from the fact that in 1893 there were 1,100 machines (of which 1,000 belonged to the peasantry) haymaking for Falz-Fein. In Kherson Gubernia there were 3.3 million dessiatines under cultivation in 1893, of which 1.3 million dess. belonged to private owners; in five uyezds of the gubernia (without Odessa Uyezd) there were 1,237 medium-sized farms (250 to 1,000 dess. of land), 405 big farms(1,000 to 2,500 dess.) and 226 farms each of over 2,500 dess. According to data gathered in 1890 on 526 farms, they employed 35,514 workers, *i.e.*, an average of 67 workers per farm, of whom from 16 to 30 were annual labourers. In 1893, 100 more or less big farms in Elisavetgrad Uyezd employed 11,197 workers (an average of 112 per farm!), of whom 17.4 per cent were annual, 39.5 per cent seasonal, and 43.1 per cent day labourers. Here are data on the distribution of crop area among all the agricultural undertakings in the uyezd, both of private landowners and of peasants.

Thus, a little over 3 per cent of the peasants (and if we count only those who cultivated, 4 per cent) concentrate in their hands more than a third of the total area under crops, for the tilling and harvesting of which masses of seasonal and day labourers are required.

There is no need, apparently, to comment on these data. We have had occasion to observe that the area described is the most typical of agricultural capitalism in Russia—typical not in the agricultural sense, of course, but in the social-economic sense.

These colonies, having developed with the greatest freedom, show us what relations could and should have developed in the rest of Russia, had not the numerous survivals of pre-Reform life retarded the development of capitalism. The forms, however, of agricultural capitalism, as will be seen from what follows, are extremely varied.

COMMERCIAL RELATIONS OF PRODUCTION

We are all familiar with the classical story of how capitalism came to dominate industrial production and how capitalist relations of production swallowed up the individual artisanal producer. We recognize the power that the capitalist mode has to infiltrate and finally transform other forms of the organization of production and exchange. We sometimes think that the power of that transformation is so great that all of the significant action already occurred in the past, at least in Europe and North America, and was essentially over by the end of the nineteenth century. In the society we inhabit, it is a fait accompli, whose dynamic we can only understand by reconstructing the past because it is not happening around us. On second thought we realize that the transition was still in progress until very recently in a few skilled domains like medical care and entertainment, where individual artisans were able to ply their trade throughout most of this century, but these fossils of early capitalist relations seem exceptional because of their requirement of special talents or of necessary skills acquired by long training. But the view that the transition to mature capitalism is essentially over except at the margins of the main body of commodity production is clearly wrong, because it ignores an immense sector of basic essential commodity production, agriculture, which is still in the throes of the transition.

PENETRATION OF CAPITAL IN AGRICULTURE

The penetration of capital into agriculture has been a long process of a different form than the classical case of industrial production usually exemplified by cloth weaving in the eighteenth and nineteenth centuries. Indeed, on the surface agriculture would seem to have been resistant to capital. After all, despite a 72 percent drop in the number of of individual farm enterprises in the United States from 6.7 million in 1930, there are still about 1.8 million independent farm producers today. This means that even though only 6 percent of these establishments account for 60 percent of the total value of farm production, there are over 100,000 separate enterprises producing more than half of all the value of the output. In the industrial manufacturing sector the four largest enterprises account for an average of 40 percent of value produced, and even in a highly differentiated product like clothing the top four companies produce over 15 percent of the value.

There has also been a major increase in the proportion of farmland that is leased to farmers who also own their own land. Roughly 55 percent of farmland is now operated by owner-renters who are for the most part small producers. Finally, despite the conventional wisdom that corporate farming is taking over, the proportion of farms and farmland operated by managers representing absentee owners has remained about 1 percent since the beginning of the century.

Thus if we are to look for evidence of the capitalist transformation of agriculture, we will not find it in the classical industrial model. We do not find a concentration of more and more productive capacity in the hands of a very small number of farmers, employing a large wage labour force carrying out its tasks under close supervision and according to a tightly controlled schedule. There are, of course, some examples of a factory-like labour process in farming, especially in the harvesting of fruits and fresh vegetables, and these are often pointed to as evidence of a capitalist transformation to factory farming. However, the vast majority of farm enterprises do not employ a large labour force, but more typically have one or two hired laborers, usually for only part of the year.

In analyzing the process of the capitalist transformation of agriculture we must distinguish between farming and the agrifood system. Farming is the physical process of turning inputs like seed, feed, water, fertilizer, and pesticides into primary products like wheat, potatoes, and cattle on a specific site, the farm, using soil, labour, and machinery. The failure of classical capitalist concentration in farming arises from both financial and physical features of farm production. First, the ownership of farmland is unattractive to capital because it cannot be depreciated, and investment in farmland has very low liquidity as a consequence of the thin farm real estate market. Second, the labour process on very large farms is hard to control because farming operations are spatially extensive. Third, economies of scale are hard to achieve beyond what has already been realized by medium-scale enterprises. Fourth, risks from external natural events like weather, new diseases, and pests are hard to control. Finally, the cycle of reproduction of capital cannot be shortened because it is linked to an annual growth cycle in plants, or a fixed reproductive cycle in large animals. An important exception to this constraint has been in poultry, where there has been considerable success in shortening the reproductive cycle, and this has had important ramifications for the development of capitalist farming as we will see. For all of these reasons we do not expect to see, and have not seen, the wholesale direct takeover of farm ownership by large corporate enterprises employing large, well-controlled labour forces.

ENTIRE CHAIN OF AGRICULTURAL PRODUCTION

The agrifood system, however, is not simply farming. It includes the farm operation, but also the production, transportation, and marketing of the inputs to farming, as well as the transportation, processing, and marketing of the farm outputs. While farming is a physically essential step in the entire chain of agricultural production, the provision of farm inputs and the transformation of farm outputs into consumer commodities have come to dominate the economy of agriculture. Farming itself now accounts for only about 10 percent of the value added in the agrifood system, with 25 percent of the food dollar paying for farm inputs and the remaining 65 percent gained by transportation, processing, and marketing that converts farm products into consumer commodities.

At the beginning of the century the value added on the farm was around 40 percent of the total food dollar, and many of the inputs were produced directly on the farm in the form of seed, draught animals, feed for the animals, manure and green manure for fertilizer, and family labour. For the most part these inputs are now purchased in the form of commercial seed, tractors, fuel, refined or synthesized chemical fertilizers, and machinery and manufactured chemical substitutes for labour. Thus, it is the production of farm inputs and the transformation of farm outputs that have provided an opportunity for industrial capital to capture profits in the agricultural sector.

Like any other industrial processes, the production of farm machinery, chemicals, and seeds, and the turning of threshed wheat into a box of breakfast cereal at the supermarket checkout counter are completely controlled by capital and its demands. The problem for capital, however, has been that sitting in the middle of the transformation of petroleum into potato chips is an essential step, farming, in the hands of two million petty producers. They cannot be dispensed with, they own certain essential means of production whose ownership cannot be concentrated (land in particular), and, while they are economically rational, they consume their surplus rather than turning it into capital. Agriculture is unique among all the sectors of capitalist production by possessing at its productive centre an essential process organized around large numbers of independent petty producers. It is as if the spinning of yarn, the weaving of cloth, and the sewing of garments were in the hands of a few large capital enterprises (as they are), but the dyeing and finishing of the raw woven material were unavoidably the exclusive province of hundreds of thousands of home producers who bought the unfinished cloth and sold their product to clothing factories.

SUSTAINABLE DEVELOPMENT OFINDIAN AGRICULTURE

India's agricultural growth has been sufficient to move the country from severe food crises of the 1960s to aggregate food surpluses today. Underlying this growth were massive public investments in irrigation, agricultural research and extension, rural infrastructure, farm credit and rural development programmes. India's agricultural sector, however, faces severe challenges for the future. Despite sizeable national food stocks (30 million tons in 1995), widespread poverty and hunger remain because agricultural and national economic growth have not adequately benefitted disadvan-taged regions and the poor.

The demand for basic staples, non-food grains, and exports is increasing. At the same time, resources are shrinking and the productivity of some resources already being utilised is threatened by environmental degradation. Growth in total factor productivity is reported to have declined slightly in major crops. Returns to investment in agricultural research and rural infrastructure are reported to be high, but these investments remain low. Most of the increase in agricultural output over the years has taken place under irrigated conditions.

The opportunities for continued expansion of irrigated area are limited, however, so Indian planners increasingly are looking to rainfed, or unirrigated agriculture to help meet the rising demand for food projected over the next several decades. Despite the historic bias in favour of irrigated agriculture in terms of research and infrastructural investments, rainfed agriculture has always been an important part of the agricultural sector.

Rainfed agriculture accounts for about two-thirds of total cropped area (Government of India 1994b), nearly half of the total value of agricultural output. Nearly half of all food grains are grown under rainfed conditions, and hundreds of millions of poor rural people depend on rainfed agriculture as the primary source of their livelihoods. Rainfed areas are highly diverse, ranging from resource-rich areas with good agricultural potential to resource-poor areas with much more restricted potential.

Some resource-rich rainfed areas potentially are highly productive and already have experienced widespread adoption of improved seeds. In drier, less favourable areas, on the other hand, productivity growth has lagged behind, and there is widespread poverty and degradation of natural resources. Even given that rainfed agriculture should receive greater emphasis in public investments, a key issue is how much investment should be allocated among different types of rainfed agriculture.

Outmigration and income diversification into the non-agricultural sector must provide the long term solution to economic development of many resource poor areas, but these opportunities currently are inadequate in relation to population growth to provide short to medium term solutions. Agricultural growth in these areas will be essential for reducing poverty and environmental problems in the decades ahead. There is a need to identify the opportunities for stimulating agricultural growth and reducing poverty and environmental degradation in rainfed areas. Likewise, there is a need to assess the opportunity costs of diverting scarce public resources from resource-rich to resource-poor areas.

The tradeoffs between investing in resource-rich and resource-poor areas in terms of their productivity, poverty and environmental outcomes need to be understood in order to guide public policy decisions towards productive outcomes. Developing strategies for rainfed areas is difficult because of their diversity in terms of agroecological characteristics, infrastructural development, and other socioeconomic variables. On an all-India scale, for example, rainfed systems include high-rainfall agriculture in the east and northeast as well as the drought-prone areas of the Deccan Plateau. Other agroclimatic characteristics such as soil types also vary, as do infrastructure development, human capital, and other socioeconomic factors. Across villages within a district, for example, there is wide variation in access to paved roads and public transportation to market centers.

Similar diversity of agricultural systems is found even at the local level. Individual villages in the semi-arid regions, for example, often contain numerous soil types with widely differing crop production potential. Irrigation wells are found in practically every village, so irrigated and rainfed agriculture co-exist almost everywhere. Diversity at both the national and local scale has implications for agricultural development strategies. At the national scale, there is a need to distinguish among regions according to their constraints to agricultural development. This requires creating a typology of rainfed agriculture that would incorporate both agroecological and socioeconomic variables in order to serve as a tool for planning agricultural research and other public investments. Local-level diversity of rainfed agricultural systems, meanwhile, implies that planners must recognise that changes in policy, technology or infrastructure may have varying impacts across small areas, and that there is a limit to the extent to which external interventions can induce finely-tuned responses. Regional or district-level planning must be complemented by local initiatives that can be more responsive to specific needs.

RAINFED AGRICULTURAL DEVELOPMENT

The overall goal of this stage is to review the important issues in rainfed agricultural development and report on the progress made in India to date. This will serve as a precursor to a detailed study to be carried out by the Indian Council of Agricultural Research, IFPRI, ICRISAT and the World Bank. That study will result in recommendations for designing a strategy to develop rainfed agriculture in India. We compare the past performance of rainfed and irrigated agriculture and of different types of rainfed agriculture, including relatively high- and low-potential areas.

We attempt to identify the factors that determine differences in performance, and we examine the possibilities for influencing those factors. Where information is not available, we recommend further analysis that may be required as a prerequisite to formulating a thorough strategy for rainfed agricultural development. We approach the problem by reviewing the relevant literature on the subject and conducting a statistical analysis of all-India district-level data. The database contains several agroclimatic and socioeconomic variables that we hypothesise to influence agricultural performance at the district level.

The district-level approach, of course, does not permit analysis of the implications of micro-level diversity of rainfed agricultural systems. Therefore we focus on broader indicators with implications for area-wide development efforts. In addition to the district level data analysis, we review the literature on rainfed agricultural performance in terms of technology adoption and performance, yield levels and their variability, natural resource sustainability, and poverty alleviation.

We examine the role of economic and social policies, area development programmes and infrastructural investments in promoting sustainable rainfed agricultural development. On some topics sufficient evidence is available to draw conclusions and make policy recommendations, and on others, additional analysis is recommended.

CHARACTERISTICS OF RAINFED AGRICULTURE

Rainfed and irrigated agriculture coexist in practically every village in India. Public investment programmes, however, usually cannot be targeted so precisely. For practical purposes, they need to be planned and implemented on a larger scale, such as at the village, taluk, district or state level. For example, public programmes that provide credit, employ people, or build roads cannot target their efforts to either rainfed of irrigated agriculture; they can only target areas that are relatively more irrigated or more rainfed. Price policies, on the other hand, can attempt to target rainfed or irrigated agriculture within a given location by targeting crops that may be more likely to be rainfed or irrigated.

But few crops are either 100 per cent irrigated or 100 per cent dryland, so some spillover will always remain. Also, every crop is grown over a large geographic area, so it is difficult to isolate the socioeconomic and agroclimatic variables affecting their performance. And while price policies are important, they are not the only approach through which policy makers can influence agricultural development.

DEFINING RAINFED AGRICULTURE

In the present investigation we use the district as the unit of analysis. We do so for two main reasons. First, through a district level focus our analysis may be relevant for public investment programmes that provide infrastructure or other social services to particular areas. Second, a district focus enables us to examine the contributions of both socioeconomic and agroclimatic variables on a nation-wide basis.

The district is the smallest administrative unit for which the required data are available. To arrive at a district-level definition of rainfed agriculture, we consider the percentage of each district that is irrigated or rainfed, and consider predominantly rainfed districts as "rainfed" and pre-dominantly irrigated districts as "irrigated." Obviously there is a certain degree of arbitrariness to any threshold we may choose to distinguish between irrigated and rainfed districts.

Several previous studies have faced this same dilemma in categorising rainfed areas. Some of them have distinguished between irrigated and rainfed districts according to certain criteria such as the amount of rainfall and the level of irrigation. Some of these studies and their definitions of rainfed areas. All of these definitions suffer from the inability to distinguish between rainfed and irrigated agriculture within districts, but we accept this as an inevitable limitation. Another problem is that both the rainfall and irrigation thresholds are defined somewhat arbitrarily. We discuss rainfall and irrigation thresholds in turn.

RAINFALL CRITERIA

Bapna et al, (1984) and subsequently Jodha (1985) used broad rainfall thresholds, which is important in order not to be too exclusive. At the same time, the 500-1500 mm range maintains a degree of homogeneity in the types of agriculture under analysis by excluding both very dry, desert areas and very high rainfall areas. Such areas may face unique constraints that limit comparability to agriculture under the more moderate conditions that predominate in most of the country.

Shah and Sah (1993) and Thorat (1993) use narrow rainfall thresholds with a relatively low maximum because they intended to focus on very dry (but not quite desert) areas. It is important to note that the impact of the level of rainfall on crop production is conditioned by both the distribution of rainfall over the course of the season and the factors that determine moisture retention in a given location.1

As a result, narrow rainfall thresholds such as those used by Thorat (1993) are likely to combine some areas with disparate moisture regimes and separate others with similar moisture regimes.

A narrow rainfall range probably makes sense only if limited to relatively uniform soil types. Incorporating soil types into the definition, however, introduces yet another variable and makes the definition somewhat clumsy.1 For this reason, our preference is to utilise a relatively broad range of rainfall levels such as used by Bapna et al, (1984), excluding only those that are either desert environments or extremely humid. We choose a range of 450-1600 mm average annual rainfall as the range for predominantly rainfed districts.

The lower bound of 450 mm excludes the desert districts of western Rajasthan as well as one district each in Punjab, Haryana and Gujarat. The 1600 mm upper bound excludes the Himalayas, the northeastern states, Kerala, all the coastal districts of Karnataka and Maharashtra, and one coastal district each in Tamil Nadu and Gujarat.

Where more disaggregated analysis is required to examine the performance of relatively moist or dry rainfed areas, we can subdivide the rainfall criteria into a low rainfall area (<750 mm per annum), a medium rainfall area (750-1125 mm), and a high rainfall area (>1125 mm), sometimes described as the arid, semi-arid and humid areas. To repeat the earlier caveat, these broad rainfall classes are heavily conditioned by the factors that determine moisture retention, particularly soil type.

IRRIGATED AREA CRITERIA

Classifying districts by irrigated area is difficult for several reasons. First, any threshold percentage area irrigated must be defined somewhat arbitrarily, and second, in most districts irrigated area has increased steadily during the period under study. As a result, we consider some alternate approaches to categorising districts by irrigated area. A single irrigated area threshold to distinguish between irrigated and rainfed districts.

In these studies the threshold ranges from 10 percent to 30 percent, with most defining rainfed districts as those with less than 25 percent irrigated area. 25 percent is the mean irrigated area for the years 1956-90, so according to this definition, rainfed areas are those with less than average area irrigated, while irrigated areas are those with more than average area irrigated. A number of arguments can be made about whether the figure of 25 percent is appropriate, but ultimately any definition based on such a threshold suffers from the problem that slight differences in irrigation levels will move some districts from one category to the other.

One approach is to use three categories of irrigation instead of two in order to more clearly identify the characteristics of lightly and heavily irrigated districts. This approach however, also has weaknesses, because more categories means more thresholds, which means that fewer districts will remain in one category over the entire period. As a result, when the three irrigation categories, nearly half of all districts shift categories at some point in the period.

When only two irrigation categories are used, on the other hand, only about one quarter of the districts shift categories. For that reason, we also conduct the analysis with only two irrigation categories, with districts with less than 25 percent area irrigated considered unirrigated, and districts with 25 percent or more area irrigated considered irrigated. We conduct the analysis twice; in one case all districts are analysed, and in the other only districts that remain in one category or the other throughout the study period are used.

Before continuing, we briefly discuss two other criteria for defining rainfed areas that we considered but rejected. First, districts could also be subdivided by the extent of different types of irrigation, in particular, canals, wells, or tanks. The justification for this concerns the quality of irrigation services delivered to each farm. Well irrigation, for example, is controlled by the individual farmer (to the extent that the aquifer yields water), whereas under canal irrigation farmers depend more on the amount of water taken by their upstream neighbours, so they incur a greater risk of drought.

As a result, farmers with well irrigation apply more inputs and have much higher yields on average. The district-level data cover gross cropped area as opposed to net cropped area, so we control for variations in the quantity of irrigation water delivered to the farm. However, the data do not control for variations in quality or differences in farmers' response to the different levels of risk under each irrigation source. When the circumstances warrant it we may examine irrigation by source, but mainly we do not, since our main focus is on rainfed agriculture, not distinctions in irrigated types.

A second alternative criterion for defining irrigation levels would be to distinguish districts by the proportion of farmers who have access to some irrigation. In many areas, water markets or shared irrigation wells enable farmers to gain access to irrigation even if they do not own a well or are not directly serviced by a canal or a tank. As a result, the number of farmers with access to irrigation can be much larger than the number who own wells. The distinction between the proportion of area irrigated and the proportion of farmers is important because it can affect the way in which most farmers manage their crops. If a larger proportion of farmers have access to a small amount of irrigation, they may concentrate their managerial and other inputs on irrigated plots, which they may perceive to be more productive and less prone to risk of crop failure than dry plots. In this case, perhaps dryland crops would be less productive (though more farmers will be better off).

Farmers without access to irrigation, on the other hand, may devote relatively more resources to rainfed crops than those with some irrigation. Unfortunately we do not have access to district-level data on the proportion of farmers with access to irrigation, and we do not know if the proportion of farmers with access to irrigation and the proportion of area irrigated vary independently of each other across districts. Therefore we cannot consider using this definition; we raise it only to draw attention to some of the issues to consider in developing a definition of a rainfed district.

DEFINITION OF RAINFED AGRICULTURE AND ITS PERFORMANCE

The definition of rainfed agriculture present will assist us in comparing the performance of predominantly rainfed and irrigated districts. We also wish to compare the performance within rainfed agricultural districts and relate differences to a range of constraints to agricultural development.

This in turn will be useful for prioritising and organising agricultural research, public investment, and policy and institutional reform.

To characterise districts according to the various agroclimatic and socioeconomic variables that constrain agricultural development, as suggested, need to construct a typology based on those variables. The typologies of Indian rainfed agriculture that already exist, the reasons why a new typology needs to be constructed, and the ways in which such a typology would be used.

EXISTING TYPOLOGIES

Current typologies of Indian agriculture are based on agroecological zones. Recently, ICAR delineated 20 agroclimatic regions based on soils and climate. 13 of these zones cover the area of this study; of the rest, 5 are in the Northeast, the Himalayas, and the Andaman, Nicobar and Lakshadweep Islands; one zone covers the high rainfall areas of the Western Ghats and the Arabian Sea coast; and one zone covers the desert in the western parts of Rajasthan and Gujarat. ICAR's agroecological zoning system is based on variations in rainfall, soil type and temperature.

Irrigation status, however, is conspicuously absent. This is a severe limitation due to the primary importance of irrigation in determining cropping patterns and productivity in most of the country. In this analysis we overcome that shortcoming by dividing zones into primarily rainfed and primarily irrigated districts. The 20-zone system is sufficiently disaggregated to enable it to keep problems of within-zone variation to a manageable level, and the number of zones remains small enough to be manageable for most uses.

Also, the zones can be easily reaggregated for particular purposes. Recently ICAR subdivided the 20-zone typology into a total of about 50 subzones; such a disaggregated typology may be useful for certain agricultural research purposes, but for policy analysis it is too large to be functional. In our analysis, using rainfed and irrigated districts in the 13 zones covered in our data would yield a total of 26 categories, which becomes unmanageable. For the purposes of our district-level analysis, we modify the 20-zone system so that it is sufficiently aggregated for our purposes.

We create a new 5-zone system in which each zone is a combination of two or more of the zones of the 20-zone system. The new zones, require some explanation. First, the 20-zone system does not follow district boundaries, but in our analysis districts must remain intact. As a result, in many cases we classify a district as lying in one zone even though part of it may actually lie in another. Districts in ICAR's Zone 18 along the Bay of Bengal coast, for example, also lie in adjoining agroclimatic zones 7,8 and 12. As a result, zone 18 drops out of the sample. Second, by combining the zones it is inevitable that some new, aggregated zones will contain substantial within-zone diversity. We find that for the case of ICAR zone 4, it makes sense to place the portion of zone 4 that lies in the Gangetic plain in one new zone, and the part that lies in upland areas of Rajasthan and Gujarat in another.

WHAT A NEW TYPOLOGY SHOULD LOOK LIKE

The existing agroclimatic typologies may be adequate for a narrow set of objectives, such as locating where certain crops are likely to be produced and which regions may be prone to certain natural resource management problems. Beyond such highly specific applications, however, the agroclimatic typologies are of limited use because they are so narrowly defined. In order to be useful for designing a strategy to develop rainfed agriculture, a typology must be constructed on the basis of the whole range of factors that affect agricultural development.

These extend far beyond simple agroclimatic conditions or even irrigation status. If a district has favourable growing conditions but lacks the infrastructure needed to support productive farming, for example, it should not be surprising to find poor performance in that district despite the favourable agroclimatic conditions. As suggested, examine the determinants of agricultural performance and demonstrate that other factors in addition to agroclimatic conditions help explain the variation in performance.

In addition to agroclimatic conditions and irrigation status, numerous additional variables can be hypothesised to influence agricultural development. Physical infrastructure such as roads and electrification, for example, and social infrastructure such as banks, markets and agricultural research and extension services, can be expected to play an important role in stimulating the agricultural sector. Demographic indicators such as population density and literacy levels also may be related to agricultural performance, as may economic policies that directly or indirectly affect input or output prices. Institutional considerations also may affect performance; they include laws governing trade, property rights, prices of inputs and outputs, etc., and the quality of services provided by government agencies.

Just as there are many determinants of performance of the agricultural sector, there also are many criteria for evaluating performance. Productivity growth is one that is commonly applied, but others include the levels of poverty and food security, the variability of production and income, and the degree of degradation of natural resources.

The ideal typology of Indian agriculture would characterise regions or areas according to all the factors that determine performance over a broad range of criteria. In this way it could serve as a valuable planning tool for public investment in agricultural research, infrastructural development, poverty alleviation programmes, policy and institutional reform, etc. While such a "super typology" might be unattainable, it presents an objective to work towards. We lack the resources to develop an acceptable typology, but it remains a high priority for future research intended to support Indian rainfed agricultural development.

We analyse the determinants of rainfed agricultural development using multiple regression analysis. As suggested, identify many of the agroclimatic and socioeconomic factors that contribute to performance of Indian rainfed agriculture according to a variety of criteria. As suggested, stop short of creating a typology, but as suggested, gain preliminary indications of the kinds of information that need to go into such a typology.

EMPLOYMENT IN AGRICULTURE

UNDERSTANDING CHANGING WORK PATTERNS IN AGRICULTURE

The IUF and the International Land Coalition (ILC) have jointly produced an analytical report on understanding changing work patterns in agriculture in the Ugandan sugar industry with regard to:

- Full-time waged workers; and
- Temporary and/or seasonal waged workers, including self-employed farmers hired as wage labourers.

The research aims to improve understanding of the rapidly changing patterns of production, employment and work in agriculture in order to help the IUF and ILC to more clearly focus their respective work programmes, better target their resources, and give clearer indications of potential partner organisations.

The report found:

- An increase in the number of waged workers on short-term contracts of employment on the nucleus plantation;

- Increased hiring of casual waged workers by self-employed farmers, producing sugar under contract as "outgrowers" to the sugar plantation companies;
- Increased use of casual waged workers on nucleus plantations;
- Increasing casualisation of employment.
- Ongoing downsising of the permanent waged workforce on sugar company nucleus (*i.e.,* directly managed) plantations;
- Outgrower associations acting as labour contractors, hiring casual waged labour to work on the farms of its outgrower farmer members;

The combined effects of these changes for waged workers are growing job insecurity, lower rates of pay, poorer working conditions, increasing food insecurity and growing levels of poverty. Agricultural workers have a range of responsibilities, from planting, cultivating, grading, and sorting agricultural products to inspecting agricultural commodities and facilities. They may work with food crops, animals, or trees, shrubs, and plants. Depending on their jobs, they may work outdoors or indoors.

Agricultural inspectors are employed by Federal and State governments to inspect agricultural commodities, processing equipment and facilities, and fish and logging operations for compliance with laws and regulations governing health, quality, and safety. They inspect horticultural products or livestock to detect harmful disease or infestations. To assist in eradicating disease, they also inspect livestock to help determine the effectiveness of medication and feeding programmes. They may collect samples of pests, or of suspected diseased animals or materials, and send such samples to a laboratory for identification and analysis.

AGRICULTURAL PRODUCTS WORK

Graders and sorters, agricultural products work to ensure the quality of the agricultural commodities that reach the market. They grade, sort, or classify unprocessed food and other agricultural products by size, weight, colour, or condition. *Farmworkers and labourers, crop, nursery, and greenhouse* manually plant, maintain, and harvest food crops; apply pesticides, herbicides, and fertilizers to crops; and cultivate the plants used to beautify landscapes. They prepare nursery acreage or greenhouse beds for planting; water, weed, and spray trees, shrubs, and plants; cut, roll, and stack sod; stake trees; tie, wrap, and pack flowers, plants, shrubs, and trees to fill orders; and dig up or move field-grown and containerised shrubs and trees. Additional duties include planting seedlings, transplanting saplings, and watering and trimming plants.

Farmworkers, farm and ranch animals care for live farm, ranch, or aquacultural animals that may include cattle, sheep, swine, goats, horses and other equines, poultry, finfish, shellfish, and bees. They also tend to animals raised for animal products, such as meat, fur, skins, feathers, eggs, milk, and honey. Duties may include feeding, watering, herding, grasing, castrating, branding, de-beaking, weighing, catching, and loading animals. They also may maintain records on animals, examine animals to detect diseases and injuries, and assist in birth deliveries and administer medications, vaccinations, or insecticides as appropriate. Daily duties include cleaning and maintaining animal housing areas.

FARMWORKERS AND AGRICULTURAL PRODUCTION

Farmworkers, agricultural production may have a wide range of duties, some of which overlap duties of other farmworkers. They tend to livestock and poultry; plant and harvest crops; and apply pesticides, herbicides, and fertilizers to crops. These farmworkers also repair farm buildings and fences. Other duties may include operating milking machines and other dairy processing equipment, supervising seasonal help, irrigating crops, and hauling livestock products to market. Some farmworkers operate tractors, fertilizer spreaders, haybines, raking equipment, balers, combines, threshers, and other equipment used for plowing, sowing, and harvesting. They also may help with the sorting, storage, and working in post-harvest treatment of crops.

Inspectors Field Work

Working conditions vary widely. For example, some inspectors do field work, and may travel frequently. Federal food inspectors may work in highly mechanised plants or with poultry or livestock in confined areas with extremely cold temperatures and slippery floors. The duties often require working with sharp knives, moderate lifting, and walking or standing for long periods. Many inspectors work long and often irregular hours. Inspectors may find themselves in adversarial roles when the organisation or individual being inspected objects to the inspection process or its potential consequences.

Graders and sorters may work with similar products for an entire shift, or may be assigned a variety of items. They may be on their feet all day and may have to lift heavy objects, whereas others may sit during most of their shift and do little strenuous work. Some graders work in clean, air-conditioned environments, suitable for carrying out controlled tests. Some may work evenings or weekends because of the perishable nature of the products. Overtime may be required to meet production goals. For farmworkers in nurseries, work is seasonal; spring and summer are the busier times of the year and hours in the cold weather tend to be fewer.

These workers enjoy relatively comfortable working conditions while tending to plants indoors. However, during the busy seasons when landscape contractors need plants, work schedules may be more demanding, requiring weekend work. Moreover, the transition from warm weather to cold weather means that nursery workers might have to work overtime with little notice in order to move plants indoors in case of a frost. Farmworkers enjoy a somewhat inde-pendent lifestyle working with animals or on the land. Benefits include the wide-open physical expanse, the variability of day-to-day work, and the rural setting. However, hours are generally uneven and often long; work cannot be delayed when crops must be planted and harvested, or when animals must be sheltered and fed. Weekend work is common, and farmworkers may work a 6- or 7-day week during planting and harvesting seasons.

About 1 out of 5 agricultural workers had variable schedules, compared with fewer than 1 in 10 workers in all occupations combined. As much of the work is seasonal in nature, many workers also obtain other employment. Migrant farmworkers, who move from location to location as crops ripen, live an unsettled lifestyle, which can be stressful. Much farm and ranch work takes place outdoors in all kinds of weather and is physical in nature. Harvesting fruits and vegetables, for example, may requiremuch bending, stooping, and lifting. Some field workers may lack adequate sanitation facilities, and their drinking water may be limited.

The year-round nature of much livestock production work means that ranch workers must be out in the heat of summer, as well as the cold of winter. Those who work directly with animals risk being bitten or kicked. Farmworkers in crop production risk exposure to pesticides and other potentially hazardous chemicals that are sprayed on crops or plants. However, exposure is relatively minimal if safety procedures are followed. Those who work on mechanised farms must take precautions when working with tools and heavy equipment to avoid injury.

Agricultural workers constitute by far the largest segment in the unorganised sector and their number according to 1991 Census was 74.6 million. In addition, a significant number, 110.7 million, are listed as cultivators (large, medium and small) of whom approximately 50 per cent belong to the category of small and marginal farmers. Many of these small and marginal farmers on account of utterly deficit, small and uneconomic holdings and low yield work on the land of others. Further, a significant number engaged in livestock, forestry, fishing, orchards and allied activities as well as small and marginal farmers work as agricultural workers in their spare time or in times of difficulty to supplement their meagre incomes.

In spite of the fact that these agricultural workers have such numerical strength, they are extremely vulnerable to exploitation on account of low levels of literacy, lack of awareness, persistent social backwardness and absence of unionisation and other forms of viable organisation. The avenues of stable and durable employment for them have been limited leading to inter-district and inter-state migration in search of better avenues of employment and wages but with a lot of dislocation of family life, dislocation of education of children and numerous other handicaps. Several measures have been taken to protect the interests of the working class and uplift the condition of agricultural workers. The very first legislation, the Minimum Wages Act, 1948 was applied to the agricultural sector also.

Subsequently, the Plantation Labour Act, 1951 was enacted to provide certain basic facilities to plantation workers. Many other existing labour laws are applicable or have direct bearing on agricultural labour. The problems of agricultural labourers have been sought to be tackled through Multi-dimensional course of action *viz.*, impro-vement of infrastructural facilities, diversification to non-farm activities, skill improvement programmes, financial assistance to promote self-employment, optimising the use of land resources, etc., through a variety of rural development, employment generation and poverty alleviation programmes.

All these efforts have not been able to adequately protect the interests of agricultural workers. This is partly on account of lack of bargaining power. Keeping in view this broad perspective, the Ministry of Labour is contemplating to bring a comprehensive legislation to safe guard the interests of agricultural workers.

Service Conditions of Agricultural Workers

The proposed legislation would provide for regulation of the service conditions of agricultural workers and provides for certain welfare measures which include financial assistance in case of death and injury, payment of group insurance premia, health, maternity benefits, old age pension, housing assistance and educational assistance to the children of agricultural workers. Special provision/welfare schemes for women workers prohibiting their employment after sunset, rest shelter with employment of 20 and above female agricultural workers for use of children under the age of six, ensuring payment of equal wages to men and women for same and similar nature of work as required under Equal Remuneration Act, maternity benefits, etc., are also provided in the proposed legislation. To meet the expenditure for various welfare measures there is provision for constitution of an Agricultural Workers' Welfare Fund at the district level to be financed by employers' contribution and contribution by the workers. The proposal is at the stage of consideration at various levels in the Government. However, Government's endeavour is to finalise the proposal at the earliest. For the benefit of the Agriculture workers Government has launched Krishi Shramik Samajik Suraksha Yojana from 1.7.2001 to provide social security to the agriculture workers.

Common Agricultural Policy

One of the principal objectives of the common agricu-ltural policy (CAP) is to provide farmers with a reasonable standard of living. Although this concept is not defined explicitly, one of the measures tracked within the policy is income development from farming activities. Economic accounts for agriculture provide information that allows an analysis of agricultural activity and the income generated by it.

This stage gives an overview of recent changes in agricultural output, gross value added and prices in the European Union (EU), and their effect on income from agricultural activity. The EU-27's agricultural industry generated EUR 125 400 million of gross value added at producer prices in 2009, which represented a 14.0 per cent reduction in relation to the previous year. There were large decreases in both the value of crop output (down 13.9 per cent to EUR 171 000 million in 2009) and animal output (down 10.9 per cent to EUR 133 000 million); these were partly compensated for by a sizeable reduction in the value of intermediate consumption of goods and services (down 10.5 per cent).

Changes in the value of agricultural output comprise a volume and price component: one important strand of recent changes in agricultural policy has been to move away from price support mechanisms, so that prices more accurately reflect market forces and changes in supply and demand. During the period 2005 to 2009 there were considerable differences between the Member States in the development of deflated agricultural output prices: such deflated prices show the extent to which agricultural prices have changed compared to consumer prices. Deflated prices rose in nine of the 26 Member States (Germany, no information available), the largest increases being recorded for the United Kingdom (average growth of 5.9 per cent per annum), Cyprus (3.9 per cent per annum between 2005 and 2008) and Romania (3.2 per cent per annum), while reductions were posted in 17 of the Member States, the most significant being in Latvia (-6.3 per cent per annum), Slovakia (-6.2 per cent per annum) and Estonia (-6.1 per cent per annum).

The development of deflated agricultural input prices showed a very different picture, as prices rose in 17 of the 25 Member States for which data are available between 2005 and 2009 (Germany and Ireland, no information). As with output prices, Cyprus (4.9 per cent per annum between 2005 and 2008) and the United Kingdom (4.7 per cent per annum) reported the highest input price increases, followed by Portugal (3.5 per cent per annum). There was an overall 9.4 per cent increase in EU output prices for agricultural products between 2005 and 2009, with a breakdown between crop output (9.0 per cent) and animal output (9.8 per cent) showing prices increasing by a similar magnitude. The overall increase in output prices between 2005 and 2009 did not occur as a stable development, as there was a considerable reduction in prices between 2008 and 2009 when the price of agricultural products fell by 13.9 per cent. The largest reductions between 2008 and 2009 were recorded for cereals (-30.2 per cent), eggs, milk, fruits and olive oil (reductions of between 14 per cent and 17 per cent).

The real net value added at factor cost of the agricultural activity per unit of labour (expressed in annual work units – equivalent to the work performed by a person employed full-time), also termed as agricultural income indicator A, declined by 11.7 per cent in the EU-27 in 2009, compared with 2008. There were stark contrasts among the Member States, with decreases in income of more than 20 per cent in Hungary, Luxembourg, Ireland, Germany and Italy, contrasting with rapidly rising incomes in Malta (7.1 per cent) and Denmark (4.2 per cent).

DATA SOURCES AND AVAILABILITY

Economic accounts for agriculture (EAA) provide key insights into:

- Agriculture's contribution to a Member State's wealth;
- Relationships between prices and quantities of both inputs and outputs.
- The economic viability of agriculture;
- The remuneration of factors of production;
- The structure and composition of agricultural production and inputs;

These accounts comprise a production account, a generation of income account, an entrepreneurial income account and some elements of a capital account. For the production items, Member States transmit to Eurostat values at basic prices, as well as their components (values at producer prices, subsidies on products, and taxes on products). The data for the production account and for gross fixed capital formation are transmitted in both current prices and the prices of the previous year.

OUTPUT OF AGRICULTURAL ACTIVITY

The output of agricultural activity includes output sold (including trade in agricultural goods and services between agricultural units), changes in stocks, output for own final use (own final consumption and own-account gross fixed capital formation), output produced for further processing by agricultural producers, as well as intra-unit consumption of livestock feed products. The output of the agricultural industry is made up of the sum of the output of agricultural products and of the goods and services produced in inseparable non-agricultural secondary activities; animal and crop output are the main product categories of agricultural output. Gross value added equals the value of output less the value of intermediate consumption, and is shown in producer prices (the producer price excludes subsidies less taxes on products). Intermediate consumption represents the value of all goods and services used as inputs in the production process, excluding fixed assets whose consu-mption is recorded as fixed capital consumption.

The Member States transmit information on intermediate consumption to Eurostat using values at purchaser prices (basic prices). Eurostat also collects annual agricultural prices (in principle net of VAT) to compare agricultural price levels between Member States and study sales channels. Quarterly and annual price indices for agricultural products and the means of agricultural production, on the other hand, are used principally to analyse price developments and their effect on agricultural income. Agricultural price indices are obtained by a base-weighted Laspeyres calculation (2005=100), and are expressed both in nominal terms, and deflated using an implicit HICP deflator.

Agricultural income indicators are presented in the form of:

- An index of real income of factors in agricultural activity per annual work unit (indicator A);
- Net entrepreneurial income of agriculture (indicator C).
- The index of real net agricultural entrepreneurial income, per unpaid annual work unit (indicator B);

Common Agricultural Policy

Significant reforms of the common agricultural policy have taken place in recent years, most notably in 2003 and 2008, with the aim of making the agricultural sector more market-oriented. The 2003 reform introduced a new system of direct payments, known as the single payment scheme, under which aid is no longer linked to production (decoupling); the single payment scheme aims to guarantee farmers more stable incomes.

Farmers can decide what to produce in the knowledge that they will receive the same amount of aid, allowing them to adjust production to suit demand. In 2008 further changes were made, building on the reform package from 2003, such that all aid to the agricultural sector will be decoupled by 2012. The Europe 2020 strategy offers a new perspective on economic, social, environmental, climate-related and technological challenges and future agricultural reform is likely to be made in relation to the goals of developing intelligent, sustainable and inclusive growth, while taking account of the wealth and diversity of the agricultural sector within the EU Member States.

PRICE POLICY FOR AGRICULTURAL PRODUCE

The government has formulated a price policy for agricultural produce that aims at securing remunerative prices to farmers to encourage them to invest more in agricultural production. Keeping this in mind, the gove-rnment announces minimum support prices for major agri-cultural products every year. These prices are fixed after taking into account the recommendations of the Commission for Agricultural Costs and Prices (CACP) - External web site that opens in a new window.

The Commission of Agricultural Costs and Prices while recommending prices takes into account important factors, such as:

- Changes in input prices.

- Cost of production.
- Demand and supply situation.
- Effect on cost of living.
- Effect on general price level.
- Effect on Industrial Cost Structure.
- Input/Output Price Parity.
- Inter-crop Price Parity.
- International market price situation.
- Parity between prices paid and prices received by farmers (Terms of Trade).
- Trends in market prices.

Public Distribution System

This system provides reasonable prices for basic food commodities through a network of 350,000 fair-price shops that are monitored by State Governments. It also keeps the situation of price rise in check. The Food Corporation of India is a public-sector Price agency that is responsible for implementing the government price policy through its procurement and public distribution operations. It procures wheat, paddy and rice for which minimum support prices have been announced well before the commencement of Rabi and Kharif Price seasons. Only Fair Average Quality (FAQ) food grains that have been previously specified by the Government of India are purchased. Surplus stock is exported.

GOVERNMENT'S PRICE POLICY

The main objectives of the Government's price policy for agricultural produce aims at ensuring remunerative prices to the growers for their produce with a view to encouraging higher investment and production. Towards this end, minimum support prices for major agricultural products are announced each year which are fixed after taking into account the recommendations of the Commission for Agricultural Costs and Prices (CACP).

The CACP, while recommending prices takes into account all important factors, viz:

- Changes in Input Prices.
- Cost of Production.
- Demand and Supply Situation.
- Effect on Cost of Living.
- Effect on General Price Level.
- Effect on Industrial Cost Structure.
- Input/Output Price Parity.
- Inter-crop Price Parity.
- International Market Price Situation.
- Parity between Prices Paid and Prices Received by farmers (Terms of Trade).

- Trends in Market Prices.

Of all the factors, cost of production is the most tangible factor and it takes into account all operational and fixed demands. Government organises Price Support Scheme (PSS) of the commodities, through various public and cooperative agencies such as FCI, CCI, JCI, NAFED, Tobacco Board, etc., for which the MSPs are fixed. For commodities not covered under PSS, Government also arranges for market interve-ntion on specific request from the States for specific quantity at a mutually agreed price. The losses, if any, are borne by the Centre and State on 50:50 basis. The price policy paid rich dividends. The Government have raised substantially the MSPs in recent years as may be seen from the statement enclosed.

IMPACT ON FOOD PRODUCTION

While it is a fact that late monsoons, drought, and floods had an impact on food production in the country, its influence on prices for commodities like rice had been nominal (as compared to other commodities). This is primarily due to excellent food grain production last year that immensely aided in boosting government stocks. In the current crop season, however, crop estimates point to a gloomy picture. India's overall food grain production in Kharif 2009 is estimated to come down by 16 percent with significant downfalls in Rice and Coarse Cereals respectively. Moreover, in the case of Pulses, estimates are down by 7.5 percent, mainly due to low rainfall in central, western and northern India.

Seasonality issues also came to the fore in the case of fruits and vegetables, notably Potato. Large tracts of Potato were destroyed in West Bengal and Bihar (two main potato growing regions) due to late blight infestation. As a result, strains on food reserves in the country inevitably become evident, and hence the inflationary tendencies. Such a scenario, besides stoking inflationary fear, is also instilling a fear that the country would be unable to manage satisfactory growth in agriculture GDP.

An optimistic counterview is being put forth repeatedly which suggests that Rabi harvest would satisfactorily suffice for the shortage of food articles and would also cover-up for the losses sustained so far. Estimates however, do not support this proposition. Experts point out that it is the third quarter, when Kharif harvest takes place and the fourth quarter (for Rabi) that are extremely important for the Agriculture GDP of the country. These two quarters alone account for nearly 60 percent of the agriculture GDP, with Kharif accounting for nearly one-third and Rabi, a little over than a quarter. As Kharif estimates points to a sharp decline, such a scenario puts forth immense pressure on Rabi season to match up.

However, this is an onerous task; the country would require substantial growth figures in fourth quarter. To elucidate, Widely consumed pulses varieties such as Moong, Tur are mainly kharif crops and their production has already declined; wheat production already has reached a record level of 81 Million tonnes last year and to make up for the loss this year, wheat production has to reach 93 Million tonnes, which is nearly impossible. Besides, oilseeds will have to grow by 26 percent to maintain overall oilseeds production at last year's level. Consequently, the substitution effect that Rabi harvest can have will be limited; it is highly unlikely that improvement in Rabi food grains would cover-up losses in kharif. Shortages in the availability of many commodities seems imminent this season and food inflation is going to have a longer horizon than expected. Here, it is equally important to present an interesting view, which states that we cannot confidently attribute the price increases beign witnessed currently to commodity shortages. It is pertinent to mention that we have been having two consequently good agriculture seasons prior to 2009; our stockpiles, especially of food-grains is at more than optimum levels.

A closer look at half yearly GDP data yields another interesting observation and brings in an element of doubt on attribution of inflation singly to poor production estimates and figures. An interesting point of view has come up, which states that in real terms agriculture GDP as a percentage of private consumption expenditure at nearly 24 percent, is constant for first half of both 2008-09 and 2009-10. Essentially, this means that agricultural supply as a share of demand in real terms is constant. It is not the price for a single commodity that is rising but all agricultural prices covering food grains and fruits and vegetables. These prices are rising when the share of output to demand in real terms is constant, it is not falling. Accordingly it is premature to state that inflation is stemming from supply constraints. On the other hand, the focus of policy makers is to attribute price rise to kharif grains, but this might be fallacious as the share of grains in both price and in the output indices is pretty low, in fact around a sixteenth. We cannot confidently say that there is supply crisis in food products, and that inflation is a result thereof.

PRODUCTION OF HIGH QUALITY FOOD AND RAW MATERIALS

Modern agriculture aims for the production of high quality food and raw materials in sufficient quantity for a wide range of customers. Further objectives consist of preservation of resources and protection of the environment. Means to achieve these goals are machines, equipment, and processes with high efficiency and effectiveness. These modern machines and processes are rather complex and consist of various cooperating subsystems.

Moreover, agricultural production takes place in an open system which has various relations to its surrounding. This means that state conditions of the surrounding systems as well as the interactions between the agricultural production process and its environment have to be taken into account. Mass or energy flows must therefore be accompanied by information flows. This has led to the introduction of an information-based agriculture, the so-called "precision agriculture".

This kind of agricultural production serves for aiming at the following targets: on one hand one strives for a production process which is in accordance with the demands of plants or animals and realises this in a site-specific or even single-plant-specific or single-animal-specific way. This results in the necessity to supply data about reference values and controlled variables in great variety, amount, and with short delay time, to transmit these data and process them. On the other hand, new knowledge, improvements and enhancements should be included in a simple and compatible way into technical equipment and production processes. Furthermore, maintenance and service of modern machines and process equipment should be handled according to their real operation times and circumstances.

This also requires the sampling, transmission, and processing of data in a compatible way, since the data may be generated, transmitted, and processed in different units. In summary, the compatible data transmission is a necessary condition for achievement of all the aims formulated above. Communication technology thus serves as the backbone of precision agriculture.

This book considers the information flows in different areas of agricultural production as well as their physical and logical realisation.

AGRICULTURE AND ITS EMBEDDING INTO VARIOUS INFLUENCES

Agriculture finds itself in a surrounding with various (mutual) influences and effects, *e.g.,* properties and state of the soil; biological effects and genetic engineering; finances and commerce; demands for quality and quantity of products; research and development; legislation and regulation; climatic conditions; storage, conservation, and further processing; employment, education and health of staff; (agricultural) engineering including mechatronics; information technology; actual temporal conditions.

Agriculture itself consists of a network of various institutions with various mutual interrelations:

- Agricultural administration (on a regional, state, federal, EU, and international level).
- Agricultural consultants, on various levels.
- Agricultural professionals' associations.
- Contractors, machine pools.
- Farms and cooperatives.

Furthermore, on the farm level with various tasks to be settled, there exist interactions between the economical and technical farm management as well as control mechanisms for plant and animal production processes.

NETWORKING REQUIREMENTS OF PRECISION AGRICULTURE

To meet the demands of precision agriculture, the production must be controlled sufficiently precisely. This leads to an intensive use of measurement and control equipment. These complex electronic systems can only cooperate efficiently if their various components are able to communicate and exchange data automatically. The use of actual information requires an electronic transmission of data.

The time scales of the information flows are very different: Consideration of Data Warehouse And Its Applications In Agriculture new regulations usually needs response times of weeks or months, while control of application processes in the field goes down to several milliseconds. These different time scales lead to the use of different transmission media. The automated use of transmitted data is possible only if the structure and definition of data objects is completely known. Here agriculture has to face the situation that another commercial supplier or another financially stronger customer is defining structure and contents of the data.

Agriculture thus has to bring its demands into line with established or evolving conventions defined by other disciplines. Only within the core of agricultural activities there is a chance to define standards that meet agriculture-specific demands. Therefore. Predominantly the Internet with its providers is already used for this purpose, or will be used in future. Within the centre of agricultural activities the situation becomes more specific. But also in this case established communication lines are mainly used; however, the contents and structures of the data may be defined specifically and can follow self-defined standards (agricultural software suppliers, agricultural machinery industry, administration, public information services like the German DAINet, etc.).

NETWORKING REQUIREMENTS ON FARM LEVEL

On the farm level, additional new functionalities are expected from the used data communication techniques. Connections between farm and non- farm institutions will be done in the same manner. Inside farms, depending on working processes, very different demands arise in terms of amount and time scale of data. At the moment, development and design of farm specific data networks have made greatest progress in the area of plant production.

Therefore the following explanation concentrates on two networks and their standards DIN 9684 and ISO 11783, which are planned for mobile agricultural machinery. These networks mainly serve to exchange process data, which are necessary for technical control, information of the operator, and exchange of data with stationary farm computers. Agricultural machinery is produced by international industry, so only international standardisation is able to guarantee unimpeded data transfer between agricultural systems. Nienhaus

(1993) reports that as early as in 1988 at request of Great Britain the establishment of an independent sub-committee for electronics was discussed in Technical Committee 23 (TC 23) of ISO.

Subsequently, an independent sub-committee, SC 19, with working group 1, the WG1 Mobile Machinery, was established. This TC23/SC19/WG1 under the actual chairmanship of Canada is responsible for the standa-rdisation of the agricultural bus according to ISO 11783. Due to the rapid progress in software design and electronics there will be some important differences between the LBS and the ISO definitions. For example, LBS uses the CAN protocol version 2.0A (11 bit identifier) and ISO the protocol version 2.0B (29 bit identifier) with the higher data transfer rate of 250 kBaud.

FIELD OF EXPANSION OF LOCAL AGRICULTURAL NETWORKS

Another field of expansion of local agricultural networks is the area of animal production. Here data communication techniques may be used, which are known from PC technology (such as standard network boards, Ethernet, Novell,....) to exchange information between the farm computer, control units of technical equipment and components such as self feeders, automatic milking systems, or animal health control.

To guarantee compatibility, protocol and data objects should be defined in a standard. Inside of a technical equipment, *e.g.,* a feeding system, only the producer is responsible for the way of data exchange between its components. If such a facility is constructed in a modular way with components of different suppliers, physical network, protocol and application should also be fully standardised. The LBS application layer (without restrictions of the CAN protocol) could be the basis for discussion of such an agricultural network for animal production.

New Data Communication Technologies

Modern data exchange techniques via different communication media such as chip card, CD, MD, mobile phone or radio will offer totally new solutions for a lot of problems in all areas of technical equipment. In agriculture, for instance, precautionary service of machinery is meaningful to avoid time consuming repair during harvesting or other critical working conditions. Integration of computer techniques can realise automatic diagnoses.

These improvements may be strengthened by remote diagnoses and services based on wireless data telecommuni-cation. Online data exchange between stationary farm computers and mobile field machinery can assist agricultural network services such as the LBS service task controller. Direct access to Internet or other global networks theoretically enables the farmer to plan, decide, and act on the tractor as well as on the farm computer. Tremendous progress in technical development will also push forward many areas of agriculture.

Here only a little number of examples may be listed. For the area of plant production with mobile machinery, agricultural enterprises are interested in sensor systems which enable to collect online (during the working processes) information about positions, soil conditions, parameters of crop, etc. Some new techniques such as GPS based yield data collection already represent state of art. Jahns *et al.* (2001) state that GPS based calculation of driving direction assisted by image based identification of tramlines will support automatic vehicle guidance. Rode and Paul (1999) report that spectral analysis of reflected radiation gives information about humidity of soil, humidity of crop, nitrogencontent of plants, etc.

Standardised transmission of processed measurement data via a network such as LBS makes the data available for many applications. Precision agriculture represents mainly an information based venture. To bring such an enterprise into action, it is necessary to make available information on different levels with variable demands. Therefore data communication in various versions has to be performed. For automatic data processing standardised machine-readable data exchange is mandatory. The actual standards defined in DIN 9684 or ISO 11783 permanently have to be expanded to meet the growing tasks and functions of precision agriculture. For the field of animal production, corresponding standards have to be created, whereby the existing ones may be a guideline.

A Data warehouse is a repository of integrated information, available for queries and analysis. Data and information are extracted from heterogeneous sources as they are generated. This makes it much easier and more efficient to run queries over data that originally came from different sources. In other words Data warehouse is a database that is used to hold data for reporting and analysis. A data warehouse is a single, complete and consistent data archive, extracted from different sources and made available to end-users in a form understandable and usable to them in the context of the business.

A data warehouse consists of a set of subject-oriented, integrated, permanent, time-dependent data providing support to managerial decision-making. Economic foundation and productivity growth depends on agricultural sectors. Agriculture is the driving force behind the way of live and source of earnings for the majority of peoples. More than 60 percents of population are living in rural areas and the majority are farmers. The rural communities as a main producer for country food productivity and food security earn only 11 percents of Gross Domestic Product (GDP). The arrival of information age guides this country to new development strategies. 2National Electronics and Computer Technology Centre (NECTEC) in collaboration with the Ministry of Agriculture, has launched "Agriculture Information Network" as a response to the unmet information requirements of the agricultural sector. Farmers should gain benefit from the contents provided which include risk assessment, agriculture warning system and agricultural knowledge base, which aim to improve technology, productivity, income and stability of India agriculture sector through the age of Information Technology.

The data warehouse consists of common databases and geo-spatial databases from various departments and organisations in the country and abroad. Farmers can get access to the contents through Internet by themselves or from groups of professional people called "Information Brokers". First step towards understanding any agricultural system is the comprehension of relationships between the system and numerous physical, chemical and biological factors influencing it. Any decision regarding such systems requires analytical exploration of the involved data.

The exploration task is to be supported by an efficient data storage and retrieval mechanism. In this stage, we have presented the case of an Agri data warehouse for this purpose. We have briefly discussed the process we adopted for establishing the data warehouse encompassing pest, pesticide and metrological data. We have also shown how implementing an Olap tool on top of the Agri data warehouse resulted in interesting findings from a decision support point of view.

Information System of Methodology

The information system will consist of several integrated sub-systems for input, storage, retrieval, analysis and output based on strong database design with its essential functions. Besides this it will include other functions such as manipulation and dissemination of information to various users. The information system, composed of set of files for use in a RDBMS and GIS will be capable of delivering accurate, useful and timely information to various applications. Design of spatial and non-spatial database will have specifications of different data fields, their logical array and inter-relationship with subsystem database. Data warehouse is a repository of an organisation's electronically stored data. Data warehouses are designed to facilitate reporting and analysis.

This definition of the data warehouse focuses on data storage. However, the means to retrieve and analyse data, to extract, transform and load data, and to manage the data dictionary are also considered essential components of a data warehousing system. Many references to data warehousing use this broader context.

Thus, an expanded definition for data warehousing includes business intelligence tools, tools to extract, transform, and load data into the repository, and tools to manage and retrieve metadata. A data warehouse is used for answer any ad_hoc, complex, statistical or analytical queries. Data warehouse is situated at the centre of a decision support system (DSS) of an organisation.

BENEFITS OF DATA WAREHOUSING

Some of the benefits that a data warehouse provides are as follows:

- A data warehouse provides a common data model for all data of interest regardless of the data's source. This makes it easier to report and analyse information than it would be if multiple data models were used to retrieve information such as sales invoices, order receipts, general ledger charges, etc.
- Because they are separate from operational systems, data warehouses provide retrieval of data without slowing down operational systems.
- Data warehouses can work in conjunction with and, hence, enhance the value of operational business applications, notably customer relationship management (CRM) systems.
- Data warehouses facilitate decision support system applications such as trend reports (*e.g.*, the items with the most sales in a particular area within the last two years), exception reports, and reports that show actual performance versus goals.
- Information in the data warehouse is under the control of data warehouse users so that, even if the source system data is purged over time, the information in the warehouse can be stored safely for extended periods of time.
- Prior to loading data into the data warehouse, inconsistencies are identified and resolved. This greatly simplifies reporting and analysis.

AN ORGANISATIONAL DATA STORE

A data mart is a subset of an organisational data store, usually oriented to a specific purpose or major data subject, that may be distributed to support business needs. Data marts are analytical data stores designed to focus on specific business functions for a specific community within an organisation. Data marts are often derived from subsets of data in a data warehouse, though in the *bottom-up* data warehouse design methodology the data warehouse is created from the union of organisational data marts.

A data mart is a data repository that may or may not derive from a data warehouse and that emphasises ease of access and usability for a particular designed purpose. In general, a data warehouse tends to be a strategic but somewhat unfinished concept; a data mart tends to be tactical and aimed at meeting an immediate need. There can be multiple data marts inside a single corporation; each one relevant to one or more business units for which it was designed. Data marts may or may not be dependent or related to other data marts in a single corporation. If the data marts are designed using conformed facts and dimensions, then they will be related. In some deployments, each department or business unit is considered the *owner* of its data mart including all the *hardware*, *software* and *data*.

This enables each department to use, manipulate and develop their data any way they see fit; without altering information inside other data marts or the data warehouse. In other deployments where conformed dimensions are used, this business unit ownership will not hold true for shared dimensions like customer, product, etc.

Reasons for creating a data mart;

- Creates collective view by a group of users.
- Ease of creation.
- Easy access to frequently needed data.
- Improves end-user response time.
- Lower cost than implementing a full Data warehouse.
- Potential users are more clearly defined than in a full Data warehouse.

PROCESSES, STRUCTURAL COEFFICIENTS AND SERVICE

SYSTEMS OF ORDER LEVELS

Structurally, the main building blocks of a whole-farm system are its enterprises; these provide its income in cash or kind. Enterprises may stand alone or be supported by resource-providing activities. The building blocks of both enterprises and their enabling activities are agro-technical processes.

DEFINITION AND NATURE

A *process* is the specific way in which a production operation is done, together with the levels or amounts of resources used in doing it. A process specifies or implies the use of some operational technology, the types and levels of resources used in its operation, and the types and levels of its resultant outputs.

Processes present two general analytical or management problems:

- To select the 'best' or most appropriate technology; and
- To operate the selected technology at its optimal level in terms of inputs and outputs.

According to the general definition of a system, a process is itself a system. Its components are its technology, its inputs and its outputs. Interaction exists in the relationships among these inputs and outputs.

The (management) objective relative to a process system is to operate it:

- At a level which is optimal for the enterprise to which it contributes; and
- In such fashion as to achieve maximum efficiency in resource use, *i.e.*, maximum output for a given input, or minimum input for a given output. The boundaries of a process are defined by the specification of the process itself and, at least conceptually, a given process system can usually be disaggregated into successively smaller subsystems.

Before looking further at these problems it will be useful to consider some examples. Table 6.1 presents a typical activity budget for maize production. While Table (and similar activity or enterprise tables such as Table) would be adequate as the basis for financial evaluation of this activity, it is nonetheless a highly generalized statement: it offers little or no structural information about any of the seven operations which comprise the activity, *e.g.*, no information is given regarding how the field was ploughed (mule, bullock or tractor?), the number of times it was ploughed or the degree of tilth aimed at. Or considering operation (2), planting, no information is offered regarding the several variations possible in this operation which could affect crop yield, *e.g.*, depth of seed placement, in-row and between-row plant spacing, seasonality of planting, the moisture level of the field at planting time etc. Nor is any agro-technical information offered regarding any of the other operations beyond the bare fact that they were done and the inputs which were used in doing them.

The seven operations shown in Table 6.1 represent seven operational subsystems, one each relating to ploughing, planting, irrigating etc. However, due to the absence of data, it is not possible to judge whether or not these subsystems consist of the best of all possible technologies to use in each operation, nor whether each one is operated at maximum efficiency. Seven kilograms of seed are specified but would it be better to use six or nine kilograms? Forty kilograms of fertilizer are budgeted but might this better be 60 or 80 kilograms? In short, Table tells nothing about the optimality of resource use. Clearly, if interest is in ascertaining whether there are better ways of performing these separate operations and whether the resources to be used in them are being used to their maximum efficiency, these operations have to be examined in greater detail.

Table. Budget of a Maize-growing Activity Inputs Per Acre

Inputs per acre				
Operation	**Materials**	**Labour (days)**	**Oxen (days)**	**Costs/returns (₹)**
1. Ploughing		5	4	200
2. Planting	seed: 7 kg	1		240
3. Irrigating	water: 1 ac ft	1		50
4. Fertilizing	fert 40 kg *N*	1		200
5. Weeding		3		30
6. Harvesting	sacks: 50	6		280
7. Drying	wood: 2 m	3		400
Total inputs and costs		20	4	1 400
Outputs per acre				
Item	grain: 1 t			3 000

The operations of Table 6.1 are listed again in Figure 6.1. This also shows, for each operation, the alternative technologies that might be employed in performing it and a range of input intensity levels at which each technology might be implemented. For example, the 'ploughing' operation could be done by tractor, by oxen or by spade; and whichever ploughing technology is chosen could be applied one, two, three or four times: further, whichever of these possible combinations is used, it could be applied to cultivate to a depth of 7, 14 or 21 centimetres. Alternative possible technologies and alternative possible technology intensities or input levels are also shown for the other of the seven production operations.

Each specific technology (*i.e.*, the way or means by which an operation is performed), operating with the application of one or more different kinds of (variable-level) inputs, is a *process.* The technology operates either as a single-variable input process or, if it is used with two, three, four... different kinds of inputs, as a multi-variable input process. In Figure, three possible technologies are shown for the planting operation: using two-row or four-row machines or doing this operation by hand. Whichever of these planting technologies is chosen by the farmer, it can be used with a variable amount or intensity level of seed (20-, 30- or 40-thousand seeds per acre). Each of the three planting technologies is thus a single-variable input process where the variable input is seed used in conjunction with a fixed input consisting of either a two-row, four-row or hand planter.

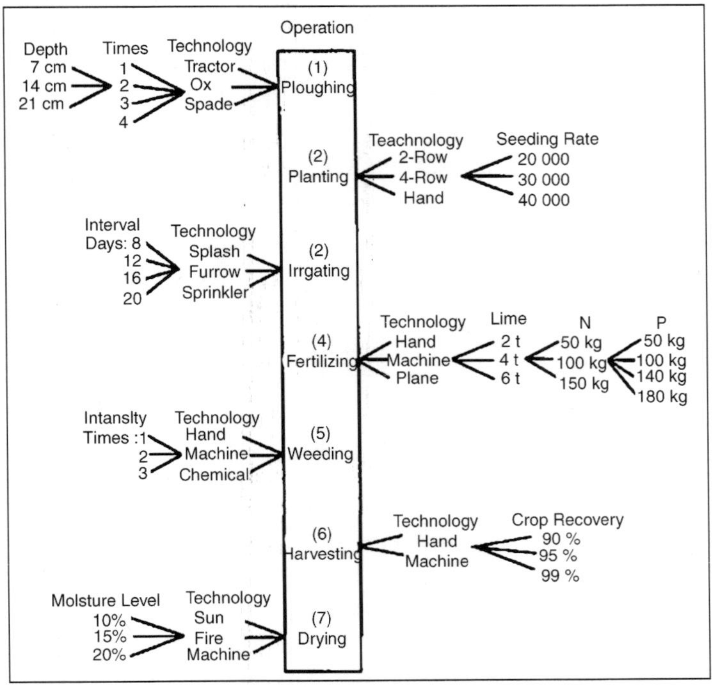

Fig. Example of Alternative Technologies in Maize Production (Per Acre Basis)

On the other hand, the operation 'ploughing' is a two-variable input process: each of the three possible ploughing technologies (doing this operation by tractor or by oxen or by hand) can be done or combined with some variable range of the two 'inputs' shown—depth to which the field can be ploughed and number of times it can be ploughed. Thus there are a total of three by three by three, or 27, combinations of ploughing technology by depth by frequency which could be applied to this operation.

Each of these 27 combinations could at least potentially result in a different crop yield as illustrated relative to number and depth of ploughings by the graphs in the lower half of Figure. For analytical purposes, such processes are usually described and quantified in mathematical terms as *response functions* or *production functions* which relate the output of a crop, livestock activity etc. to the inputs used in producing it. For a single-variable input process, they are specified by the general functional form $Y = f(S)$ which states that, *e.g.*, crop yield per ha (denoted by Y) is some function of the amount of seed used per ha (denoted by 5); or more realistically as a multi-variable input process, $Y = f(S, C)$ which states that yield is significantly determined by both the amount of seed and the number of times the field is cultivated (denoted by C); or more realistically still, $Y = f(S, C, N, P)$ where the effects of nitrogen fertilizer (N) and phosphate fertilizer (P) are also considered.

Figure 6.1 illustrates the concept of production functions. In the top figure, crop yield per ha (for some particular set of climatic, soil and husbandry conditions) is graphed as a function of the single input-variable seeding rate over the range from 10 000 to 50 000 seeds per ha. This depicts the response or production function $Y = f(S)$. In the lower figure, crop yield per ha (again for some particular set of climatic, soil and husbandry conditions - including seeding rate but excluding ploughing frequency and depth) is shown as a function of the two variable inputs depth (7, 14 or 21 cm) and number of ploughings (1, 2, 3, 4 or 5). This depicts the production function $Y = f(D, K)$ by the set of three single-variable input-output graphs $Y = f(K/D)$(for D respectively equal to 7, 14 or 21) where D and K respectively denote depth and number of ploughings and the symbolism K/D indicates that K is variable while D is fixed at some specified level.

NUMBER OF RELEVANT PROCESSES

The number of separate *operations* in an activity can be large (seven in the above example of Figure 6.1). The number of *processes* in an operation can also be large; *e.g.*, in the Figure three technologies are shown for the irrigation operation (the alternatives of splash, furrow or sprinkler application), each of these operating over some intensity range (days' interval between water applications). One could, if it were appropriate, list many more factors relating to irrigation which would have an effect on crop yield, *i.e.*, other dimensions in which irrigation could operate such as the amount of water applied at each irrigation, the quality/salinity of water used, the time of day at which irrigating is done etc.

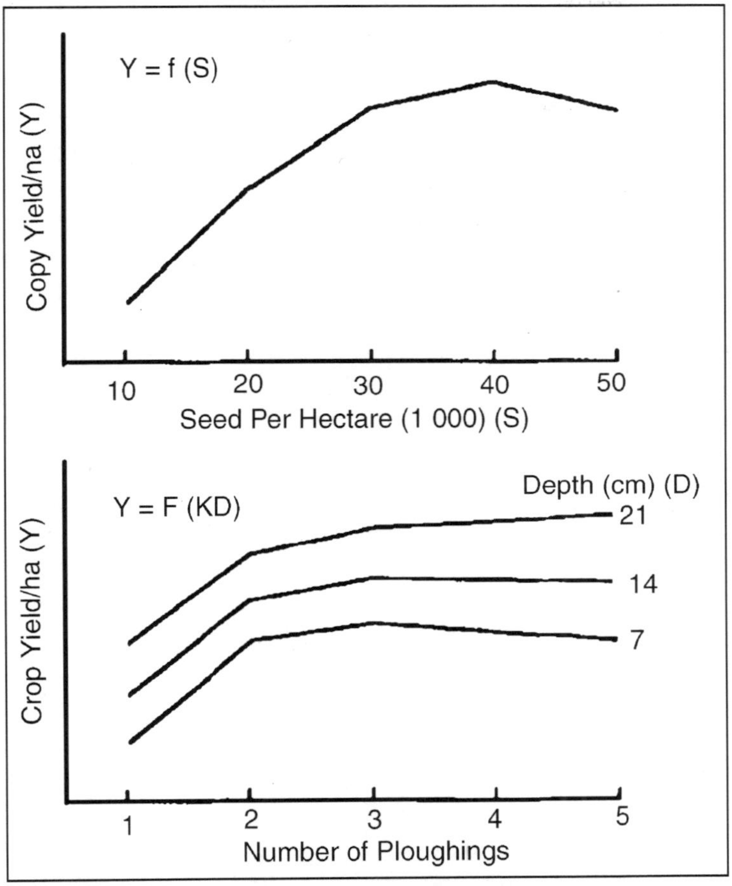

Fig. Graphical Examples of Single-variable Input and Two-variable Input Production Functions

However, such an examination of an operation in greater-and-greater detail by defining more-and-more dimensions in which it exists, if done for all operations in all farming environments, would be not far short of defining the total scope of all agricultural science. (Thus relative to the operations listed in Figure, 'planting' would encompass the realm of agronomists; 'harvesting' and 'drying' that of engineers; etc.) From the very large number of physical processes which do exist, farm management is concerned with selecting and analysing only that relatively small number which are of practical economic significance; or, in terms of the example of Figure, only those processes which have or are thought to have a significant (economic) impact on crop yield. Just which of these processes are 'significant' and thus to be subjected to economic analysis via *response analysis*, will depend on analytical circumstances. As a practical guide, farm management analysis would be confined to processes which have a relatively large effect on output or which are expensive or which require large inputs of scarce resources. In short, in such activities as those shown in Table 6.1 and Figure 6.1, there might be only two or three processes of sufficient importance to warrant full economic analysis.

Types of Processes

In agricultural production there are three broad types of processes:

- *Biological processes* are those in which the stimulus or input operates *directly* on the biological system of an animal or plant. Irrigation water applied to a crop root zone, feed digested by a dairy cow are examples. The great majority of economically relevant agricultural processes are of this type.
- *Bio-mechanical processes* are those in which the stimulus or input operates *indirectly* on a plant or animal, its direct or immediate effect being on the physical micro-environment in which the plant or animal exists. An example is the number of times a field is tilled. This will affect subsequent plant growth/yield, but will operate indirectly through changing the physical/mechanical conditions in which plant growth occurs - *e.g.*, through changes to clod size, particle cohesiveness, water infiltration and soil moisture storage capacity etc. At a practical farming level these bio-mechanical processes are usually not distinguished from direct biological processes.
- *Mechanical processes* do not exist as part of a plant/animal biological system, but act as physical/mechanical support to such systems. Some of them can be operated at varying intensity levels, such as the delivery of feed to a herd of cows by a conveyor belt driven at varying speed. Here there might be some non-linear relationship between, say, fuel consumption and amount of feed conveyed by the belt, and the relationship would appear. In consequence, determination of optimal belt speed would be economically relevant. Many types of mechanically powered equipment—tractors, trucks, stationary motors—have such an optimal operating rate. But with others the relationship between fuel input/speed and work output is linear over some specified range; if the machine is operated beyond this range, it might simply disintegrate.

Shape of Input-output Process Relationships

Figure 6.3 illustrates some differently shaped production functions for the case of a single-variable input production process. Each graph shows the physical input-output relationship or total physical product curve as the level of the single variable input is increased with all other input factors held constant. Note that, in graphs A and B, the law of diminishing returns (sometimes called the law of variable proportions) prevails—beyond some point, as the level of the variable input increases with no change in the level of other input factors, increases in output occur at a diminishing rate (the marginal product is decreasing) and eventually, beyond the point of maximum output, output declines in absolute terms (the marginal product becomes negative).

In graph A of Figure 6.3, which is the classical depiction of a production function, all three theoretical stages of production are to be seen as the level of the variable input increases: first, an initial stage of increasing returns with output increasing at an increasing rate—maximum efficiency would never be achieved by operating the process in this stage since the marginal product is increasing; second, a middle stage of decreasing returns with output increasing at a decreasing rate (*i.e.*, marginal product is positive but declining); and, third, beyond some maximum level of output, a final stage where output declines (*i.e.*, marginal product is negative). Graph B is more realistic in showing only the second and third stages since increasing returns are not found in practice.

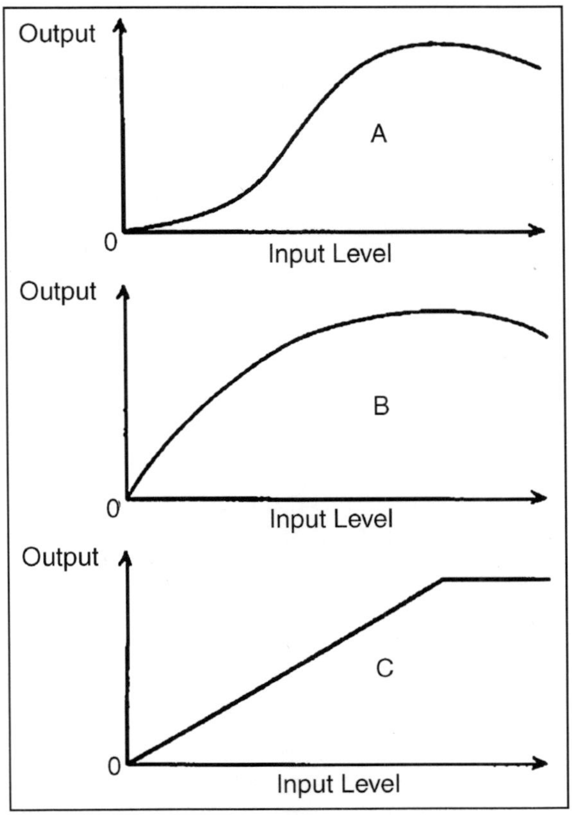

Fig. Stylized Production Functions or Input-Output Relationships for a Single Variable Input.

Graph C depicts a process in which output increases at a constant rate (*i.e.*, linearly) up to some maximum level and then remains constant (at least within the input range covered by the graph - it must be expected eventually to decline). While graphs A and B are non-linear, graph C is of (segmented) linear form. Note also that as depicted in all three graphs, output is zero when none of the variable input is used. This indicates that the variable input under consideration is essential to production (as, *e.g.*, seed in crop production). Often, however, some output may still be obtained when none of the variable input is used. In this case the input is to some extent optional (as, *e.g.*, chemical fertilizer in crop production).

The reasons why the use of some kinds of inputs beyond a certain level causes a decline in output will be intuitively obvious. As more and more water is added to a crop, keeping all other inputs constant (especially drainage capacity), the field will eventually become waterlogged and yield will decline; or as a crop is weeded with greater and greater frequency (*i.e.*, weeding labour inputs are increased), the point will be reached where workers will cause more damage in trampling the crop than benefit. Or again, as in curve C of Figure 6.3, offering more feed to a cow than she can consume might not cause actual milk output to decline, but beyond a certain level feed will be uneaten and go to waste (and the value of output will decline relative to the increasing cost of inputs).

ANALYTICAL PROBLEMS PRESENTED BY PROCESSES

As noted, processes present two problems in farm systems analysis:

- Selection of the 'best' technology or method of performing an operation; and
- Determination of the optimal level of intensity at which the process should be operated.
- *Technology:* Usually, selection of the 'best' process is not difficult on small farms; it is often determined by the socioeconomic environment. Selection of a two-row or four-row mechanical grain planter might present a real management problem in South Dakota, but there would be no such alternative possibilities among the hill farmers of Nepal where all field operations are done by hand. Where a farmer does face a management choice in technology selection, decisions can be made by budgeting out the costs and returns of the alternatives.
- *Optimization of input or intensity levels:* The second problem of operating the 'best' process at the 'best' level can be a little more complicated. If the choice is between two, three, four... discrete alternatives, this also can be made on the basis of comparative partial budgets. If the process is of such economic significance as to warrant more precision and if it relates to a continuous type of input, then

it might require the more sophisticated methods of response analysis.

INTERRELATEDNESS OF SYSTEM COMPONENTS: STRUCTURAL COEFFICIENTS

The next element of a system to be examined is its structural coefficients. From the system definition, a necessary property of any system is the existence of interrelatedness among its components. In farm-household systems this takes the form of structural coefficients of two kinds. *Internal structural coefficients* exist and operate within individual production activities or other subsystems and define explicitly or implicitly the interrelatedness which exists between/ among their several sub-components.

External structural coefficients are also often relevant for a given system, such as a production activity/enterprise, but their function here is to quantify relatedness between the given system or subsystem and other related systems or subsystems.

INTERRELATEDNESS WITHIN AN ACTIVITY INTERNAL STRUCTURAL COEFFICIENTS

Internal structural coefficients are those which 'tie together' or link the various components of a (crop, livestock or whole-farm) system. They are an especially important characteristic of those farm production activities which generate part of their own resources, *e.g.*, mixed livestock activities. The budget for one such activity, annual maintenance of a sheep flock to produce wool and lambs, is shown in the lower section of Table.

This flock budget would probably be adequate if the purpose is to evaluate the financial results of sheep production and perhaps compare such results with those of other activities.

Table Internal Structural Coefficients and Annual Activity Budget for a Self-sustaining Flock of 100 Ewes

Internal Structural Coefficients	
Ewe mortality rate	0.05
Lamb birth rate	0.90
Lamb mortality	0.09
Rams: ewes	0.05
Ewe and ram replacement rate	0.20
Activity Budget	(₹)
Input costs	
Replacement rams	(bred)
Replacement ewes	(bred)
Feed	8000
Veterinary	300
Shearing	1900

Labour	2000
Marketing	800
Total direct costs	13000
Output returns	
Culled ewes and rams	9000
Male lambs	10000
Female lambs	5000
Wool	8000
Total returns	32000
Gross margin	19000

On the other hand, however, the budget tells practically nothing about the techno-economic structure of the activity, *i.e.*, how the various internal components of ewes, lambs and rams, and the technical performance of each, impact on each other and on the overall budget results.

Such interrelatedness must, of course, exist but in the budget itself it is only implied. To be of use for some analytical purpose - *e.g.*, analysis in problem-diagnostic mode—the implied coefficients have to be stated in explicit form. The relevant internal structural coefficients are shown in the upper section of Table.

They indicate that in this example the normal death rate among ewes is five per cent annually; 90 lambs are born annually per 100 ewes; nine per cent of lambs do not survive; five rams are run per 100 ewes; 20 per cent of the (old) ewes and rams are replaced (by retained lambs) annually.

There are three main reasons for taking explicit note of these internal structural coefficients. First, they show at a glance the techno-economic conditions under which the results of an activity are achieved (in this example the results are a self-sustaining flock of 100 ewes yielding an annual gross margin of ₹19 000).

Second, they are essential information if the budget is intended for activity problem diagnosis. Third and of primary interest here, they provide a basis for closer examination of the interrelatedness of the various components of the activity—in this example between populations of and returns from the lamb and ewe components of the activity.

The objective might be to quantify the separate effects of sheep losses and sales on the annual maintenance of a constant-size flock of 100 ewes. Assuming that this particular aspect of the sheep system is to be examined, a flowchart such as that of Figure would be prepared showing the interrelatedness of components, in terms of animal numbers, in more detail. This is an elaboration of the relevant parts of the budget table. As noted, this flowchart refers to sheep populations.

If some other aspect of interrelatedness is of interest (*e.g.*, feed supply *vs.* births/deaths etc.), a flowchart based on the relevant parameters would be prepared analogously to Figure 6.4.

STRUCTURAL COEFFICIENTS AS CRITICAL PARAMETERS

From the previous discussion of parametric budgets, most of the internal structural coefficients of Table will be recognized as 'critical parameters'. Such coefficients as lamb birth rates etc. are critical in the sense that any significant change from their present level would obviously flow through to alter the final result (sustainability and gross margin) of the activity. Such changes would be evaluated by making conditional or parametric extensions to the budget of Table.

However, it might be noted that while internal structural coefficients are similar to critical parameters, they are not exactly equivalent. Some factors, *e.g.*, lamb mortality rates, are both coefficients and critical parameters. But others, such as the amounts of wool cut from ewes and lambs and the prices received for these, are critical parameters although they might not involve interrelatedness among the several elements of the system and are therefore not internal structural coefficients. Similarly, some activity input/cost items such as labour and feed might be economically 'critical' but would have nothing to do with interrelatedness among activity components.

INTERRELATEDNESS AMONG ACTIVITIES

EXTERNAL STRUCTURAL COEFFICIENTS

The second type of system interrelatedness, that which is quantified in terms of external structural coefficients between activities or enterprises, is illustrated by the example of Figure 6.4. This presents budgets for four integrated coconut activities: growing coconuts for direct sale, or alternatively using the nuts and by-products as inputs to the three related activities of making copra (from coconut flesh), making charcoal (from shells) and making coir fibre (from husks).

From the previous discussion, it is here useful to distinguish, on the one hand, between this set of four coconut-based operations as an enterprise and, on the other hand, each of the product-specific subsets of operations as activities. Note also that Figure 6.4 encompasses only a small set of the great number of coconut activities that are possible.

Activity budget 1 of Figure. which relates to producing 4000 nuts annually from the standard 64 palms per acre, would apply if these nuts are simply to be grown and sold. Budgets 2, 3 and 4 apply if instead the nuts are retained on the farm for further processing.

They show operations, inputs, costs, outputs, gross returns and net returns for the respective activities (all of which are possible components of the overall coconut enterprise). For present purposes what are of interest are the external structural coefficients which link these several activities together. These coefficients are briefly explained.

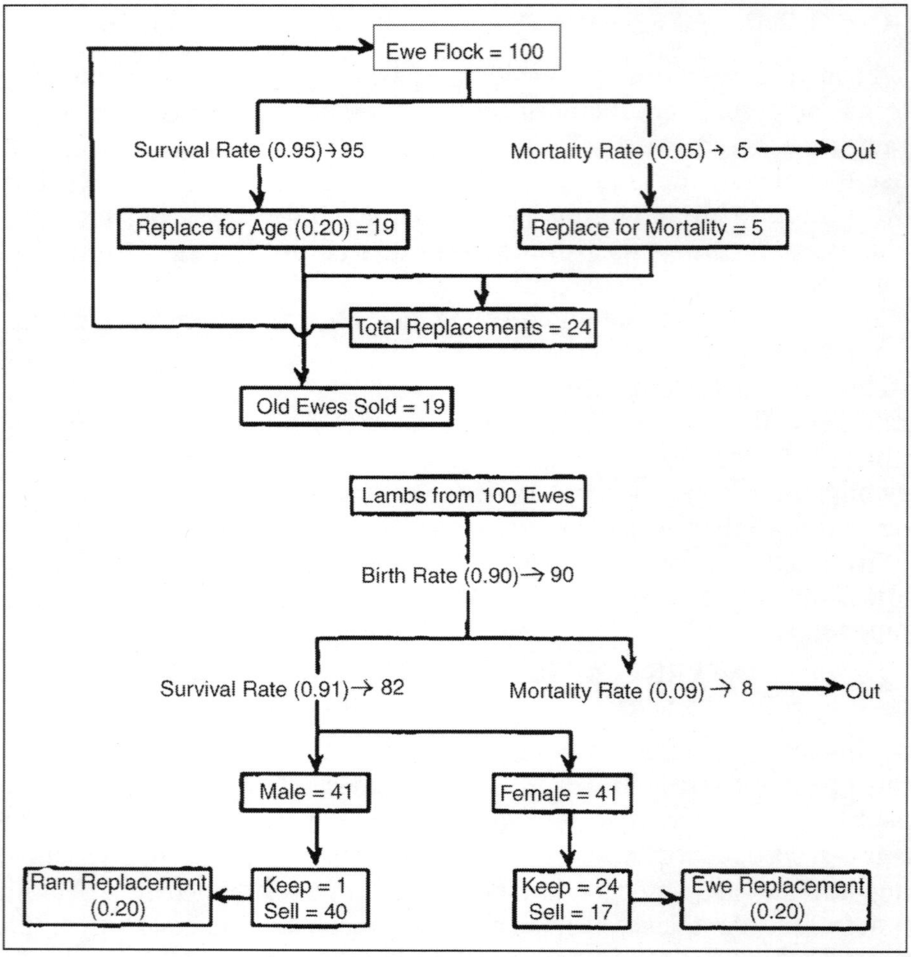

Fig. Flowchart depicting Role of Internal Structural Coefficients in Annual Maintenance of a Self-sustaining Flock of 100 Ewes

In Figure the first relationship between Activities 1 and 2 is through the output of nuts in Activity 1 as this determines the raw material available for Activity 2, copra making. This linking coefficient has a value of 1.0—all nuts are used for copra. But on some other farm the coefficient could be, say, 0.75 if three quarters of the nuts are processed and one quarter sold as nuts. This would occur, *e.g.*, if 25 per cent of nuts are first grade and sold as food, while all second-grade nuts are processed as copra.

In Activity 2, copra making, the first operation is husking 4 000 nuts, which produces 4 000 clean nuts plus 4 000 husks. The clean nuts are then split into halves which contain the (future) copra. These are first sun-dried for half a day then loaded into a fuel-burning drier for five days. After unloading, the cured copra is hand-extracted from the half-shells and is then subjected to the further operations shown under Activity 2. The now-empty shells, on the other hand, are disposed of in two ways: two thirds of them are recycled back as dryer fuel for curing some future batch of copra (*i.e.*, two thirds of the shells from any batch would provide sufficient heat to dry the copra of that batch). This is shown in Figure 6.5 as a coefficient value of 0.67 (of 8 000 half-shells) so that 5 360 half-shells are cycled back as fuel into the copra-drying operation.

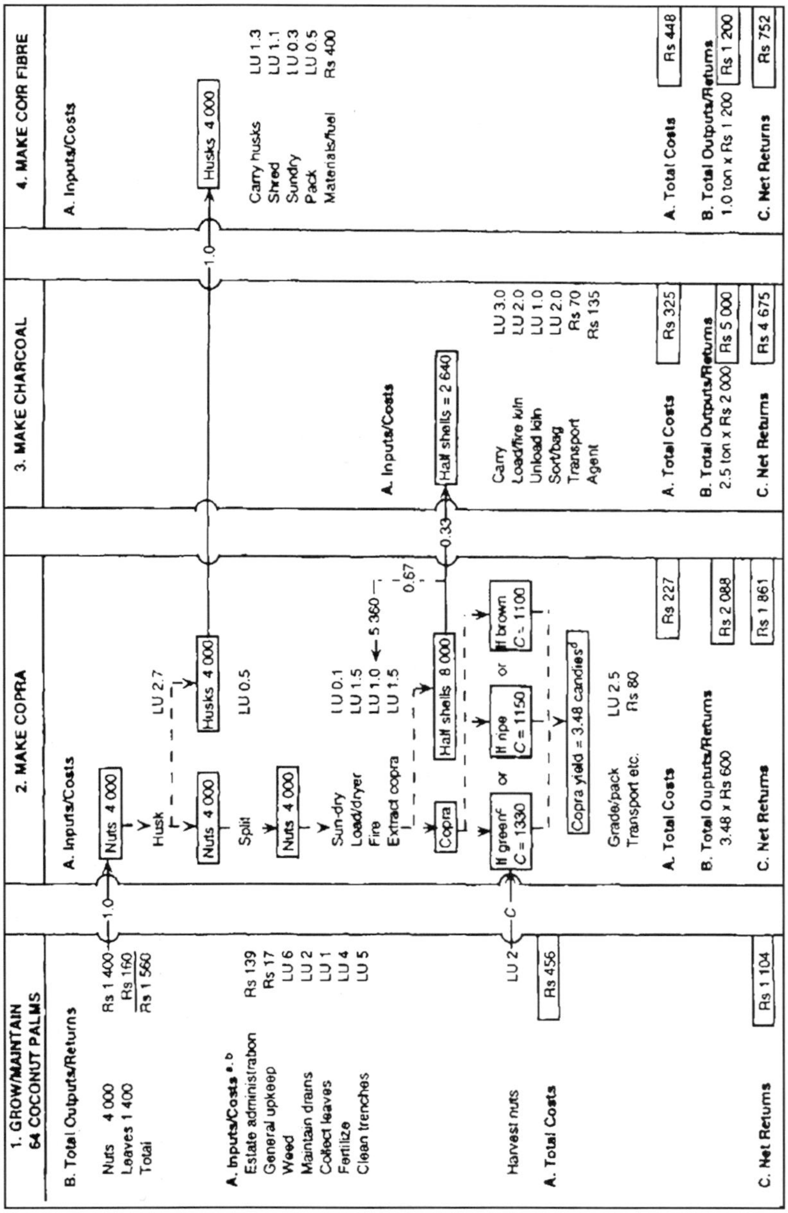

Fig. Structural Relationships among Four Coconut Activities (Per Acre Basis)

The remaining output of one third of the half-shells, *i.e.*, 2640, now becomes raw material input for the next activity, charcoal making. Thus the output of charcoal in Activity 3 is governed by the (shell) fuel requirements of Activity 2. Note, however, that these coefficients of two thirds and one third are subject to some variation. Firing the half-shells in copra curing requires considerable skill, the degree of which can be directly measured in terms of the copra-shell fuel requirement coefficient: if this rises much above 0.67, say to 0.75 (leaving only 25 per cent of the shells available for processing to charcoal), it would indicate unskilled workmanship or poor management.

To return to the second structural linkage between Activities 1 and 2: the size of this external structural coefficient is determined by the degree of maturity of the nuts at harvest time (coconut is usually harvested at two-month intervals). Maturity level affects the rate of recovery of copra. The recovery or nuts-to-copra conversion rates for three maturity conditions are shown as structural coefficients in Activity 2, but they are determined by the timing of the harvesting operation in Activity 1: the conversion rate, denoted here by C, will be 1 330 nuts required to make one 'candy' of copra (480 pounds, 218 kilograms) if nut harvesting is at the still-green stage. For ripe nuts, C = 1 150, and for brown nuts, C = 1 100. (Of course, other management practices such as palm fertilizer applied, weeding etc. will also affect the absolute level of nuts-to-copra conversion, but the relative recovery rates due to the maturity effect will still hold.)

Finally, Activity 4 consists of making coir fibre from the husks by-product generated in Activity 2. The structural coefficient relating these two activities has a value of unity since each nut for copra production provides one husk for making coir fibre.

This is the only structural coefficient shown as providing linkage between Activity 4 and the other activities. However, on most estates another important linkage does in fact operate between Activities 1, 3 and 4: it consists of the common practice of retaining some proportion of the husks generated in Activity 2 and using them (buried in trenches alongside the palms) as a source of potash in the fertilizing operation of Activity 1. The proportion of husks used for this purpose, which will depend on the potash status of soils on any particular estate, will then govern coir production output in Activity 4. (The deciding factor between using husks as fertilizer or as an input to coir production will be the cost saved by using husks instead of artificial potash versus the income foregone by not making coir.)

In summary, the external linkage coefficients shown in Figure quantify the interrelatedness which exists between the various activity subsystems of this total coconut enterprise. Any full analysis of any one of these activities would also require consideration of its effects on the others.

FARM SERVICE MATRIX

The next element of a farm-household system to be considered is its farm service matrix. This is a system of Order Level 9. It consists of some set of material, labour and cash inputs which enables the farm-household to function as a system, but which is not specific to any particular production activity of the system. (If they are activity-specific they will be treated as costs of the appropriate activity.) This section thus continues the discussion of resources, capital and costs begun.

In their financial dimension these system-service inputs are referred to as *whole-farm overhead, common* or *farm fixed costs.* Such fixed costs must be included in the economic evaluation of a farming system for the two reasons that they influence both the profitability and the sustainability of the system.

There are two broad categories of overhead costs, *general charges* and *capital fixed costs.* General charges represent an actual money expenditure and as such, when included together with the aggregated direct costs of the production activities of the system, will determine its profitability. The second category of fixed costs (capital fixed costs, below), while not directly affecting immediate system profitability, will affect its sustainability.

GENERAL CHARGES

General charges are those fixed costs incurred in obtaining service inputs of an institutional nature which logically cannot be assigned to any specific production activity of the farm and which must be paid for. They represent an actual financial outlay. Some examples are: land tax payments, taxes on general-purpose livestock, water licence fees and vehicle registration fees.

Table provides an example of the general charges and capital fixed costs making up the annual fixed costs on a rubber estate. It illustrates the importance and wide range of general charges.

CAPITAL FIXED COSTS

Capital fixed costs are those costs incurred in the use of non-activity-specific physical farm capital and pertain to its maintenance, operation (in non activity-specific uses only) and provision for its eventual end-of-life replacement. Their payment is not mandatory—at least in the short run—and 'payment' is often in the nature of an internal bookkeeping transfer which is designed to provide—if indeed at all—only for the long-term sustainability of the system's fixed capital and for the eventual replacement of such capital as it wears out. Typical of these capital fixed costs are 'payments' or provisions for the maintenance, use and replacement of farm buildings, houses, fences, pumps and other machinery, paths, roads, farm bridges, ponds, irrigation and soil conservation systems, and breeding livestock.

Table Example Listing of Annual Total Fixed Costs on a Rubber Estate

Cost Item	Amount
General charges	`
Salaries	18 757
Staff allowances	600
Staff provident fund	1 012
Workers provident fund	11 462
Wage adjustment	673
Labour holidays	6 454
Food for functions	708
Medical, sanitation	3 635
All insurance	2 852
Office supplies	1 771
Commissions paid	1 005
Visiting agent	750
Rents, taxes	2 231
Vehicles	10 000
Watchmen	1 373
Retirement gifts	2 478
Capital fixed costs	
Housing upkeep	9 264
Labour-lines upkeep	1 857
Minor buildings	390
Roads, water supply	950
Total fixed costs	78 222
Total production (pounds weight)	276 600
Fixed cost/pound weight	0.28

The essential difference between general charges and such capital fixed costs is that payment for the former is mandatory, while cash disbursement for the latter is not. (The alternative, if no funds are put aside for capital replacement and no replacement is carried out, is to run down the farm capital structure, in which case it sooner or later ceases to be sustainable.)

RELATIVE IMPORTANCE OF TOTAL FARM FIXED COSTS

On most small farms, expenditure on fixed costs of both categories will be very low. Most fixed-capital costs (*i.e.*, for capital maintenance) will be 'paid' for in the form of family labour used to repair and eventually reconstruct fences, ponds, ox gear etc. Obviously, the importance of farm fixed costs will thus vary according to the farm type under consideration. The forest-garden farms of Kerala and Sri Lanka can practically ignore capital fixed costs (but not general charges such as land taxes), simply because apart from their trees, a few hand tools and the land itself, they have little capital. On the other hand, on the intensively operated mixed crop-livestock farms of Sind, capital fixed costs (and total farm fixed costs) might be significant - but still much less so than on commercial estates.

The typical situation on these latter is summarized in Table which shows annual average direct, fixed and total Cost of Production *(CoP)* per pound of made rubber on a sample of 148 Sri Lankan estates. Total estate fixed costs (general charges plus capital costs, but, as noted, mainly general charges) are very significant and amount to about one third of total costs.

Table Average Annual Costs of Production of Made Rubber for a Sample of Sri Lankan Rubber Estates (` per Pound Weight)

Sample	Direct costs			Fixed costs	Total *CoP*
	Cultural	Factory	Marketing		
36 sheet estates	0.402	0.088	0.030	0.249	0.769
86 crepe estates	0.430	0.147	0.045	0.293	0.915
26 mixed estates	0.450	0.117	0.049	0.289	0.905
All 148 estates	**0.430**	**0.138**	**0.044**	**0.289**	**0.901**

DETERMINATION OF CAPITAL FIXED COSTS

Obtaining the general charges of a farm or estate will usually present no problems. Table is an adequate guide to the types of cost items which may occur.

On the other hand, the evaluation of capital fixed costs will require a little arithmetic as exemplified by the illustrative schedule of Table. This is for a particular farm whose operating budget is presented later in Table. The schedule consists of a complete inventory listing of all the farm's fixed-capital items (including land) and their capital values as shown respectively in columns (1) and (2). The inventory is then assessed to obtain the annual fixed costs of replacing/repairing/operating these capital items as respectively listed in columns (4), (5) and (6).

These costs are aggregated in column (8) to give the annual fixed cost of each capital item. Column (7) is not needed immediately; it will be required later for economic evaluation of a farming system.

In calculating annual capital fixed costs as per Table, the values given to capital items in column (2) and hence their depreciation charge in column (4) should not be based on their initial purchase or construction cost. Capital items should be valued at their current *expected replacement cost.* The tractor, *e.g.*, might actually have cost ₹ 8 000 five years ago, but today the cost of replacing this five-year-old machine with a new one might be ₹10 000.

Whatever the initial cost or value might have been is of historical interest only and, except by coincidence, will no longer be of relevance in making provision for eventually replacing the item when that becomes necessary. Column (3) contains estimates of the years of useful service which can be expected of each item from the time of its initial purchase by the farmer. These are inevitably somewhat arbitrary. Land is assumed to be used sustainably and thus to have an indefinite useful life. Columns (4), (5) and (6) of Table show the individual components of the fixed-capital cost of each capital item, based on columns (2) and (3). Value based on current expected replacement cost. *'Land' includes all fixed improvements (drains, levelling, earthworks etc.) and permanent tree crops in house yard.*

Table. Farm Capital Investment Inventory and Schedule for Calculating Annual Capital Fixed Costs.

Capital investment inventory							
(1) Capital item	(2) Item value[a] (₹)	(3) Useful life (years)	(4) Deprec'n[b] (₹)	(5) Repairs (₹)	(6) Operating costs (₹)	(7) Interest at 10% (₹)	(8) Total (4)+(5)+(6) (₹)
Land	50 000	-	-	-	-	5 000	-
House, sheds	15 000	25	600	200	-	1 500	800
Tractor	10 000	10	1 000	400	-	1 000	1 400
Hand thresher	2000	6	330	50	-	200	380
Cultivators	3000	5	600	100	-	300	700
Livestock gear	600	3	200	50	-	60	250
Barn	5000	20	250	200	-	500	450
Fences	6000	30	200	400	-	600	600
Dam/pond	8000	40	200	-	-	800	200
Water pump	4000	8	500	200	800	400	1 500
Oxen	3000	5	600	-	200	300	800
Total	106 600		4 480	1 600	1 000	10 660	7 080

Note: [b]Here the straight-line method of calculating depreciation is used and it is assumed that the capital items have no residual value at the end of their useful life.

Depreciation is the decline over time in the capacity of a capital item to provide the service expected of it and for which it is held. Depreciation is usually measured on an annual basis. Ideally, it would be measured in actual terms but that would involve inordinate record keeping. Instead, simpler rule-of-thumb procedures (as outlined are used. As well as through *wear and tear* arising from use of the capital item, depreciation also occurs through *technical obsolescence* as more modem machines or other items providing the same service but at lower unit cost become available. While wear and tear may be relatively predictable and approximately constant over time, technical obsolescence may not be. In consequence, to be as correct as possible, annual depreciation should be calculated afresh each year. Whether or not it is economically worthwhile to do so will depend on the particular situation.

Column (4) of Table 6.5 provides some examples of depreciation. These amounts are measured as a constant pro rata proportion over each item's life of its expected replacement cost. In percentage terms this depreciation cost corresponds to 100 divided by the item's useful life. Consider the tractor valued at ₹10 000 which is estimated to have a total useful life of ten years. On a pro rata basis, the annual cost of obtaining this service is ₹10 000/10 or ₹ 1 000. Or to put it another way, based on the present assessment, if the farm's fixed capital is not to be depleted, a sum of ₹ 1 000 per year should be set aside to enable the tractor to be replaced when it finally wears out or, due to technological advance, becomes obsolescent (in five years' time if it is five years old now). (Hence the preference for basing item value in column (2) on current expected replacement cost rather than past/historical actual cost.)

Repairs refers to the sum of money which normally must be spent on maintaining each capital item in good repair. Note, however, that in spite of such repairs, the item (tractor, thresher, fences etc.) will sooner or later wear out or become obsolete, hence the need for its depreciation as well as its routine repair.

Operating costs are the costs of actually operating a capital item: *e.g.*, ₹ 800 for water-pump fuel, ₹ ₹ of feed and veterinary expenses for the oxen. In Table the tractor would, of course, also incur fuel and oil operating costs but in a typical farm situation it would be fairly easy to charge these against the separate specific activities (paddy, cotton etc.) which actually consume this fuel or incur such operating costs, rather than against the farm as a whole. Often, however, some capital operating costs will be incurred in non-specific farm work, in which case they should be included in column (6).

Interest as listed in column (7) of Table 6.5 is a bookkeeping charge levied on total farm capital - *i.e.*, all capital invested in the farm - in order to assess the productivity of the several farm resource categories or factors of production (land, labour and capital). It is not a 'cost' in the conventional sense of detracting from the value of farm net output (or family income). For the moment, only the procedure of obtaining this item is of concern. Briefly, some appropriate rate of interest, here ten per cent, is applied to the assessed value of each/all of the capital investment items as listed in column (2) of Table 6.5. The appropriate interest rate is determined by the opportunity cost of similar capital items in their 'most likely most profitable most prudent' other use. Thus if the best alternative investment available were for the family to sell the farm and put the proceeds in a bank earning ten per cent annual interest, this would determine the *opportunity cost* of farm capital and thus the appropriate interest rate to apply in obtaining column (7). To conclude, one might state the obvious: these procedures for obtaining the interest costs of column (7) are full of practical pitfalls.

Is the replacement value of an item a proper representation of its value in use? If not, a more appropriate value should be used. Or, as is not infrequently done, items might be valued at the mid-point of their useful life with allowance made for any residual value they may possess at the end of their useful life. Thus the oxen of Table with a useful life of five years and, say, a residual value of ₹ 800 as meat would be valued at ₹(3 000 + 800)/2 = ₹ 1 900.

Is it sufficient to apply some rate of interest (say ten per cent, as above) uniformly to all capital items, or are the opportunity costs of some capital items greater than of others? (Probably yes, but precision must be weighed against the extra work required in obtaining the necessary information.) What is an appropriate alternative investment? Could money, instead of being put in the bank at ten per cent, be lent to a speculator in the souk at 50 per cent and still be regarded as a prudent alternative investment? (Probably not.).... Anyway, do realistic alternative uses of farm investment capital actually exist?

On the other hand, when concern is with small farms,

These practical difficulties are largely removed by the facts that

- The value of farm capital itself, and thus the level of fixed costs associated with it, will not be very great; and
- Most capital can be maintained and replaced by using (largely 'free') farm-generated resources and family labour. In short, while the effort that goes into the construction of Table must inevitably be considerable if later analysis based on it is to be technically satisfactory, the actual data obtained within and subsequently from Table might not make much practical difference in the evaluation of small-farm performance.

To summarize the discussion of Table 6.5: total capital fixed costs on this farm, column (8), are the sum of the previous cost-item columns (4), (5) and (6)—in the example ₹ 7,080 annually. Total farm fixed costs are the sum of this item and the farm's general charges.

MANDATORY *VS.* OPTIONAL FARM FIXED COSTS

It was noted previously that payment of general charges is usually mandatory. Taxes and licence fees must be paid. It was also noted that payment of capital fixed costs might be considered optional, at least in the short run. In fact it would be more correct to say that some of the components of capital fixed costs are mandatory while others are optional. Again referring to Table 6.5, payments for running repairs and operation (*e.g.*, fuel, feed for the oxen) are in a large sense mandatory, while provision for depreciation is largely optional (in any one operating year). Depreciation (column 4) might be provided for in practice by setting aside ₹ 4,480 per year; or such an amount might be re-invested in the business to generate the necessary future replacement funds; or no provision at all might be made.

This third case implies that:

- Farm capital stock is being run down or depleted;
- To the extent that such depletion is occurring, real farm net income is being overestimated; and
- Sooner or later the farm will cease to be a sustainable system.

DEPRECIATION METHODS

Ideally, the annual depreciation of a capital item should be measured in terms of its actual wear and tear due to usage and the change in its degree of obsolescence. This would imply much inconvenient record keeping not worth its cost. Instead, it is assumed that usage of the item and the accompanying flow of service from it follow some regular pattern and depreciation is estimated accordingly. Thus there are four main methods of calculating annual depreciation 'cost' or the annual rate at which a capital item provides services and is thereby used up or becomes obsolete. Three of these methods are briefly discussed here.

Straight-line depreciation assumes a constant flow of service with consequent wear and tear and/or obsolescence during the item's useful life so that the value of the item will therefore decrease by a constant uniform annual amount over its life. This is the easiest method to apply. The formula for obtaining the annual straight-line depreciation amount, denoted by D, is $D = (PV - SV)/L$ where PV is the item's present value (*i.e.*, its expected future replacement cost at the moment of analysis), SV is its expected salvage or residual value at the end of its useful life and L is its expected total years of life. Thus annual depreciation on a cultivator with an expected replacement cost of ₹1 000 and which has an expected total useful life of ten years and can then be sold for ₹ 200 as scrap would be ₹ (1 000 - 200)/10 = ₹ 80; or if it has no salvage value, ₹ 1 000/10 = ₹ 100.

This method is probably most appropriate for small Asian farms where most capital items (pumps, cultivators, livestock gear etc.) suffer no loss in value due to obsolescence, are entirely used up in the production process, and do not have a residual value (*e.g.*, as the basis for trade-in on a new model). The results of applying this method are shown in the lefthand-side graph of Figure.

Declining-balance depreciation assumes that the item is used up and/or becomes obsolescent at a constant percentage rate of its annual starting value. Applied to the previous example with a zero salvage value and assuming an annual depreciation rate of ten per cent, this would result in an annual depreciation amount of ₹1 000 x 0.10 or ₹100 in year 1 of the item's life, ₹(1 000 - 100)0.10 or ₹ 90 in year 2, ₹ (1 000 - 100 - 90)0.10 or ₹ 81 in year 3, ₹ 73 in year 4, etc. With declining-balance depreciation, the formula for calculating the annual depreciation 'cost' in year t, denoted by D_t is:

$$D_t = (V_{t-1})d$$

where V_{t-1} is the item's depreciated value at the end of year t-1, $V_{t-1} = (V_{t-2} - DT - 1)$, $V_0 = (PV_0 - SV)$ where PV_0 is the item's expected replacement cost at time zero, *i.e.*, at the start of the depreciation analysis, and d is the constant annual rate of depreciation.

Obviously, as illustrated by the middle graph of Figure 6.6, the procedure results in a lower and declining depreciation loss in later years. This is appropriate where the value loss is due to the 'planned obsolescence' of modem equipment (which is reflected in dealers' secondhand machinery and vehicle-buying price schedules as these are used in the West). Such obsolescence hardly exists on small Asian farms where, as noted, value loss is due to wear and tear from physical use. Note also from Figure 6.6 that, unlike straight-line depreciation, the declining-balance method does not lead to full write-down of an item at the end of its useful life.

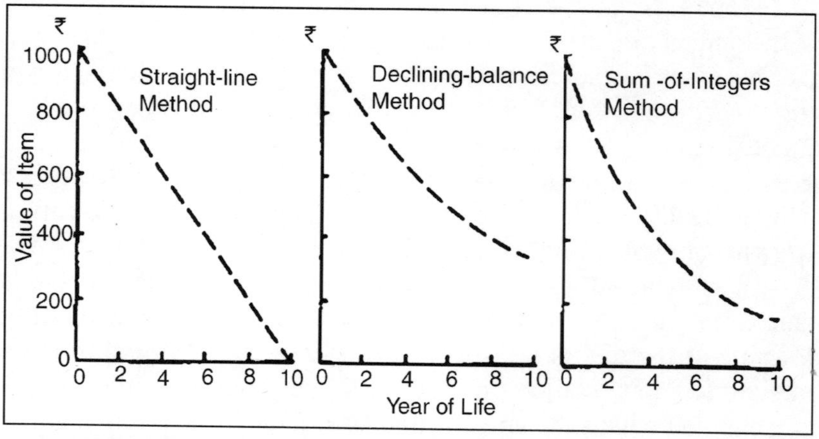

Fig. Example of Straight-line, Declining-balance and Sum-of- Integers Depreciation Methods Applied to an Item with an Initial Value of ₹1 000, a Ten-year Life and Zero Salvage Value

Sum-of-integers depreciation is essentially similar to the declining-balance approach in that this method also results in less than full write-down and in a declining annual depreciation 'cost' which eventually becomes zero in the last year of life as shown by the righthand-side graph of Figure. Compared to the declining-balance and straight-line methods, the sum-of-integers method implies a more rapid initial depreciation but slower later depreciation. The formula for sum-of-integers depreciation is:

$D_t = (PV_{t=0} - SV)$ [Remaining years of life/Sum of integers of total life]

where D_t is again depreciation for year t and $PV_{t=0}$ is the expected replacement value of the capital item at time zero, *i.e.*, at the start of the depreciation analysis. Using the previous example of the cultivator with a life of ten years and no salvage value (*i.e.*, $SV = 0$), the 'sum of the integers' would be (1 + 2 + 3..... + 10) or 55, and the annual depreciation 'cost' would be:

Year 1: ₹ 1 000 x 9/55 = ₹ 164
Year 2: ₹ 1 000 x 8/55 = ₹ 145
Year 3: ₹ 1 000 x 7/55 = ₹ 127
... ...
Year 9: ₹ 1 000 x 1/55 = ₹ 18
Year 10: ₹ 1 000 x 0/55 = ₹ 0.

Comparing the three depreciation methods outlined above, the straight-line approach is generally to be preferred on the grounds that it is less complicated and ensures full depreciation or write-down of the item.

Bibliography

A.D. Kajlag, T.A. More and S.N. Mate: *Dryland Agriculture*, Agri Biovet Press, 2014.

A.K. Nayak: *A Textbook of Internet Technologies and Applications*, Dominant Publishers, Delhi, 2011.

Ajoy Gangopadhyay: *Assessment of Improved Crop Production Technologies*, Gene Tech Books, 2007.

Andrew Boss and George A. Pond: *Modern Farm Management: Principles and Practice*, Biotech Books, Delhi, 2005.

Anita Stephen: *Communication Technologies and Women Empowerment*, Rajat, Publication, Delhi, 2006.

B.L. Jana: *Appropriate Technologies for Drought Prone Areas*, Agrotech, Publication, Delhi, 2005.

Chen: *Bioinformatics Technologies*, Springer, Publication, Delhi, 2004.

Cheuk H. Lam and Eiji Oki, H. Jonathan Chao: *Broadband Packet Switching Technologies A Practical Guide*, Wiley India, Delhi, 2011.

Chung: *Composite Materials: Functional Materials for Modern Technologies*, Springer, Publication, Delhi, 2004.

G F Warren: *Farm Management*, Arise Publication, Delhi, 2008.

Ghulam Mohyuddin Wani: *Animal Agriculture Biotechnology: Biotechnologies, Policy, Planning, Reviews and Visions*, Satish Serial Publication, Delhi, 2009.

Indrani Gupta, Mayur Trivedi and Subodh Kandamuthan: *Adoption of Health Technologies in India: Implications for the AIDS Vaccine*, Sage, Publication, Delhi, 2007.

J.M. Dhaka: *Economics of Agricultural Production and Farm Management*, Aavishkar Publication, Delhi, 2009.

Jagannath Adhikari: *Decisions For Survival: Farm Management Strategies in the Middle Hills of Nepal*, Adroit, Publication, Delhi, 2000.

K.R. Chowdhary and V.S. Bansal: *Bioinformatics and Computational Technologies*, Scientific, Publication, Delhi,l 2010.

Laxmi Lal Somani: *Agri-Business and Farm Management*, Agrotech, Publication, Delhi, 2010.

M. Put and M.P. van Dijk: *Government and NGO Interventions in Dryland Agriculture: A Study of Two Projects in Andhra Pradesh*, Manohar, Publication, Delhi, 2000.

Mohapatra: *Ad Hoc Networks: Technologies and Protocols*, Springer, Publication, Delhi, 2004.

P.P. Joglekar and Pankaj Goyal: *Animal Husbandry and Allied Technologies in Ancient India*, Pentagon Press, Delhi, 2015.

Pawan Kumar Jha: *Communication Technologies in Higher Education*, Rajat, Publication, Delhi, 2005.

R. Murugesan: *Energy Use Efficiency in Dryland Agriculture*, Kalpaz, Publication, Delhi, 2010.

R.L. Adams: *Farm Management*, Srishti Books, Delhi, 2006.

R.P. Singh: *Sustainable Development of Dryland Agriculture in India*, Scientific, Publication, Delhi, 2007.

Rajveer Singh: *Modern Farm Management Principles and Practice*, Oxford Book Company, 2007.

Reji D. Nair: *Farm Management: Theory and Practice*, Concept, Publication, Delhi, 2011.

S C Panda: *Dryland Agriculture*, Agrobios, Publication, Delhi, 2004.

S L Verma: *Advanced Modern Political Theory: Analysis and Technologies*, Rawat, Publication, Delhi, 2008.

S. Felix: *Aquaculture Technologies for India*, Narendra Publishing House, Delhi, 2014.

Sameer Kumar: *Connective Technologies in the Supply Chain*, T and F/Routledge, Delhi, 2008.

Satish Kumar Mehla: *Biodiesel Production Technologies*, Pointer, Publication, Delhi, 2007.

Somasundaram Rajarathnam and Ramesh Shyam Ramteke: *Advances in Preservation and Processing Technologies of Fruits and Vegetables*, New India Publishing Agency, 2011.

Srinivas C. Rao and John Ryan: *Challenges and Strategies for Dryland Agriculture*, Scientific Publication, Delhi, 2007.

Syed Zahoor Qasim and Malti Goel: *Sequestration Technologies for Clean Energy Awareness and Capacity Building*, Daya, Publication, Delhi, 2010.

T I Khan: *Atmosphere and Air Pollution Control Technologies*, Aavishkar, Publication, Delhi, 2004.

V.M. Mayande, Y.S. Ramakrishna, C.R. Thyagaraj, G.R. Korwar and I. Srinivas: *Mechanization of Dryland Agriculture*, Agrotech, Publication, Delhi, 2012.

Y V R Reddy; K P R Vittal; C R Thyagaraj; Y S Ramakrishna and L L Somani: G Subba Reddy: *Dryland Agriculture*, Agrotech Publication, Delhi, 2008.

Index

Data Warehousing 238